Understanding
FEMALE SEXUAL HEALTH

Understanding
FEMALE SEXUAL HEALTH

Dorothy Baldwin

HIPPOCRENE BOOKS
New York

For information, address:
HIPPOCRENE BOOKS, INC.
171 Madison Avenue
New York, NY 10016

Library of Congress Cataloging-in-Publication Data
Baldwin, Dorthy.
Understanding female sexual health / Dorthy Baldwin.
        p.   cm.
Includes index.
ISBN 0-7818-0072-2 : $19.95
1. Gynecology—Popular works.   I. Title.
RG121.B245   1992   92-21486
        618.1—dc20   CIP

Printed in the United States of America.

Contents

Foreword

by Natalie Blagowidow, M.D.

Understanding the changes in the female sexual organs during a lifespan is a vital part of self-care. That self-care should begin before puberty. Appropriate hygiene is outlined for girls approaching puberty, and the problems of body image and self-esteem which often accompany puberty are discussed in detail. Parents will find the information invaluable as they educate and cope with their teenage daughters.

Reproductive function and dysfunction are reviewed, including a sensitive discussion of the causes and treatment of infertility.

The modern management of gynecologic diseases is described. Whereas hysterectomy was the only option twenty years ago, several medical therapies and conservative surgical procedures are now viable alternatives. The management of conditions such as uterine myomas, endometriosis and ovarian cysts are reviewed.

Important issues surround the climacteric and life after menopause. For example, every woman faces the difficult decision of whether to take hormonal replacement. Estrogen therapy has been shown to reduce the risk of osteoporosis and heart disease and can provide relief from the hot flashes and mood swings of the climacteric. However, the therapy may increase the risk of breast cancer and can worsen some medical conditions. The author weighs the risks and benefits of hormonal therapy, allowing the reader to make an informed decision.

Sexual satisfaction is a health component that is often overlooked. There are many misconceptions about sex. Here, the reader is educated about the components of the orgasm—including how to achieve an orgasm, how to overcome inhibition of orgasm, and the distinction between achieving orgasm and achieving sexual satisfaction.

For couples deciding on a contraceptive method, the safety, and efficacy of the many options is explored.

Dorothy Baldwin does not forget the importance of seeking appropriate medical advice. A woman who has read this book will know *when* and *why* she needs a medical examination. She will know what facts to report to her doctor and what questions to ask. She will be able to critically evaluate the answers she receives. And, if there is poor communication with her physician, she will know it.

I hope many of my patients will read this book. I always look forward to seeing a well-informed patient. Such a patient is more likely to come in with a problem that can be identified early and therefore may be easier to resolve. Her ability to bring complete information about herself will aid in diagnosis and treatment.

Most importantly, understanding and appreciating one's body is the first step in caring for oneself and one's health. Good self-care can prevent many problems from occurring in the first place.

Introduction

Why do my breasts hurt sometimes?
At what age should my daughter do breast self-examination?
It hurts when my breasts are touched. Is this normal?
My sister has breast cancer. What is my level of risk?
What are the cancer risks from having a mammogram?
Why do some orgasms feel better than others?
Can a woman have orgasms after a hysterectomy?
How can I cope with vagina problems of lubrication?
What is meant by the "sweating phenomenon"?
My labia appear uneven. Are there health risks to this?
Is douching advisable after a period?
Are there any methods to avoid urinary tract infections?
Can I avoid surgery for my fibroids?
What are the symptoms of cancer of the ovaries?
How can I help my daughter avoid early sexual activity?
Why is self-esteem considered important for little girls?
What is meant by precocious puberty?
Is nymphomania a medical condition, or a subjective opinion?
How can I avoid surgery for a mild urine leakage?
Can you explain Kegels exercises, and how they are done?
Is taking the Pill advisable for older women?
Are there health risks with the new underarm implant?
How can an old and cured PID problem now block my tubes?
My periods are irregular? Are there any health implications?
Are there any new methods to help cope with cramps and PMS?
What are all the different types of in vitro fertilization?
Which self-care methods reduce the symptoms of menopause?
My doctor thinks I'm a difficult patient. What can I do?

The answers to these and many more questions are to be found in this book.

Change Around Me...

A woman's reproductive years involve a series of changes. The critical times for many of her health concerns are related to hormone activity. Puberty can be perceived as the first major change, when the girl's body becomes *feminized*. During this time, she must learn to adapt and adjust to her newly emerging frame, and to the monthly flow. In late adolescence, she faces critical choices over contraception. Which type of fertility control will provide her with the greatest protection against pregnancy, while offering her the least health risks?

Later, can come pregnancy, birthing, and nursing. During these events, her entire hormone system is radically altered. She must adapt to these changes for at least a year, and it takes some time afterwards to adjust to her pre-pregnancy state. Then, at menopause, she needs information on how to adjust to the reduced output of her own hormones, and to adapt to the effect of her "male" hormones now being able to show through.

Freud's statement about women, "Anatomy is destiny," is viewed with distaste by many feminists. Nevertheless, in terms of a woman's health, these major reproductive life stages to which she must constantly adapt and adjust are hormone-related. The modern edict, "Change is good; change makes you grow," is almost a tautology for women, who learn how to be flexible in their reproductive years.

Which Type of Patient?

One ongoing study in Nashville suggests that not all children benefit from being told what to expect during a hospital stay. It appears that there are three separate types of coping behavior which children exhibit. Some are *avoiders*; they feel more in control if they have very little information about their surgery, or the potential risks of therapy. Others are *vigilants*; they cope by seeking as much information as they can, the more they know the more confident they feel. The third group are *combiners*; they want to know the details of surgery, but nothing about potential risks or post-operative complications.

In much the same way, some women feel more in control if they have very little information about their condition. They prefer to take their physician's word on all aspects of their illness and therapy. They put their faith and trust in their physician, and wish to be told precisely what to do to get well. For these women, remaining untroubled about the details of their illness prevents them from suffering unnecessary distress.

Other women prefer to gain more control. They want to find out everything they can about their condition. They need to know all the different therapies, what are the potential complications, and the chances of the outcome of one therapy over another. They buy books, research in libraries, and join local groups which offer information and support. They quiz their physician at each stage of the healing process, and deserve frank and open answers.

Still others may be too busy to do research, or not want to overload themselves with information. They do not want to hand over total control of their illness to the physician, but learning all the possible complications would frighten them. One way around this is to keep up to date on the latest health news, which is generally well reported in the press and magazines. Then, if illness occurs, there is a background of information on which to evaluate the physician's advice.

Illness brings sufficient stress on its own. To avoid adding distress, work out which type of coper you are, and stick with it. Studies show that physicians who are caring and patient, and explain problems to their patients, get sued far less often than those who are cold, or curt, or respond to the problem as if it were too trivial for medical help. The relationship between a woman and her physician is very important. If there is antipathy on either side, it might be appropriate to seek a change of doctor.

At the Physician's Office

Some women take their health problems directly to their gynecologist. Others prefer to visit their primary care physician first. The most valuable work of a primary care physician — of all medical doctors — is *accurate diagnosis*. If the condition is rare and not easily diagnosed, a first rate physician will know the best medical specialists who need to be contacted. *Ask for a second opinion.* Huge advances in hormone therapy have reduced the likelihood of surgery as a first option. A second opinion helps to reassure the woman that she has received the best therapeutic advice for her condition, reproductive life stage, general state of health, and so on.

Not all physicians are first rate. Be wary of one who:

- Is always in a hurry, and cannot listen carefully.
- Does not explain the medication or other therapy clearly.
- Withholds facts on the risks or side-effects of therapy.
- Promotes the sensation of not being taken seriously.
- Believes that breast pain, PMS, or cramps are psychic pains.
- Prescribes only tranquilizers for the above conditions.
- Recommends getting pregnant to "cure" the above conditions.
- Considers rest is the only therapy for urinary infection.
- Suggests adoption before offering fertility information.
- Does not have a nurse in the room during an examination.
- Infers that there is shame attached to certain conditions.
- Makes any non-medical, personal judgment on behavior.

In the 4th century BC, Hippocrates, the father of medicine, advised physicians to conceal most issues from their patients. He also advised them to reveal nothing of the patient's present and future condition, because the prognosis could turn out to be incorrect. Physicians today usually take care to inform a woman of her condition, and the potential risks and outcome of therapy. Yet it is not always easy to understand information when it is presented in the office, and many physicians do not explain the issues clearly enough. Before an appointment, write down all the symptoms and the questions you want answered. Then go through the list and shorten it. Keep everything as clear and simple as possible.

- The pain is — where?
- It comes on — when?
- It lasts — how long?
- It is stabby, short, slow — which?
- It is severe, moderate, mild, just a nagging worry?
- It seems associated with — eating? sleep? exercise? periods?
- It is better — when?
- It is worse — when?
- It is not exactly pain, yet it needs to be investigated.

How To Avoid Your Physician

Try to make time for your own health needs. This is not always easy. Many women spend their years between 20 and 50 caring for the needs of their family. After age 50, almost as many find that they take up the caring reins once again to look after elderly parents or other kin in need.

The result is that women can neglect their health. They become powerhouses of strength and effective caring for others, and push their own health concerns into the background. Keep in mind the three known preventive measures against ill-health: diet, exercise, and sufficient sleep. In 1991, American women had a life expectancy of 78.6 years, way behind the 82.5 years for Japanese women. Diet may have a major impact on these figures.

The aims of this book are to help women care for their own reproductive health. For example, many minor infections which plague the genitals could be *avoided* with appropriate preventive measures. Various methods to keep the reproductive organs healthy and free of infection are listed in some detail. Other problems, including certain infections, respond to self-care, and so do not require a visit to the physician's office.

Infections and many surgical procedures are named by their site, with the following suffixes.

- itis — means an inflammation, as in cystitis, vaginitis.
- ectomy — means to cut out, as in hysterectomy, mastectomy.
- otomy — means to cut open, as in episiotomy.

The high incidence of *breast cancer* is a major concern for women. Cancer of the ovaries is often a fatal disease. As yet, nobody knows what causes cancers to develop in the first place, so methods to reduce the risk remain theories only. However, a number of population studies looking for clues to cancers point to a protective role for a diet rich in vegetables, particularly vegetables high in *beta carotene*, the pigmented nutrient which makes carrots orange. Other good sources of beta carotene include dark-green leafy vegetables such as kale, collard greens, spinach, watercress, mustard greens, broccoli, endive, beet greens, dandelion and turnip greens.

In 1990, some 250,000 women died of *coronary artery disease*, also known as atherosclerosis. A continuing study among 22,000 American physicians suggests that those taking a beta carotene supplement to test its anticancer potential suffered only half the expected number of cardiovascular problems, such as heart attacks. Another study found that the risk of developing angina (chest pains due to insufficient oxygen to the heart), was nearly three times higher among men with low levels of *vitamin E.* Yet another study found a link between low blood pressure and high levels of *vitamin C.*

America's most popular fruits and vegetables include apples, oranges, iceberg lettuce, and corn. These are not high in beta carotene. Fruits which are good sources include cantaloupes, apricots, mangos, and papayas. Squashes and sweet potatoes also provide beta carotene. Most of these foods are good sources of vitamin C as well, especially broccoli, cabbage, turnip greens, cantaloupe, citrus fruits and juices. Vitamin E is provided in wheat germ, whole-grain cereals and bread, dried beans, and green leafy vegetables.

Vitamins (and minerals) are best consumed in foods. Check your diet for foods rich in beta carotene, vitamin C, and vitamin E.

Mothers of the World

In 1900, life expectancy at birth in the U.S. was 47 years. In 1988, it was 75 years. (This dramatic reduction was, in part, due to the equally dramatic reduction in infant and maternal mortality.) The 1988 figures break down into 78 years for women, and 71 years for men. One study into the 1988 data found that, on average, men have a life expectancy of 60 years in good health. Women have a life expectancy of 63 years in good health. Estimates suggest that men lose the equivalent of 12 well years of life. Women lose the equivalent of 16 years of well life.

One theory for these findings suggests that women are more subject to chronic, but not life-threatening, diseases. Conditions such as allergies or arthritis can seriously reduce the quality of life, but are not fatal. Men are more susceptible to fatal diseases, such as heart attack. Another theory suggests that when men are ill, they get sicker because they take less good care of themselves than do women. These theories appear to ignore the fact that after menopause, a woman's risk of heart disease is the same as a man's, and that women are prey to specific illnesses, due to their function as "mothers of the universe."

In the past, a woman's sexual health depended upon how healthy she was as a child, which depended upon how healthy her mother was, which depended upon her grandmother, and so on, going backwards, on and on. Today, a woman's sexual health is like a tree-lined avenue, going forward, on and on, into the distance. Improved diet, exercise, health information, and a knowledge of self-care makes each daughter off-shoot stronger and healthier.

Advances in medical therapies, especially hormone therapy, reduce the risk of being felled by gynecological disease. Today's women are healthier and fitter than their grandmothers, and intend to stay that way.

"The health of the world depends upon the health of its mothers."

CHAPTER 1

The Genitals

The Modest Vulva

The word *vulva* means a covering. It refers to the genital area which is covered by pubic hair. The genitals are the external sex organs, those which can be seen. In men, these are the penis and testicles. In women, only the vulva can be seen. It forms two plump folds of tissue which meet to protect the inner organs of the genitals. These are the clitoris, and the openings of the vagina and urine tract.

The vulva is also known as the *pudendum*. It comes from Latin, and means "that which brings shame." The word pudendum is used to refer to the genitals of both women and men. Today, it is used only for the female genitals. Is this sexist? Do women's genitals "bring shame," and not those of men? Yet pudendum also means "that which demands privacy, modesty," and the female genitals do seem designed to be naturally modest. The external folds cover the clitoris and vagina, and so they remain private, hidden from view beneath the vulva. Male genitals have no such covering.

The Mountain of Love

The *mons veneris* comes from Venus, the goddess of love. It is the cushion of fatty tissue which covers the pubic bone in front. In some thin girls and women, the pubic bone under the mons veneris can be very prominent. When wearing a tight skirt, the bulge can look almost like the bulge of male genitals.

The mons veneris is covered with *pubic hair*. This hair forms a straight line across the lower abdomen in 75 percent of women. It makes up the "love triangle" of hair descending between the legs. In the other 25 percent of women, the hair marches in a neat line up to the naval. It can grow down the inner thighs. In fact, this is body, not pubic, hair. There is no health significance in having a straight hair line, or not.

The growth of pubic hair is one of the first signs of puberty. The hair is scant at first, then slowly grows bushy. Later, it thins out again after menopause. The color and thickness of pubic hair reflect the owner's head hair. Caucasian women have coarse, curly hair; it is fine and straighter in Asiatics. It used to be shaven for surgical procedures. This is rarely done nowadays.

At puberty, *apocrine* glands in the groin and armpit begin to function. These are special sweat glands which secrete fluids during sexual excitement. The fluid gives off a characteristic sea odor. A few women consider it offensive. Men, however, often find it highly erotic and stimulating.

In fact, the function of pubic hair is to act as a scent trap. The odor is caught in the hair, which slows down its evaporation. It lingers much longer than it would otherwise. Shaving pubic hair, or removing it by other means, destroys this function. The same is true for armpit hair. In fact, many women worldwide do not shave underarms. Their menfolk would be distressed if they did. It is mainly in industrialized countries that removing body hair has become the custom, and then only for women. Men do not shave their underarms, though they may begin soon.

All body sweat, when fresh, has a distinctly personal scent. Underarm sweat, when unfresh, quickly turns sour and offensive. Armpit hair traps this smell, and keeps it lingering on. This is why hair removal is considered hygienic. It is *not* the same as the scent from apocrine glands. Apocrine sweat is secreted when a woman is sexually aroused, whether she has underarm hair or not.

Hot Lips

The *outer lips* (labia majora) are two folds of skin with pubic hair on their surface. In never-pregnant women, the folds meet in the middle. In others, they can be slightly open, more relaxed. The skin can be dark, or pink. The outer lips are plump with fat tissue. These soft, squashy pillows act as cushions during the act of love. They protect the delicate inner structures, and keep the vulva moist. They react to temperature; the lips pucker and shrivel when cold, rather like the scrotum in men.

The *inner lips* (labia minora) are smaller and thinner, and enclosed by the outer lips. Usually, one lip is slightly larger than the other. In some cases, both lips can be large enough to protrude through the outer folds. There is no health significance in either kind, though there may be some erotic value in lips which protrude. Their color ranges from light pink to brownish black, and their texture can be smooth or wrinkled.

The inner lips join together to form the hood of the clitoris. Like the outer lips, they are rich in sebaceous glands, apocrine sweat glands, blood vessels, and nerve receptors. Both outer and inner lips contain tissue which swells up at sexual arousal.

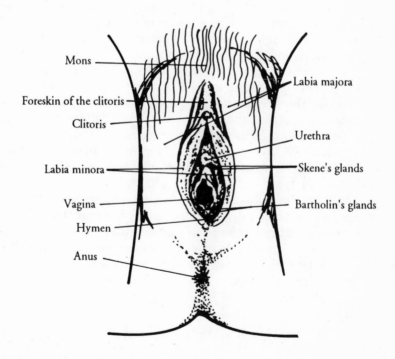

The Key to Love?

The word *clitoris* is from Greek for a "key," and a splendidly apt name it turns out to be. Because the clitoris is the key to unlock the door of sexual arousal. There are more nerve receptors here than any other part of the body. Combined with a plentiful blood supply, they enable the clitoris to become erect.

The clitoris is the equivalent of the male penis, though in miniature. The penis is made of a long root, a shaft, and the glans. The clitoris has two long roots, a shaft which can feel rubbery, and a glans about the size of a pea which looks like a pink fleshy knob.

Like the penis, the shaft is made of two spongy tubes which can erect. Running along the top of the shaft is the main vein, which drains blood away from the organ. When engorged with blood, the shaft and glans erect and almost double in size. The rounded glans is the most exquisitely sensitive part of the clitoris.

Again like the penis, the sensitive glans is protected from normal everyday friction by a *foreskin* (prepuce). This is a small hood which fits snugly over the glans. *Smegma*, a cheesy cream, is made under the foreskin. It keeps the glans comfortably oiled in times of high friction, i.e., love making. Smegma can cause itching or inflammation if it is not removed by daily washing.

In male circumcision, the foreskin is pulled back from the glans and cut off. This is a common, and usually unnecessary, surgical procedure in affluent industrialized societies. Female circumcision is not a Western custom. It can involve the removal not only of the foreskin but the inner labia too. With growing awareness of *circumcision as mutilation*, many parents now protect their babies boys from these procedures. In rare cases, minor female circumcision is required (see Chapter 14).

According to the well-known sexologists, Masters and Johnson, "The clitoris is a unique organ in the total of human anatomy. Its express purpose is to serve as a receptor and transformer of sensual stimuli. Thus, the human female has an organ system which is totally limited in physiologic function to initiating or elevating levels of sexual tension. No such organ exists within the anatomic structure of the human male."

Bartholin's Glands

Bartholin was a physician who first described the tiny glands at each side of the vagina, (like Montgomery of the breasts). These glands are two small sacs at either side of the vagina. They function like Cowper's glands in men, which make drops of moisture to lubricate the tip of the penis before penetration. Bartholin's glands produce drops of mucus which moisten the vulva prior to penetration. The drops ooze from the glands through tiny ducts.

Sometimes, one of these ducts becomes blocked for no known reason. (In rare cases, it is due to gonorrhea). The gland goes on producing fluid which cannot get out. The result is a swollen Bartholin's cyst. The cyst usually gives no symptoms, and does not require therapy. However, if it interferes with penetration or if it forms an abscess, it may then be necessary to have the cyst drained.

The G Spot?

The mysterious G spot has ardent fans and ardent scoffers. Most doctors keep quiet about the G spot because they do not know exactly where it is. Dr. Ethel Sloane, professor in the biological sciences at the University of Wisconsin has written the following in her excellent book *Biology of Women*:

"On either side of the midline, just posterior to the external urethral orifice, are the openings from the paraurethral or *Skene's glands*, the female homologue to the prostate glands in the male. They secrete a small amount of mucus and, along with the secretion of small mucus-secreting glands in the wall of the urethra, function to keep the opening moist and lubricated for the passage of urine.

"When Skene announced his discovery of the glands that bear his name in the nineteenth century, they had already been described by de Graaf 200 years earlier as the producers of *female semen*, the lubricating fluid discharged during sexual stimulation. That in some women these glands may produce a secretion emitted from the urethra during coitus was momentously rediscovered in 1982 by Alice Ladas, Beverly Whipple, and John Perry. The three reported in their instant best-selling book *The G Spot: & other Recent Discoveries about Human Sexuality* that the secretion, dubbed the female ejaculate, occured in response to stimulation of the Grafenberg spot, located on the anterior wall of the vagina....

"[Ernst Grafenberg's] 1950 description of a *zone of erogenous feeling located along the anterior vaginal wall* was largely ignored, but the publication of Ladas', Whipple's, and Perry's book revived the controversial inquiry about the phenomenon. The G spot aroused a flurry (some would say frenzy) of interest on TV talk shows and in newspapers and magazine articles, but whether it has profound implications for female sexual response remains to be demonstrated. Some women may be concerned about expelling what seems to be a small gush of urine during intercourse. They are probably experiencing a greater discharge from the paraurethral [Skene] and vulvovaginal [Bartholin] glands..."

In short, the female ejaculate is lubricating fluid from the sex glands around the urethra. The "G spot" is the place on the front vagina wall which, when pressed, stimulates these glands to secrete fluids.

The God of Marriage?

The *hymen* is called after Hymena, the Greek god of marriage. It is a membrane which partially covers the entrance to the vagina. It used to be known as the maidenhead, and was thought to guard the vagina. On her wedding night, a young woman had to bleed as proof that she had not lost her maidenhead. The stained sheet was thrown over the balcony for both families to witness. This was not only proof of the woman's virginity, but proof that her young husband could comport himself like a man.

Many were the tales of parents smuggling in ox blood for their daughter to smear on the wedding sheets. Young boys, ill-equipped for the marriagebed, also had blood smuggled in for the same reason. Yet the mythology of deflowering a virgin remains very strong. In large cities, there are still brothels which pander to such male tastes. The girl is usually somewhat older and more experienced than the man could possibly guess. Nevertheless, if this is what the punter pays for, that is what he thinks he gets.

An intact hymen can be perceived as a sweet and delicate structure in a young girl. It marks a definite rite of passage to lose her virginity at betrothal. The idea of deflowering that which has been intact obviously holds appeal. (Consider the delight of stepping on untrodden snow, or making new footprints on a cleanly-washed beach.) To borrow from the sonorous tones of *Star Trek* and in a somewhat humorous vein, "to boldly go where no man has gone before."

According to most textbooks, "The hymen is normally perforated during childhood when cycling, playing games, horseback riding, and so on, to allow the escape of menstrual flow at puberty."

This is not so. At birth, the hymenal ring surrounds the vagina opening but does not completely block it. Virgins can, and do, insert tampons with ease. The hymen is *not* an imperforate structure.

The deflowering of a virgin can be perceived as male fantasy. It is linked to that other male fantasy of longing for a larger penis. A virgin, having no intimate knowledge of other men, would be impressed by the male organ, whatever its size. She would be in no position to make comparisons. Nowadays, most men have more respect for women; indeed, many prefer not to be responsible for a girl's first sexual encounter.

Hymens vary. Some appear more intact than others. If there is resistance to penetration, the usual cause is lack of desire on the woman's part. However, if a hymen does appear unyielding when a first attempt is made to insert a tampon, this problem can be overcome. Dilate the skin gently a little each day with the fingers until it will yield comfortably to the tampon. A more intact hymen is not proof of virginity. Nor is a ruptured one proof of sexual intercourse. There are many other sexist notions about the hymen too numerous to list.

The Stubborn God

In rare cases, a baby girl is born with a hymen to fit male fantasy. The membrane stretches right across the vagina, completely closing it off. Now, any woman can work out what will happen when the girl's periods start. The menstrual flow will pool in the vagina. It will not be able to get out. Over the next months, the blood will back up to flood the uterus and oviducts. If not detected, it would pass out of the tubes and into the pelvic cavity, causing pain. The condition is usually detected early, and corrected by minor surgery; *hymenectomy* removes the membrane and *hymenotomy* opens it by cutting.

The Sheath

The name *vagina* comes from Latin for *sheath*. The associated name for the penis is *shaft*. Shaft and sheath; sword and scabbard. What a delightful fit! However, students of etymology might like to explain why, in slang terms, "to shaft someone" means to do that person a wrong.

The vagina is a moist passageway leading from the vulva to the cervix. It is 3 to 5 inches long (7.5 to 12.5 cm). The walls are normally collapsed upon themselves, but can widen to accommodate three fingers. During sexual arousal, the vagina can lengthen another 2 inches (5 cm), and stretch to 2 inches in diameter. At birth, it can dilate to a full 5 inches across to accommodate the passage of the baby.

Moist and stretchy, the vagina has been called "endlessly accommodating," and perhaps it is. For in spite of those tales of prodigious sized male organs, the vagina can take almost any penis with ease. In young girls, this is not always the case. A man who is over-endowed must pay special attention to foreplay to ensure that she is really aroused. Even then, he must proceed at her pace, not his.

A tall, well-built woman does not necessarily have a larger vagina than a petite woman. (Nor does a tall, well-built man have a larger penis than a shorter man.) Though the hands and feet can be related to general body size, the vagina and penis cannot. For some mysterious reason, there is no relationship between the size of genital organs and general body size.

In a never-pregnant woman, the vagina has many folds and the walls are firm. After the birthing process, the walls become smoother, though they retain their firmness, especially near the vagina entrance. This is not always the case for women who have born many children, and/or had an *episiotomy*, the cut used to ease the passage of childbirth.

Vagina Size

"I feel large," Mrs. Jones told her gynecologist. "Sort of baggy inside."

"When do you feel large?" he inquired. "When you wake up? At work? Exercise? When?"

"Not *then*." She grinned at his question.

The gynecologist pressed, "Precisely *when* do you feel large?"

"When we make love, of course," she stated the obvious.

"Ah!" he sounded thoughtful. "Tell me more about that."

Mrs. Jones sighed. "He's always been a bit, you know, small. My husband. We didn't mind before we had the kids. My muscles were strong. Now he's complaining. Says he feels lost inside me."

"*He* complains, does he?" the gynecologist stressed the word.

"Tell me, if your husband had a larger penis, would you still think that your vagina is too large?"

She smiled, "I see what you mean." Then added, "But over the years, I've stretched."

"Let's have a look at you," the gynecologist said.

After the examination, he explained his findings. "Repeated childbirth can stretch the vaginal walls. The muscles lose some degree of elasticity, the walls become smoother, and the vagina feels more relaxed. A nulliparous (childless) woman does not undergo this stretching, even if she leads a very active sex life. It is only the extreme duress of *repeated* childbirth which stretches the vaginal walls..."

"Five kids," she nodded.

"A baggy vagina is a fairly common complaint from the late thirties onwards. You have also a slight sagging at the vaginal entrance. That was probably left over from an episiotomy. You could try adopting new positions at coitus."

She interrupted, "We've done all that. Can you tighten me up inside? By surgery?"

"Yes, indeed. But I would not recommend the procedure at this stage. Surgery is always a risk, it leaves scar tissue."

"When?"

"Not until menopause. At that time, there could be minor sagging of the ligaments which support the uterus. Prolapse. Mild leakage problems. That sort of thing. We can tighten everything up together."

"But that's almost ten years away," she cried.

His thoughtful manner changed. He became almost bossy. "Mrs. Jones, in reproductive terms, your body has had a hard life. Now your children are in school, give *yourself* quality time. Each day. Every day. *Care* for your body. Do exercises to tighten up the pelvic muscles, Kegels they are called. Rest. Get your body in shape before menopause. Eat well. Exercise."

She was disappointed. She had fantasized he would promise her a virgin-sized vagina. "My husband — "

"If we could perform surgery to enlarge the penis, Mrs. Jones, would you want your husband to have such an operation?"

"Him?" she laughed at the notion. "He would *die* before he let a doctor touch his thing with a knife."

"I rest my case," the gynecologist replied.

* * *

Corrective plastic surgery is an option for women who wish to restore the size of the vagina. The procedure can be performed through the vagina walls, so there are no external scars. The loose tissue is pulled together and cut away, and the edges are sewn up. The surgery is done in hospital, usually with general anesthesia. Intercourse must be avoided for some while, depending upon the healing process.

The operation is invasive surgery, and requires considerable thought. It can be regarded as a more appropriate option when other problems appear at midlife, such as mild urine leakage due to prolapse. However, if an over-stretched vagina does cause a woman distress, the surgery can be done as a single procedure.

The Sweating Phenomenon

The vagina is kept naturally damp from its own fluids. This moisture is not sufficient for the act of love. The friction from penetration and thrusting demand that the vagina be really wet. Extra lubrication is provided from tiny blood vessels in the vagina walls. Early in sexual arousal, they become engorged with blood. The pressure from the engorgement forces drops of moisture out of the veins and through the vagina walls. The drops run together and coat the vagina with fluid. The sexologists, Masters and Johnson, thought that this looked like beads of sweat running down a hot forehead. Hence, the somewhat inelegant name: "the sweating phenomenon."

Extra lubrication is essential. Without it, the friction of a thrusting penis would soon become unbearable. Tiny lesions in the walls would occur, and the vagina would be at risk of *secondary infection;* other germs could get in. If the vagina feels dry, the sweating phenomenon has not occurred. If it has occurred, then some time has elapsed, and the woman no longer feels aroused. *Stop all movement the moment the vagina feels dry.* If wishing to continue, a break for more external loving should do the trick. A woman does not have an unerect penis to signal her lack of excitement. However, a dryish vagina is a clear sign to her partner that she is not sufficiently aroused.

The sweating phenomenon lasts into old age. At menopause, there may be less blood flow to the vagina, and so less fluid is passed through. A dryish vagina after menopause does not necessarily mean lack of desire. Just as a less-than-fully erect penis does not mean lack of excitement. These things just require a little more time and attention. For the vagina, some external lubrication, such as K-Y jelly, will do the trick.

Men and Vagina Size

Men tend to fantasize about the size of their penis. They long to fill the vagina to a stretching point, to reach deep inside their beloved and batter against the *cervix*. A few psychologists have lurid reasons for this. Yet it seems a reasonable enough and harmless myth, because the cervix can escape penile battering. At sexual arousal, the inner two-thirds of the vagina increase in length a further two inches. They widen to stretch to a full two inches in diameter. The uterus with its cervix is pulled right up and out of harm's way. This is known as "the ballooning effect."

At the same time, the outer one-third of the vagina swells up. This is due to *vaso-congestion*. Sexual arousal causes extra blood to enter and fill up the tissues. The result is a narrowing and tightening inside the entrance to the vagina. There is a clamping of tissue around the penis as it thrusts. This is known as "the gripping effect."

If the average erect penis is 6 1/4 inches long and 1 1/4 to 1 3/4 inches wide, the average aroused vagina will sheath it to mutual satisfaction. The myth of a tiny, tight vagina *during* the act of love is just that, a myth. The ballooning effect helps the vagina stretch to accommodate the penis in comfort. Only an "unaroused" vagina can offer resistance to deep penetration, (or one which is sore from repeated love making or infection). If the vagina does feel tiny and tight, then it is *not* ready for penetration. The woman lacks sufficient desire at that time.

The cervix projects into the upper part of the vagina, with a dip like a tiny trough running around it. This dip has front, back, and side parts called *fornices*. The back fornix is another mechanism to protect the cervix from battering. It takes the brunt of penile thrusting, and so prevents injury or jarring.

The walls of each fornix are thin, and the uterus, ovaries, and oviducts can be felt through them on a pelvic exam. They assist in fertility if, after making love, the woman remains lying on her back. The semen can then pool in the posterior fornix, and bathe the cervix. This allows more time for sperm to enter the *os*, the tiny opening of the cervix which leads to the uterus.

Tough Baby

The lining walls of the vagina are thick, being made up of 20 to 40 layers of cells. These overlap like the tiles on a roof. They are similar to skin cells (epithelial), but with no hair follicles, sweat or sebaceous glands. So there are no pores, no *external orifices*, through which germs can enter. The vagina has a robust, tough, resilient, protective lining.

Like all skin tissue, the bottom layer grows and pushes up the middle layer, which pushes up the top layer, which eventually dies and is sloughed off (shed). The female hormone *estrogen* stimulates this constant cell growth and replacement. Before puberty, the lining of the vagina is immature: pale, delicate, and very thin. (Sexual intercourse with a little girl damages the walls; it is physical as well as sexual abuse.) Some time after menopause, the lining can start to thin out again.

The vagina walls help support the bladder and rectum, and hold them in place. If they are stretched by repeated childbirth, or damaged in other ways, they lose some of their natural tension and strength. When this happens, there can be prolapse, a small portion of the bladder, rectum, or uterus dips down into the vagina. This problem can occur later in life. (see Chapter 5).

The vagina has its own carefully balanced ecology. It produces a constant supply of moisture from blood fluids in the walls. During the reproductive years, this fluid is acid-based. It contains mucus, sloughed-off dead cells, helpful bacteria, yeast, and other microbes. The acidity, the tough lining, and the bacteria all protect against infection. They are essential for vaginal health.

To Douche or Not?

To quote Dr. Ethel Sloane again, "Douching is a procedure of vaginal *irritation* in which fluid in a bag is permitted to run through a tube, entering the vagina under slight pressure and ballooning it out slightly. As the fluid runs out or is expelled through muscular action, the vaginal contents are washed out. Douching to prevent pregnancy after intercourse is totally *ineffective*, since it has been determined that sperm can be recovered from the uterus within seconds after being deposited in the vagina — and no woman can get the douche bag apparatus set up and going that fast."

So much for douching as a method of birth control. If sperm can be recovered from the uterus within seconds, so can the germs of sexual disease. What of douching as a cleansing and freshening routine? Does it really work? "Douching is seldom essential for normal health because the vagina is self-cleansing through the process of normal discharge... To douche more than every 4 or 5 days is *excessive*, however, and it will *destroy* the normal physiology of the vagina."

These are strong words from Dr. Sloane: "Excessive... Destroy the physiology of the normal vagina." The risk is that douching upsets the carefully balanced ecology of the vagina. Just as saliva helps to fight mouth infections, so vagina fluids help to fight internal infections. If there is a constant tide of water washing them out, this valuable mechanism of self-cleansing could become less effective.

However, with repeated love making, and/or repeated use of spermicides which feel sticky when they dissolve, the vagina can become uncomfortably damp. Some women only feel fresh when they have douched. Others douche if they believe the advertisements for commercial douche products, which imply that the natural sea odor of the vagina is somehow "unclean."

Studies show that at least 60 percent of women douche occasionally. The following are suggestions which can help:
- Use lukewarm water, never hot.
- Keep the bag low, no more than two feet above the hips.
- Wait till the fluid is flowing before inserting the nozzle.
- Consider having a douche while sitting on the toilet.
- Insert the nozzle, then hold the vulva lips tight.
- Never squeeze the bulb-type bag hard.
- Reduce douching to once a week at the maximum.
- If the vagina is clogged with semen, use condoms inbetween.
- Avoid douching if there is any chance of pregnancy.
- Avoid if blood spotting appears after douching.
- If pain and/or fever starts, see the doctor the same day.
- Avoid heavy douching if there is infection; it can force the germs up into the uterus and tubes.
- Douching can encourage an infection; it strips away the protective coating and kills normal, infection-fighting bacteria.
- One quart water to one tablespoon of vinegar or bicarbonate of soda works as well and costs less than commercial products.
- A vinegar douche helps restore the vagina's acidic PH.

CHAPTER 2

Care of the Genitals

Underwear

Choice of underwear is a personal issue. Smart, silky lace; fluffy, ribboned tucks; tiny, snappy thongs — they all look charming. Underwear can be so pretty that it is hard to remember these garments play an important role in hygiene. Factors such as fiber content, fit, and absorbency should be taken into account.

Germs breed best in an environment which is warm, moist, and low in oxygen. The crotch through to the buttocks provides these three factors. Synthetic fibers such as nylon mix in underwear and pantyhose retain heat and moisture. The material clings to the skin, cutting off air. Underwear should be loose in the crotch and not too tight around the thighs and buttocks. Ideally, French knickers with their soft draped folds are the most appropriate. Cotton is porous; it absorbs moisture and allows air to circulate. Try to keep the genital environment as cool and dry as possible.

Self-Care

- First, wash the hands and fingernails thoroughly.
- If using a body cloth, it should be fresh from the laundry.
- Otherwise, avoid wash cloths; they tend to harbor germs.
- Work up a rich lather with warm water and plenty of soap.
- The water must be hot enough to soften and melt vulva grease.

- Plain soap breaks down the oils; it emulsifies them.
- Avoid scented soaps which can cause contact dermatitis.
- Begin by washing the outer skin, back to the anal area.
- Wash hands again before opening and cleansing the lips.
- Slide the clitoris hood back; gently cleanse all crevices.
- Rinse really well. Avoid leaving any soap on the genitals.

Good general health helps maintain the health of the genitals. Being run down, lacking sleep, or otherwise over-stressed lowers the immune response to disease. This drop in resistance is a gradual event; it does not happen overnight. Many women are unaware that they are exhausted until an illness finally sends them to bed. Often, they cannot remain there long; there are too many calls on their time. It is not always easy to care for the self. Try to put genital health high on the list of priorities.

A Tart's Wash

There are occasions in the day when a busy woman has no time for a bath or shower. The French call the quick cleansing routine which can be used when in a hurry "a tart's wash." It involves freshening those parts which produce smegma and apocrine sweat: the armpits and groin. The reason for this crude name is because the prostitute wants to remove the pungent odor of sex before her next "trick."

Tiny glands around the *anus* (bowel opening) secrete a cheesey, waxy cream. This keeps the anal area softened and comfortably damp. The cheesey odor can become trapped between the cheeks of the buttocks. It is more noticeable in both women and men after a night's sleep, or after a hectic day with no time to shower.

If the couple are unaware of the source of this smell, the cheesey waft can be mistaken for vaginal odor. Yet it occurs in both genders. When there is time only for a quick cleansing routine, make sure a tart's wash includes washing the anal area.

Vaginal odor can be extremely exciting; a deep-sea aroma. If it becomes stale, it can be a sexual turn-off. One effective way to clean the genitals is by a bath or a bidet. Many women prefer to douche, though physicians do not generally recommended this.

Hygiene

From puberty onwards, the vulva and vagina are bombarded with female hormones. These trigger different levels of different fluids and secretions during each month. A few women are plagued by soreness, itching, and discharge. This is hardly surprising, when the following events are taken into account:

- Sebum and sweat are secreted from the glands in the vulva.
- Fluids from the vagina walls keep it clean and damp.
- The "sweating phenomenon" occurs at sexual arousal.
- Copious mucus flows from the cervix at mid-cycle.
- The monthly flow occurs from puberty to midlife.
- Semen is deposited in the vagina during male orgasm.
- Spermicides dissolve and clog up the vagina.
- On top of which, consider the position of the vulva between urine outlet and fecal waste from the bowel.

The mixture of secretions from the sebaceous and sweat glands is *smegma*. Together with the vagina fluids, it forms a slippery coating, rather like the proofing of a mackintosh, to protect the genitals. Menstrual blood, urine, feces, semen, and bacteria slide off the skin's surface rather than penetrate it. If smegma collects between the foreskin and glans, *and* an infection forms, scar tissue can cause clitoral adhesions.

A penis is a large obtrusive organ. So are the testicles. Both are seen by men at regular intervals during the day. The opposite occurs for women. Unless they do personal checks, the vulva stays modestly hidden beneath its covering of hair. Germs can hide in the labia folds, under the clitoris hood, inside the vagina, or on the cervix itself. Some produce no symptoms, while others cause infections which are *asymptomatic*. In either case, the woman in unaware that she has a disease. These factors are the reasons why the female genitals are sometimes known as "silent reservoirs" of disease.

The Proper Study of Womankind

Keep a regular date for genital self-examination (GSE). This should be before a bath or shower. Cleansing the area first can cause redness or other reactions which confuse the findings. Wash *the hands thoroughly.* Spread the pubic hair apart with the fingers. Use a mirror, if desired. Carefully examine the mons and both sides of the outer lips. Look for red patches or swellings. Feel for areas of unusual tenderness. Check for bumps, spots, cysts, sores, or blisters. In the early stages of infection, they can be nearly impossible to detect with the unaided eye. So *feel* for any bumpy growth, or other suspect patch. Continue the search right back to the anus. *Wash the hands before continuing.*

Become familiar with the size and site of freckles or moles on the skin. Blackheads, whiteheads, or infected hair follicles can occur here just as anywhere else on the body. They are self-healing, and soon clear with appropriate genital hygiene. If desired, they can be popped out with clean fingers, and a *very mild* astringent dabbed on.

A *sebaceous cyst* is due to a blocked pore in the sebaceous glands. The sebum is trapped, and hardens into a yellow, cheesey lump. The cyst grows to the size of a pea. If rubbed by the edge of underwear, it hurts. It tends to be self-healing; within a few days, the blocked sebum drains and the cyst disappears. A small one can be popped out, if desired. If the cyst grows large and/or becomes infected, avoid self-therapy. An infected cyst requires surgical excision. This takes only a few moments in the physician's office.

Spread the outer lips and examine the hood of the clitoris. Gently ease it up to have a closer look. Examine both sides of the inner lips, the urine opening, and vagina. Keep looking for the same things: swellings, blisters, sore patches, bumps. Be familiar with vagina fluids. Any change in them is an important clue. A few women check the taste. This is not advisable if there is reason to suspect an infection. It has been known for yeast to spread to the mouth from absentmindedly licking the fingers. Take care not to spread an infection which may be present. *Auto-inoculation* can occur during GSE.

Sebaceous cysts also develop on the *inside* skin of the labia, and around the urine and vagina openings. *Avoid self-diagnosis of any pimples, spots, cysts, or strange bumps which develop here*. Though they are usually harmless, visit the physician promptly to ensure that all is well.

Yeast Overgrowth

Yeast is a fungus which grows in harmless amounts in the vagina. If something happens to disrupt the ecology, the yeast spores go crazy. They multiply and spread at a very fast rate, because the other organisms which held them in check have been destroyed. The symptoms include a thick, whitish discharge, mild to severe itching, soreness and redness around the labia which can spread to the upper thighs. If the yeast spores spread to the anus area, the symptoms can flare up there.

The itching is more intense at night. It can become maddening, and interfere with sleep. Some women wake to find that they have scratched the area raw. Others experience an increase in sexual desire, but this tends to be itch-induced rather than amorous. The growth irritates the clitoris, stimulating it to a state of heightened tension. Another side effect can be a tendency towards urine leakage. If already present, an outbreak of yeast makes the condition worse.

Yeast flourishes best under conditions of moisture, heat, and lack of oxygen. The vulva is a classic example of these. Choose cotton underwear, which is porous and allows air to circulate. If appropriate, avoid pantyhose, or wear those with cotton insets. Change out of restrictive clothing as soon as possible; leotards and bathing suits should not be worn for a prolonged stretch of time. The aim is to keep the area well-ventilated and cool.

Home Remedies include douching at the very first hint of an itch. A mild vinegar solution can be made of one quart of water to one to three tablespoons of vinegar, or use a yogurt solution of a thin mixture of plain yogurt and water. Lactinex tablets are another route; insert one or two daily in the vagina. Also garlic suppositories; peel one whole clove, wrap it in gauze, insert this in the vagina, and leave for twelve hours.

Over the Counter preparations contain fungicides: nystatin in Mycostatin or Nilstat; miconazole in Monistat; clotrimazole in Gyne-Lotrimin. Follow the instructions carefully. *Finish the entire course!* An antifungal cream can be spread over the mons and hair around the anus. It should *not* be used *near* the vagina. It can be applied to the penis as an extra precaution.

Not all physicians are comfortable when women self-diagnose and self-treat. They strongly advise a clinical exam to rule out more serious conditions, which have the same symptoms. Yeast is a local irritation, with burning and itching, but not severe pain. If there is severe pain or pain in the abdomen, it could be herpes, chlamydia, or some other serious problem with overlapping symptoms. Keep in mind that these diseases can be present *at the same time*.

Yeast is regarded as an infection. Yet, in most cases, nothing is "caught" from an external source. Yeast can overgrow under the influence of female hormones. Outbreaks are common if taking the Pill, and during pregnancy, because the balance of hormones has changed. Some women are more vulnerable to yeast immediately after a period. Certain antibiotics upset the ecology, and a flareup can occur. Yeast also flourishes in high blood sugar. Visit the physician to rule out diabetes, or a prediabetic condition. The clinical names for yeast are *Monilia* and *Candida albicans*.

Yeast can occur after anal sex if waste products from the bowel are transferred to the vagina. This happens with lax hygiene; the penis and hands must be thoroughly washed after anal sex. It is rare to transmit yeast, though the penis can be affected at the glans. The symptoms show as a red skin irritation, which is tender to the touch. Penile yeast is cleared with oral fungicide drugs and/or topical creams. Use condoms to be on the safe side for the next few months.

Infections

The ecology of the vagina can be easily upset. Harmless fungus or bacteria turn harmful, and multiply at a rapid rate. Though the vagina is robust and self-cleansing, the odds are fairly high that an infection will occur at some time in life. The agents for disease include bacteria, viruses, protozoans, insects, even yeast. The point of entry and/or exit is the penis, vagina, mouth, anus, and more rarely, a sore on the skin. Each woman has unique strengths and unique weaknesses in her defense mechanisms. This is why some women who are exposed to infectious agents avoid disease, while others succumb every time.

The first line of defense against infection is an intact skin. If the germs are virulent, or in high concentration, they can break through this defense. They set up an inflammation, and the immune system becomes activated to destroy the invading germs. If a woman is run down, overworked, or otherwise stressed, her immune response can be lowered. When these defenses fail, the disease begins to spread further into the system.

The first symptoms of infection are soreness and itching. With sexual disease, the vulva and vagina fluids, and the cervical mucus, can quickly become infected. Unlike other infections, STDs do not clear up without professional help. Visit the clinic or physician at the first sign that something is amiss.

Take care with "tough" sex. It carries a risk of breaking open the skin's defense at the vulva. It can cause tiny lesions in the vagina walls, making them less robust and more vulnerable to disease. Researchers have recently discovered that certain cells in the cervix are particularly vulnerable to the human papilloma virus which causes genital warts. If the virus lands on a healthy cell, it remains there harmlessly. If the cell has suffered an injury, like the tiny cuts and abrasions found on cervical cells after making love, the virus can invade. The human papilloma virus has emerged as the primary suspect in nearly all cases of cancer of the cervix. It is also known as condyloma, and genital warts. Appropriate care of the genitals involves making certain that no object can enter the vagina unless it is really clean.

Male Sexual Hygiene

Some prostitutes ask a client to wash before sex. (Nowadays, the brighter ones insist that he wears a condom, too.) Yet many women in a love relationship would not dream of asking their beloved to wash his genitals first, *even when they are unfresh*. It might spoil the moment. It might kill the romance.

The male organ produces smegma from tiny glands on the skin's surface. The penis has a rim of fleshy skin at the *corona*, where the glans and shaft meet. It has a *frenulum*, a band of stringlike tissue under the glans, which leads up to the corona. Smegma slides into the folds of the frenulum, and slips into the creases of the corona. Germs can be present in these places, and breed on smegma if it is not removed daily. A partner should take equal care over hygiene.

The uncircumcised penis has a large foreskin which completely covers the glans. It rolls back a short way at urination. It retracts right back to the corona at erection. Men with an intact penis need to pay special attention to hygiene. The foreskin must be pulled right back for washing away the smegma which collects underneath.

Some men are more conscientious over changing the oil in their auto than in removing the oily smegma from their penis. This is because, as boys, they are rarely taught personal hygiene in any intimate detail. "Keep yourself clean, boy!" is about the sum of information they receive. Other men pay attention to genital hygiene *after* making love, not *before*. They are then scrupulous in removing the pungent odor of sex from their skin. This strange order of priority is usually due to lack of information, not lack of attention. If appropriate, give a partner the hygiene facts he needs.

Cancer of the cervix is far more common in the partners of uncircumcised men. This suggests that there is some agent *on* penile skin which is infectious (the germs of other sexual diseases breed *inside* the penis). It is now known that condyloma, the human papilloma virus, which attacks the cervix and can cause cancer is found on penile skin. Often, the infection cannot be seen by the unaided eye. It may cause no symptoms; the man is an asymptomatic carrier of disease. How much greater is the risk if there is lax hygiene? A particular tragedy of this cancer is that many young girls are infected.

Cancer of the cervix is now considered a sexual disease. Women need to be very aware of this, and very particular about genital hygiene in their man. Herpes and syphilis are also transmitted on the skin of the penis. Most other sexual diseases breed in the urinary tract and are passed in the male ejaculate. Where there is risk of infection from a male partner, the appropriate genital care is avoidance of any contact with partner skin or semen (see Chapter 15).

The Hidden Epidemic

Sexual infection used to be called *venereal disease*, VD. The name came from Venus, the Goddess of Love. Attitudes have changed, in part due to the steep rise in these infections, and they are now called *sexually transmitted diseases*. STD is used for short. Physicians who specialize in STDs are *venereologists*.

STDs are the second most common infection; the cold is first. Gonorrhea, chlamydia, condyloma, and herpes top the list. In 1988, one U.S. report estimated that there were 38,000 new STD infections each day! It is not possible to get precise data because many cases go unreported. A more recent estimate put it at 10 million Americans contracting an STD every year. The media concentrate on AIDS, and our community forgets that there is a raging epidemic of all other sexual diseases.

When AIDS was first diagnosed in the early 1980s, certain individuals considered it to be the wrath of God. The disease was regarded as an appropriate punishment, not only for male homosexuals, but for heterosexuals who did not lead monogamous lives. This wishful thinking would have wiped out most of the adult population, regardless of sexual preference. Monogamy in the strict sense means only one sexual partner in life. Data show that this is no longer the norm.

When Magic Johnson contracted the HIV virus, the telephone lines to STD clinics were jammed with calls from people wanting to know what special things you did to have "heterosexual sex!" It seems a proportion of the population do not understand that heterosexual sex is simply two people of the opposite gender.

Health professionals hoped that the fear of AIDS would encourage all sexually active people to choose mutual *monogamy*. Data from STD clinics show that many male homosexuals have done just this. However, the number of heterosexuals attending STD clinics has not changed since the last decade. In spite of the fear of AIDS, other STDs remain at epidemic levels. It is estimated that most adults will have a sexual infection (other than AIDS), at some point in their lives.

Silent Reservoirs

When a man has an STD, he knows he is infected. He can *see* the drip of pus on his penis from chlamydia or gonorrhea. He can *feel* the stinging pain they cause when he urinates. Not only are the male genitals prominent, but most men develop symptoms of disease very soon after contact. One survey estimates that only 5 to 15 percent of men with STD are *asymptomatic*; they have no symptoms.

The opposite holds true for women. Between 50 and 80 percent of those with chlamydia or gonorrhea are asymptomatic in the early stages of infection. *They have no symptoms of disease*. The data are worse for syphilis: 90 percent of women are asymptomatic if the sore is in the vagina or on the cervix. By the time they learn that something is amiss, these diseases may have wreaked havoc within their reproductive organs.

Women are far more vulnerable to the effects of STDs than men because they are more often asymptomatic. This leads to the other unfortunate problem for women; they become the main carriers of disease. It is women who are the silent reservoirs of STD.

In every community, there is a pool of sexual infection. If therapy is sought at the first signs of disease, most STDs can be speedily cured. Men have early and obvious symptoms. They have the chance to reduce the pool of infection in each community. They should:

- Stop sexual contact at once.
- Seek prompt medical help.
- Inform their partners.

Women have no such choices. They need a health check at each new sexual encounter to find out if they have been infected.

Strangers in the Night

Prostitutes and those who travel overseas for war, business, or pleasure are often blamed for the spread of STD. Yet the facts seem otherwise. There is now growing evidence that these groups, though at higher risk, are not the main source of infection in a community. It is young people between the ages of 15 and 30 who are the top transmitters of sexual disease.

"Casual sex" is the term for sexual activity with a partner who may be a stranger, or one who is hardly known. A young woman is at high risk of STD if a new boyfriend does not use a condom. Because of the silent reservoir syndrome, he is at an even greater risk. Parents can inform their teens of these bitter facts. However, to focus on only one group is to ignore the fact that STDs are *multi-linked* throughout a community.

Familiarity Breeds Contempt

Familiarity also breeds STD. Antibiotics work so well at curing STD that some young people develop a careless attitude. They regard sexual disease as little more bothersome than catching a cold. This is particularly so with a type of young man who boasts how often he has had the "clap" or "drip," and been cured. He shares these boasts with his male friends, not with the girl who is to be his next conquest. Nor does he bother to wear a condom; what is the point when an STD can be so quickly cured?

These are not tales simply to frighten girls into being more selective. Such stories rarely work, and can be counter-productive. It is ironic that the efficiency of antibiotics, which have saved untold millions of lives, have given rise to contempt for STD. Educate teen boys and girls in one simple fact: *Antibiotics cannot kill viruses.* They are powerless against condyloma and AIDS, both of which are linked to fatal cancers. Other STD viruses can cause PID, infertility, birth defects, joint disease, and chronic, progressive health problems.

Advise young people against self-medication with antibiotics. They may not bother to complete the course, or they may take the drugs in doses which are too low to be effective. The symptoms of STD vanish, but they remain infectious. With repeated use, bacteria have time to develop resistance, and the drugs lose their power. In 1988, the U.S. Surgeon General reported a 75% increase from 1987 in penicillin-resistant gonorrhea and syphilis. This was one year alone in which the killer AIDS was rampant!

All Is *Not* Fair in Love and War!

This is one of the harsh biological facts of life. A woman is far more vulnerable to sexual disease than a man. Due to her anatomy, she is less likely to be aware that she has an infection. She is more likely to have a wider internal spread of disease, and for the problem to persist. This can lead to serious and painful infections of the pelvic area called *PID*. Seventeen percent of women known to have gonorrhea develop PID. Of these, 15 to 40 percent become sterile after just one episode.

Most infections are not easily transmitted *between* women. Lesbian women have a much lower risk of contracting STD, and cannot be equated with gay men concerning the occurrence of STD. Lesbians, at least those who are not bisexual in preference, have a virtual absence of gonorrhea and syphilis. On average, they also have fewer infections than heterosexual women.

In issues of sexual health, women suffer far more than men. Though it may sound extremely old-fashioned, advocate abstinence or monogamy to a teenage daughter. This advice will not ruin her life, as pregnancy and sexual disease can. Besides, she will pay no attention if she does not wish to. Studies show that girls can begin sexual activity before they really want to, due to pressure from their peers. If a daughter wishes to put off early activity, parental words do help.

Contraception as Protection

One reason for the STD epidemic is thought to be a drop in the use of barrier methods of contraception: the diaphragm, cap, condom, and spermicides. Yeast, trichomonas, chlamydia, herpes, and gonorrhea are *less common* in women who use barrier methods than in women who use the Pill or IUD. There is growing evidence that barrier methods protect against cervical cancer and its earlier stage, dysplasia. One long-term study shows a marked drop in cervical cancer and precancerous dysplasia among diaphragm users compared to users of the Pill or IUD. (Diaphragm users show a somewhat higher rate of urinary tract infections.) Other studies suggest that spermicides reduce the risk of gonorrhea. The rate was only one eighth to one fourth as high among diaphragm users as in women who use other contraceptive methods.

Many women are very happy with the Pill. They do not want to return to the diaphragm with its messy spermicides. They dislike the condom. If they are in a mutually monogamous relationship, there is no problem. However, if there is a change of partner, or some reason to suspect infection, it is appropriate to keep a spare diaphragm handy, and insist on condom use as well.

Condoms as Protection

Health professionals promote the use of condoms as *safer sex*. In an epidemic of AIDS and sexual disease, this is of enormous benefit. Condoms offer women a great deal of protection. They avoid both skin contact and the transmission of semen. However, not all condoms are perfect. If more than 4 out of 100 are found defective, the FDA rejects the entire batch. In the year ending April 1988, 41 out of 204 batches of latex condoms failed to meet government-approved standards, just over 20 percent. Just under a third of these were made in the U.S.

Passion in action has a habit of not conforming to laboratory procedures. How to gain accurate data on the failure rate of condoms which were put on improperly under passion's spell is a problem. And even when put on properly, a condom can break. It may not be worn *before* sexual contact; it may not be worn right through until all sexual activity ceases. And whether it is worn properly or not, a defective condom is worse than useless.

This is not to deny condoms their value as protection against disease. Yet women must not be lulled into a false sense of security. It is important to know what health workers in this field know: "Condoms do not provide *total* protection against sexual disease, AIDS, unintended pregnancy, or anything else."

Symptoms of Disease

The symptoms of STDs vary. Visit the physician or clinic if any of the following appear:

- Abnormal discharge, or any unusual fluid from the vagina.
- Pain, burning, frequency, urgency at urination.
- Itching anywhere on the vulva or around the anal area.
- Vulva sores, blisters, or bumps, whether painful or not.
- Enlarged lymph glands in the groin area.
- Pain or bleeding during, or after, intercourse.

None of the above necessarily signify STD. They are warning signs that something is amiss. If there is a recent change of partner, or if there is high risk behavior, the problem could be an infection. The sooner an STD is diagnosed, the easier it is to treat, and the sooner it is cured.

Cancers

Cancers of the vulva and vagina are rare and easy to detect. This makes them highly curable in the earliest stages. Yet women die from them every year. Perhaps this is because these cancers do not usually appear until the late 60s or early 70s. At these ages, women and/or their physicians sometimes avoid Pap smears and pelvic exams, regarding them as unnecessary and embarrassing, particularly if the woman is no longer sexually active.

Only 5 women in a million develop cancer of the vagina. Like cancer of the vulva, they are well past menopause. The exception to this are young women whose mothers were given the hormone drug diethylstilbestrol (DES) during pregnancy to prevent miscarriage. DES is linked to unusual tissue formation in the vagina and cervix. A rare type of vaginal and cervical cancer has been found in a small number of DES-exposed daughters. The peak incidence seems to be around age 19, with about 1 out of every 1,000 women exposed now being affected. This shocking finding has made many women wary of taking hormones for any reason whatsoever.

As cancer of the cervix is now considered a sexual disease, the most effective care of the vagina is care over what is put into it.

Summary

- Try to keep the genitals as cool and dry as possible.
- Wear cotton pants which are not tight around the groin.
- Nylon-mix underwear and pantyhose retain moisture and heat.
- Avoid sharing towels or washcloths.
- Avoid "feminine" soaps, sprays, and so on.
- Always wipe the anus from front to back.
- Wash before making love. Check that a partner does the same.
- Wash afterwards. Urinate as well.
- Douching washes away normal germ-fighting secretions.
- Stop making love as soon as the vagina feels dry.
- If lubrication is needed, use a water-soluble jelly.
- Spermicides can be used; they may slow the growth of STD.
- Yeast is often due to non-STD factors. Check these first.
- Take care with "tough sex." It can result in lesions.
- Avoid putting objects in the vagina which are not clean.
- Keep in mind that STDs are persistent and likely to spread.
- Unprotected sex can bring a risk of cancer of the cervix.
- If at any risk, insist on a partner using a condom.
- Barrier methods offer some protection against STD.
- Keep in mind that women can be asymptomatic for disease.
- Have a checkup to make sure that all is well.

CHAPTER 3

The Monthly Cycle

Facts About Periods

- The average menstrual flow lasts 3 to 6 days.
- Some women flow up to 8 days; others stop after 2 days.
- Periods can occur like clockwork, from puberty onwards.
- Periods can be infrequent, or very irregular.
- Most cycles are between 25 and 30 days.
- The "monthly" 28 days occurs only 16 percent of the time.
- Anywhere from 21 to 35 days is within the normal range.
- On the extreme edges are cycles every 17 or 45 days.
- Blood loss can be between 50 and 175 cc per period.
- This is between 3 to 9 tablespoons, or 2 to 6 fluid ounces.
- The average blood loss is less than 4 fluid ounces.
- There is no such phenomenon as an "average" period.
- Hemorrhage is bleeding; any loss of blood.
- Menorrhagia is abnormally heavy bleeding during a period.
- Amenorrhea is having no periods, a complete absence.
- Primary amenorrhea is having no periods by age 18.
- Secondary amenorrhea is periods stopping after at least one.
- Polymenorrhea occurs when cycles are shorter than 21 days.
- Oligamenorrhea occurs when cycles are longer than 40 days.
- Dysmenorrhea is a generic term for any dysfunction concerned with periods. More specifically, it refers to period pain.
- Premenstrual syndrome, PMS, is a group of pre-period

problems, including an increase in tension, irritability and lethargy.

About Sex Hormones

The menstrual cycle is controlled by female hormones, which are powerful chemicals made in the *endocrine* glands. Hormones travel in the bloodstream to various parts of the body, where they act as triggers for certain functions. A physician who specializes in hormones and diseases of the endocrine glands is an *endocrinologist*. The nervous and endocrine system interact. The study of this interaction is *neuroendocrinology*.

The female hormone *estrogen* was discovered in the 1920s. Not all of its very complex functions are yet completely understood. The name comes from Greek and Latin. *Estrus* refers to the monthly period. *Gen* means born or generated. *Menses* is the actual flow. *Menarche* is a girl's first period. In America, the average age is 12.3 years.

Estrogen is a generic term for female hormones like estradiol, estrone and estriol. At puberty, estrogen feminizes the body of a girl: breasts, wider hips, fat layer under the skin, and so on (see Chapter 13). Estrogen is produced mainly in the ovaries, with a huge surge on days 12 to 14 of the monthly cycle for the release of an egg at *ovulation*. There is another surge on days 22 to 24.

Estrogen is also produced in the adrenal glands, fat cells, and the placenta at pregnancy. Women (and men) with a high-fat diet tend to have more estrogen in the blood and less in the urine. Too much estrogen can bring pre-cancer changes in the breast, cervix, uterus, and ovaries; a very fat woman would do well to diet. A very fat man who produces excess estrogen can develop gynecomastia (male breasts). Estrogen protects women from early heart disease. It raises the good kind of cholesterol, HDL, and lowers the bad kind, LDL. Avoid over-slimming; a certain amount of fats cells are necessary to support estrogen activity.

Progesterone works with estrogen to ripen the egg. It prepares the uterus lining for pregnancy. If the egg is not fertilized, progesterone output drops and the uterine lining sheds. This is *menstruation*. Progesterone is produced in the ovaries, with only one surge on days 22 to 24 of the monthly cycle.

Testosterone is the hormone of the *libido*. This is the medical term for the sex drive in both men and women. Women produce testosterone in the ovaries and the adrenal glands; men mainly produce it in the testicles and less in the adrenals. When the ovaries slow down at menopause, testosterone continues to be produced in the adrenals (and a little in the ovaries). This is why the female sex drive does not shut off at midlife.

Women are beautiful, homely, or plain. They are tall, medium, or short. Their sex drives are as individual as their looks or their height. Some female libidos are powerful, others are mild. In the strength of the sex drive, women are more like men than they are like one another. As far as the libido goes, the genders are much the same.

Male hormones are called *androgens* because they support and maintain the growth of male tissues, not because they are made by men. Estrogen supports and maintains the growth of the softer, plumper, moister, female-specific tissues. Men also make estrogen in their testicles. Obviously, they need greater amounts of the male hormones to sustain the masculine characteristics. The typical range of testosterone circulating in the blood (ng/dl) is:

- Men 385-1000
- Women 20-80
- Children 20-80
- Pubertal boys 120-600

Spots which appear prior to a period are due to the drop in female hormones which allows the male hormones to have a greater effect. Testosterone stimulates the sebaceous glands and is linked to acne in both genders. If acne is troublesome or persists, visit the physician. Various medications, including the antibiotic tetracycline, can clear acne. Women using the Pill find that their spots clear up.

Sex Hormones at Puberty

The signal to start puberty comes from the *hypothalamus* in the brain. It comes when the hypothalamus reaches a certain degree of maturity. In girls, this level of maturity is weight-related. On average, a plumper girl will start puberty earlier than her slimmer but same-age sister.

The signal acts on the *pituitary* gland, also in the brain. Once it receives this signal, the pituitary releases the sex hormones *FSH*

and *LH*. These control sexual development. FSH is a follicle-stimu-
lating hormone, and LH is a luteinizing hormone. Because the
ovaries and testes are *gonads* (producers of seed), the hormones
which stimulate them, FSH and LH, are called *gonadotrophins*.

The pituitary releases gonadotrophins into the blood stream.
FSH stimulates the ovaries to produce estrogen. FSH and LH work
together to stimulate the release of the egg. LH "springs" the egg at
ovulation, and stimulates the empty follicle to produce progesterone. If there are disorders of the hypothalamus *or* the pituitary, this
complex chain to trigger sexual development cannot begin. The girl
cannot become *feminized*. Her body grows taller but remains that of
a large overgrown child.

It takes at least a year for the levels of FSH and LH to build up.
Then, it is all systems go; puberty begins in earnest. Breasts blos-
som, hips widen, the genitals enlarge, and so on. Periods begin.
Feminization usually occurs between ages 10 and 13.

Quality Control

It is important that control is kept over sexual development. If
the ovaries produce too much or too little estrogen, it would have
a disastrous effect upon feminization. So FSH (and LH) are produced under negative feed-back controls. Estrogen production
goes rather like this:

- Estrogen rises to its correct level in the blood stream...
- This fact is fed back to the hypothalamus...
- Which stops stimulating the pituitary to make FSH...
- Which stops the ovaries producing more estrogen...
- When the level of estrogen in the blood drops...
- This fact is fed back to the hypothalamus...
- Which re-stimulates the pituitary to produce FSH...
- Which re-stimulates the ovaries to make estrogen...
- Which causes the estrogen blood level to rise again...
- And so on, round and round, from puberty until menopause.

If only it were that simple! A baseline of estrogen and progesterone is produced monthly. FSH stimulates the rising estrogen. This
peaks by day 12, and stimulates the pituitary to release a huge and
sudden surge of LH, which causes *ovulation*; an egg is sprung from
the ovary. At the same time as LH goes up, day 14, FSH and
testosterone levels go up. All the sex hormones surge at mid-cycle.

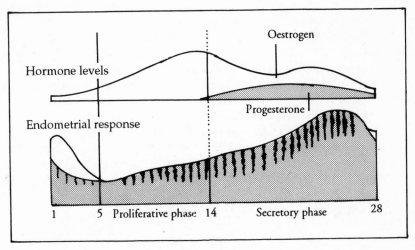

THE MENSTRUAL CYCLE

The slight rise in testosterone gives a boost to the libido. Studies suggest that women are more likely to initiate love making at mid cycle (when most fertile) than at other times. Some women report that they feel sexy during a period. Even those with cramps can experience an increase in desire once the pain slackens off.

Estrogen and progesterone have little effect on the sex drive. Instead, they affect all female-specific tissue, keeping it moist and plumped up. They stimulate the breasts to swell, cervical mucus to increase, the uterus lining to thicken, and so on. This is why therapy for many female problems is to increase or reduce female (or male) hormone production. Hormone drug therapy can be directed at controling gonadotrophin output, and/or estrogen and progesterone production.

The Two Cycles

Think of the reproductive system as two cycles. The first occurs in the *ovary*; an egg is matured and released at ovulation. The second is in the *uterus*. The lining, which is called the *endometrium*, builds up for pregnancy each month, and breaks away if none occurs. Estrogen controls the egg cycle. Both progesterone and estrogen control the menstrual cycle. Each cycle depends upon the other for smooth and efficient function.

In the first half of the cycle, as the endometrium is building up, the lining is called *proliferative*. It is hard, thick, and spreading without any particular direction. From day 14, (second half of cycle), progesterone turns that hardness into a soft, lush lining. It is now called *secretory*; it stops spreading and becomes specialized to secrete products which nourish a fetus.

If there is no pregnancy, the softened endometrium can break away easily, and is lost in the flow. It does this cleanly and smoothly; in youth, the flow is heavy at first and tapers off to spotting at the end. This smooth pattern changes slightly at age 30, and can become irregular near menopause. The important point is that the uterus is completely emptied. Each month, it has a fresh start.

If something is amiss in the ovary cycle, the uterus cycle is thrown out of balance. It is one of the main causes of irregular periods.

The Timing of Periods

When Maya, age 14, went to summer camp, her periods became scanty for three months.

When Janice, age 16, learned her parents were divorcing, her periods stopped altogether.

At boarding school, girls who are close friends often have their periods at the same time.

Women who date frequently tend to have a shorter time between periods than women who date less frequently.

Stress and emotional factors: These play a large role in the monthly cycle. Emotional upset seems to upset the hypothalamus, and an upset hypothalamus may not send strong signals to the pituitary to produce FSH and LH. With less FSH and LH, there are lesser surges in estrogen and progesterone. In extreme cases, this may result in amenorrhea, a complete lack of periods. The syndrome of friends having periods at the same time is common enough to have its own name: "boarding school synchrony." One theory suggests that it is due to sexual body odor, *pheromones*.

Age-related changes: By the early 30s, periods can be shorter and heavier. A flow which used to last 7 days may now be only 4. Periods tend to become very regular, though the time of heaviest flow changes. Instead of being on the first day, it can be on the morning of the second or third day. By age 40, periods often become irregular again. They can come 17 or 40 days after the last one. Irregular periods at this age are often due to estrogen withdrawal, and may be the first sign of approaching menopause.

The three times in a cycle when blood spotting can appear, and be perfectly normal are:

- At midcycle, ovulation
- Just before a period
- Just after a period

Any other blood flow requires medical investigation. A flow which starts for a day or two, then stops, then flows again, should be checked. It may be due to polyps or fibroids. It could be something more serious. *Visit the physician promptly for blood flow or spotting which occurs at unusual times.*

Painful Periods

Dysmenorrhea can range from mild to severe cramps in the lower abdomen, pulling pains at the inner thighs, backache, fainting, nausea, actual vomiting, hot and cold flushes, diarrhea, or dizziness with headaches. *Prostaglandins* are hormones made in abundance during menstruation. They are produced by the uterus and other body tissues, and control the contractions of blood vessels and smooth muscle in the uterus and gastrointestinal (digestive) tract.

If a specific cause for pain is found, the dysmenorrhea is said to be secondary. If no specific cause is found, it is primary dysmenorrhea. This is not an insignificant term. Women with primary dysmenorrhea tend to be extra-sensitive to prostaglandins. The uterus contracts too strongly and cramping pains are felt. Because prostaglandin constricts the blood vessels, it can upset blood flow and cause the headaches, hot and cold flushes, diarrhea, and nausea of dysmenorrhea.

One interesting point: the male ejaculate, *semen*, is rich in prostaglandins. However, the uterus is protected from any undue effects. After male orgasm, semen pools in the fornices at the top of the vagina. It remains here while the sperm struggle through the cervix. The seminal plasma does not flow through into the uterus.

"Where the hor-mones
There moan I"

The author, Aldous Huxley, made this waspish little joke in the 1930s about women who suffered cramps. It typifies the attitude at that time. Only a few physicians now believe that period pain is psychogenic. Yet there remains a tendency in older physicians to consider the girl an "hysterical" type "who reacts badly to pain." (Who reacts well?) Women who do not suffer from dysmenorrhea can be equally dismissive. These unhappy attitudes only add psychic pain to an already distressing situation.

Pain Relief

According to Dr. Penny Budoff: "of the 85 million women in the U.S. who menstruate, nearly half have menstrual discomfort with some regularity. Of these, approximately 10 percent, or 3.5 million women, are *completely* incapacitated for one or two days each month because of pain." These data come from 1980. It is to be hoped that fewer women now suffer needlessly as pain relief is available. One well-known home remedy for mild cramps is pennyroyal leaf *tea*; (not the oil, which can be toxic). Brew no more than one teaspoon per cup.

Over-the-counter drugs for mild to occasional cramps include:
Aspirin is a drug which reduces inflammation and fever. More important here, it is a mild antiprostaglandin; it cuts down the amount which is produced. It is also an anticoagulant; it stops blood clots forming which might hurt as they pass through the os (cervix opening) if it is infected. Last, but by no means least, aspirin is an analgesic (pain reliever).

However, aspirin can irritate the stomach lining. This is no real cause for concern if it is only used for one or two days each cycle. The drug *acetaminophen* is the active ingredient in non-aspirin pain relievers such as Tylenol.

Over-the-counter drugs for moderate pain include:

Antiprostaglandin inhibitors such as *Ibuprofen* are available in 200 mg tablets. Women with moderate dysmenorrhea require between 400 and 800 mg for effective relief of symptoms. They are taken some days before the period begins, to reduce prostaglandin levels and prevent them from circulating in the blood. They must *not* be taken if there is any chance of being pregnant. Their side effects are not known if used over prolonged time. Keep up-to-date on recent news about antiprostaglandin inhibitors.

There is now real choice in over-the-counter drugs for effective relief of menstrual symptoms.

Prescription drugs for moderate to severe pain include:
Narcotics such as *codeine* or *oxycodone* (Percodan) work for moderate pain. They allow the sufferer to function, though there can be sleepiness and dizzy feelings. They do have other side effects, and narcotics can be addictive. The physician will work out a safe, effective dose. Follow the instructions absolutely.

Menstrual symptoms do not begin until after ovulation starts. Stopping ovulation is one way to "cure" them. The Pill "cures" dysmenorrhea by preventing ovulation *and* by thinning the uterus lining, which cuts down on prostaglandin production. It regulates erratic periods. Tranquilizers were once offered to help a woman in pain relax, but they afford no pain relief.

As each woman is unique, so each drug affects her differently. Shop around until a pain relief is found which really works. If no analgesic works, prostaglandins may not be the problem. Consider endometriosis, fibroids, or ovarian cysts (see Chapter 6). Ask the physician for a complete investigation.

PMS

Premenstrual syndrome is not the same as dysmenorrhea. The symptoms appear well before a period and the more usual age is the late 20s to mid 30s. Some researchers believe that PMS can strike at any time in a woman's reproductive life. Others believe it is a first signal of approaching menopause, and the symptoms are due to estrogen withdrawal.

Premenstrual syndrome used to be called premenstrual tension. The main symptoms, *depression, irritability, and lethargy,* are linked to tension. A sudden mood swing can be the first sign of PMS. (A syndrome is a group of signs and symptoms which together make up a disease or abnormal condition in which the cause is unknown. This is why there is no one accepted therapy for PMS.)

Other symptoms can include: panic attacks, poor concentration, food cravings, crying for no reason, suicidal thoughts and/or attempts, rage and violence, child or partner abuse. Physical symptoms include: fluid retention and swelling, headaches, joint or muscle pain, enlarged and tender breasts, backache, heart palpitations, chest pains, clumsiness, inability to wear contact lenses, weight gain, weakness and lack of energy, craving for sweet foods. In fact, many of the physical symptoms of PMS are the same as those which occur during a period.

Researchers have found that women who suffer depression as a symptom of PMS secrete lower amounts of *melatonin* while they sleep. Melatonin is a hormone secreted by the pineal gland in the brain at night. They also found some evidence that disturbances in circadian rhythms, which are upsets in the body's biological clock, may contribute to premenstrual depression in some cases. The study suggests there is a hormonal and possibly circadian difference between PMS women and their controls.

The release of melatonin varies in rhythm with the dark-light cycle. It is suppressed by bright light. Melatonin comes from another brain hormone, *seratonin*, which has also been linked to PMS. The biological clock is the internal timing mechanism which regulates functions such as the different stages of sleep, body temperature fluctuations, and hormone production.

The research showed that timed exposure to bright light, and forced sleep extension or deprivation, can reset some biological clocks which are off their normal rhythms. Serotonin, the precursor chemical for melatonin, might be involved in both the behavioral and carbohydrate craving symptoms of PMS. Eating sweets and starches increases levels of serotonin in the brain, inducing sleep while also relieving depression.

As yet, there is no one theory on how melatonin, serotonin and perhaps other brain chemicals work to contribute to PMS. The study's results were published in early 1991. It concluded: "It is not unreasonable that some form of light therapy may be useful in treating PMS symptoms."

In 1991, an Italian study of 32 women with PMS suggested a deficiency of magnesium in the diet may be implicated in some women. The researchers reported that undesirable mood changes before the onset of menses were significantly reduced in women who took 350 milligrams of magnesium supplements three times a day from the fifteenth day of their menstrual cycle until the flow began.

Magnesium is an essential mineral in the diet. National food consumption studies show that most Americans, with the exception of preschool children, do not get enough magnesium. Like other nutrients, it is best obtained from foods such as raw leafy green vegetables, nuts, especially almonds and cashews, dried beans like soy beans, whole grains, and seafood. The recommended daily intake of magnesium for women is 300 mg. One cup of cooked spinach supplies 157 mg, one cup of cooked lima beans has 100, one ounce of almonds has 86 mg, and one cup of cooked oatmeal has 56 mg. Check that the diet contains sufficient magnesium.

Philosophy of PMS

In Britain, women were loudly cheered by feminists when their sentences for violent acts committed pre-period were reduced to one year's probation. The court lent its considerable weight to the view that all women with PMS should stay off the roads. This was in the 1960s. In 1991, in America, a woman physician whose work included some surgery, was involved in an altercation when she was stopped for drunken driving. Apparently, she assaulted the arresting officer and swore at him. At her trial, she pleaded PMS, and got off.

It seemed PMS had come of age. It was officially recognized as a disease which caused women to suffer deep disturbances. So deep, in fact, that women were *not responsible for their acts* at certain times of the month. Everyone seemed pleased with this breakthrough in new understanding — Hurrah!

Yet consider. A hundred years ago, women with PMS were said to suffer *"temporary insanity while under menstrual influence."* They went "berserk" and were capable of acts of "great violence." Some British physicians believed that they should be locked up during their menstrual years for their own good, and for the safety of society. From 19th century "temporary insanity" to 20th century "loss of responsibility for actions," has PMS really come of age? If so, is this a step forward for women? Do they, when entering the 21st century, wish special laws to be framed to allow for their irrational behavior? In short, do women want to be considered by men as out of control for some ten days each month?

It is estimated that only 2 percent of women with PMS actually become violent; it is not known why. In most cases, they have underlying psychiatric disorders and either have been, or are now, in prison. It is understandable that normal and otherwise healthy women feel more aggressive with PMS. Yet they do not abuse police officers, nor try to kill their lovers as these women did. The issue is one of self-discipline, personal control. To accept that women must respond to increased aggressive feelings with violence is as pernicious as to accept that men must respond to increased sexual feelings with rape.

Self-Care

The perception of pain is an individual issue. Stress has been shown to increase pain perception by about 30 percent per hour. Tension, whether mental or physical, makes any pain feel worse. A woman who is worried and has cramps will almost certainly feel more pain. Some find they are less aware of PMS irritability if they have a number of specific things to do. Put exercise high on this list.

The following suggestions may not work for all women. They may not work for all PMS or dysmenorrhea. Yet they have helped many girls and women reduce the need for analgesics.

- *Exercise*: Vigorous exercise releases *endorphins*, the body's natural pain killer. Higher endorphin levels may be the reason why exercise can be effective against dysmenorrhea and PMS.
- *Heat*: A warm bath can be effective against cramps. A heating pad or hot water bottle cradled at the sore spots often helps.
- *Massage*: Massage helps practically everything. The rhythmic strokes soothe and ease tension, reducing the bunching up against pain.
- *Supplements*: Some physicians recommend vitamin and mineral supplements. Others believe that these chemicals should be obtained only through a varied diet.
- *Diet*: Eat small, high-protein snacks every few hours to combat fatigue and weakness.
- *Caffeine*: Reduce tea, coffee, or chocolate intake to reduce mild dysmenorrhea and PMS.
- *Salt*: Follow a low sodium diet for seven to ten days before the start of a period to reduce water retention.
- *Yoga*: The gentle stretching and strengthening of yoga brings soothing relief. Enroll in a class, or learn from a book.

- *Sleep*: Teen girls and busy women often do not get enough sleep. Shakespeare wrote wisely that sleep "knits up the ravel'd sleeve of care."

Loss of Periods

Dear Doctor Jones: My 20 year old daughter is a fitness freak. She jogs once a day, sometimes twice, and works out with weights in the evenings. On weekends, she swims and plays tennis. Her periods have stopped. She is pleased because she used to suffer cramps. I am not. In fact, I worry because she looks half-starved, with not an ounce of fat on her bones.

Dear Mrs B: Moderate exercise is excellent for sexual health. One follow-up study on college females found non-athletic women had twice the rate of breast cancer and two and a half times the rate of cancers of the reproductive system in later life than the women who had been athletic at college. And the women who were athletic had reduced lifetime risks of diabetes and benign tumors of the breasts, cervix, uterus, and ovaries.

However, over-exercise, as in your daughter's case, is now known as *exercise abuse*. It is serious, and may well be the cause of her secondary amenorrhea. Too little body fat, any rapid weight loss of 10 to 15 percent below the average healthy minimum, has the same effect. A certain amount of fat cells are necessary to support hormone activity. When serious hormonal changes occur in a young woman, there are usually other signs, such as growth of body hair or extra fuzziness on the arms and legs. Your daughter should check out the absence of menstruation. It is clear evidence of a change in hormone cycles and should be investigated promptly.

Crash diets are also implicated in secondary amenorrhea. And yo-yo dieting, losing weight and regaining it, can do more harm than being a little overweight. Blood cholesterol levels, blood pressure, and blood sugar change with seesawing weight, and may end up worse than before the diet. Anemia (lack of iron) can cause temporary secondary amenorrhea.

More complex problems include birth defects, pituitary disease, cysts or tumors of the reproductive organs, chromosome abnormalities, and hormone imbalance. Keep in mind that hormones are very powerful. Only the tiniest change in output can cause serious problems. Dysmenorrhea can be alleviated with medication.

Though periods can be painful, and loss of them seem desirable, they are essential to sexual health. Visit the physician if secondary amenorrhea occurs.

Irregular Periods

Keep in mind that up to day 14, the uterus lining is proliferative, thick and hard, and dividing in no particular direction. After mid cycle, the lining is secretory; it stops dividing and becomes soft and lush. Estrogen and progesterone control this. In turn, they are controlled by the pituitary hormones. These, in turn, are controlled by the hypothalamus. If there is a disorder at any point in this chain, the cycles are thrown out of balance. The hormones receive incorrect feedback and periods become irregular.

For example, if an egg is not ripened, or one is not released, estrogen production stays high, and progesterone is not produced. This is *unopposed estrogen*. The endometrium stays proliferative and hard. At period time, it cannot tear away easily and only fragments break off. The result is scrappy or scant periods, sometimes followed at a later month by a very heavy flow.

In other cases, the build-up of the lining goes on for weeks, until the estrogen-producing cells simply wear out. When this happens, the lining becomes so thick that it finally breaks down and a period starts. Bleeding is usually severe; heavy and prolonged. In fact, periods which come only two or three times a year may be shedding menstrual debris built up over many cycles. The uterus is never completely emptied. It does not get a fresh monthly start.

In other cases, the ovary goes through its normal cycle, yet for some unknown reason, it speeds up. The egg is ripened too quickly, ovulation is early, the thickening and softening of the lining are all speeded up. So periods come rapidly, every two or three weeks, though the amount of flow is the same. It can be due to physical or mental stress, or after pregnancy when the pituitary is still adjusting. This type of "polymenorrhea" or "dysfunctional bleeding" is not serious. Periods usually settle down after a few months.

In a mature woman, irregular periods with or without heavy bleeding are often a sign of approaching menopause. In a younger woman, they may not have settled down and are *normally* erratic. However, irregular periods can be a sign of the following:

- Ectopic pregnancy.

- A growth in the uterus: polyps or fibroids.
- Endometriosis, an overgrowth of the uterus lining.
- Precancer changes in the reproductive organs.
- Problems with fertility

Visit the physician promptly to make sure that all is well.

Toxic Shock Syndrome

Earle Haas, an American doctor, invented internal protection. He said, "I just got tired of women wearing those damned old rags... it was designed to absorb. It didn't block. It followed the natural contour of the vagina..."

This was in 1936. The first tampons were thin. Later, they were designed to be superabsorbent. They not only soaked up the flow, but expanded in the vagina to block it. In 1980, newspaper headlines blazoned reports of a new female illness which could be fatal: *Toxic Shock Syndrome*, TSS. Forty-two women had died and 890 cases were reported to the Centers for Disease Control. The symptoms included sudden high fever, vomiting, diarrhea, skin rash, and a drop in blood pressure — the shock part of the syndrome.

In 1982, a report from the Institue of Medicine advised women, especially young women between ages 15 and 24, to avoid high absorbency tampons to reduce the risk of developing TSS; to avoid all-sized tampons for 6 to 8 weeks after childbirth; to avoid all-sized tampons if the woman had previously suffered TSS.

Many women really appreciate tampons. It is unlikely that they will stop using them entirely. Once again, it is a risk/benefit issue. The following are suggestions which might help:

- Use tampons only when the flow is heavy.
- Avoid using them for the entire period.
- Use panty liners when the flow is light.
- Use sanitary napkins or panty liners at night.
- Use regular size tampons rather than the super size.
- Change regular size tampons more frequently.
- Avoid using tampons between periods to mop up discharge.
- Stop using tampons if the vagina feels dry or sore.
- Stop using tampons if there is an infection.
- Stop using them if there is reason to suspect an infection!

Though the vagina is designed to be robust, it may not adapt well to tampons. At insertion, unclean fingers, sharp nails, or the cardboard edge of a tube, can damage the walls. Maybe harmless bacteria can turn harmful if constantly pressed into the walls by the tampon. Tampons absorb the protective vagina fluids, so the self-cleansing mechanism cannot function. (It can be more clearly seen why douching during a period is not advised).

A few women use a diaphragm to collect menstrual flow, or to absorb discharge. *Be Aware!* To date, 23 cases of diaphragm-related TSS have been reported, and one over-the-counter contraceptive sponge has been linked to TSS. Sperm are protein-rich. If trapped by the diaphragm or sponge, their presence *might* contribute to the growth of bacteria. These are theories, and have not been proven. One factor seems clear: *Leave nothing in the vagina for longer than is necessary.*

Summary

- There is no such phenomenon as an average period.
- Self-care can reduce the effects of menstrual cramps.
- Cramps can be due to an extra sensitivity to prostaglandins.
- There is a wide choice of effective medication.
- Exercise can help reduce PMS and menstrual cramps.
- Visit the physician promptly for any abnormal bleeding.
- Loss of periods is a sign of serious hormone problems.
- Use sanitary napkins rather than tampons, when appropriate.
- Leave nothing in the vagina for longer than is necessary.

CHAPTER 4

A Healthy Urinary Tract

The Urethra

A faucet is designed to allow water to flow out in a steady stream. One of the functions of the labia is to help direct urine in a similar steady stream. If the fingers are placed on each side of the outer labia and the vulva area gently pulled upwards, urine can be passed when standing upright, as a man.

The *urethra* is the passageway for urine from the bladder to the outside. It is two inches long, very short in comparison with the eight inches in men. Any germs which arrive at the vulva have only a short way to travel to reach the bladder. This is why infections of the bladder are much more common in women than men. The opening of the urethra is the *meatus*. The urethra is lined with delicate mucus membranes, which are highly sensitive and easily irritated.

There is only a thin wall between the vagina and rectum. The wall between the vagina and bladder is even thinner; a fraction of an inch thick. Any undue pressure on the "ceiling" of the vagina causes pressure on the bladder. There can be an instant urge to urinate. Some women have this sensation when inserting a tampon. The thinness of the wall between the urethra and vagina is responsible for the G-spot, and for "honeymoon cystitis."

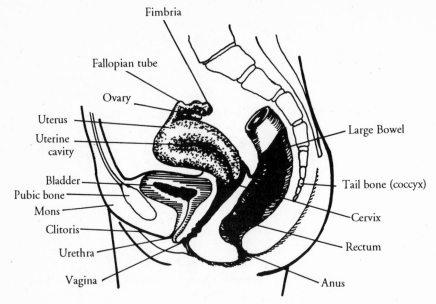

Fimbria

Fallopian tube

Ovary

Uterus

Uterine cavity

Bladder

Pubic bone

Mons

Clitoris

Urethra

Vagina

Large Bowel

Tail bone (coccyx)

Cervix

Rectum

Anus

A SIDE VIEW OF THE FEMALE REPRODUCTIVE
SYSTEM: NOTE THE POSITION OF BLADDER

Urinary Tract Infection

Urinary tract infection, UTI, refers to any infection of the urethra or bladder. UTI is the most common of all bacteria infections in women. The three classic symptoms of UTI are:

Frequency: It is the need to urinate very frequent, much too soon after the last time?

Burning: Does the urine feel unusually hot, with a burning or stinging sensation?

Urgency: Is the need to urinate very strong? It cannot wait?

If these symptoms are mild, they are due to a minor episode of UTI which can clear up with self-care. If the symptoms are severe, they require speedy medical help. In severe cases, UTI can be both painful and exhausting, with feelings of lethargy *and* tension at the same time. However, UTI is not usually considered a serious infection. Treat the first attack promptly to stop the condition from becoming recurrent and chronic.

Prevention Is Better Than Cure

Urea is made of the waste products of protein metabolism. It is blisteringly strong, with that familiar ammonia smell. Before leaving the kidneys, it is diluted in 95 percent water to become *urine*. This dilution prevents the strong urea from damaging the delicate linings of the bladder and urethra. Urine is normally a pale straw yellow in color. If it is darker *and* smells more strongly of ammonia, there is not sufficient water in the body.

Increase water intake to 8 tall glasses daily.

Healthy urine is *sterile*; it is free of germs. It drips down from the kidneys into the stretchy pouch of the *bladder*. It pools here until the level slowly rises and stimulates nerve receptors in the wall of the bladder. These send messages to the brain which translates them into the urge to urinate.

Obey these messages as soon as the time is appropriate.

Urine which pools in the bladder is static. Static urine can quickly become infected. In that case, the germs can travel up to the kidneys and cause serious damage. To avoid static urine, the bladder has a defense mechanism called "the wash-out effect." At each urination, it can almost completely empty itself. Any germs which have traveled up the urethra are regularly "washed out."

Allow time for the bladder to completely empty itself.

The bladder walls are stretchy and elastic. On average, they hold between 10 to 12 ounces of urine, about the same volume as a can of soda. But the stretchy walls can balloon out to hold a great deal more. Avoid this. Repeated over-stretching can reduce their elasticity. Eventually, the connective tissue frays and loses its ability to shrink back to its previous size.

Urinate when the urge is mild to moderate.

There are rings of muscles at the neck of the bladder; these are *sphincters* to control the flow of urine. Most women will be aware of these sphincters at some time in their life. They can go into spasm for no known reason. This is *hesitancy*, the urine flow takes some while to start. Bladder sphincters can weaken later in life, or from the weight of a fetus during pregnancy.

Avoid unnecessary challenge to the bladder sphincters.

Honeymoon Cystitis

Men suffer a curious condition called prostatodynia. Its slang term is "sailor's disease" because it flares up after a prolonged time of no sexual activity followed by very vigorous activity. It rarely occurs with one sexual episode. There has to be prolonged and vigorous activity after prolonged abstinence. The symptoms are similar to UTI: burning, frequency, and urgency.

Honeymoon cystitis is much the same phenomenon. It is due to prolonged and sudden sexual activity. Keep in mind the very thin wall between the vagina and urine tract. Prolonged thrusting can *bruise* the delicate lining, and set up inflammation inside the urethra. Deep penetration can irritate the bladder. *Always empty the bladder before making love.*

Honeymoon cystitis is not limited to brides. It can occur at any time when prolonged and vigorous sexual activity follows prolonged abstinence. The symptoms of honeymoon cystitis are the same as for UTI. When they first start, the woman may suspect a sexual disease. Though this could be possible, consider bruising first.

Cranberry Juice

It is official! What grandmothers said about cranberry juice was proven in Israel in 1991. New research studied seven fruit juices to find out if they contained compounds known to prevent bacteria from sticking to the wall of the urinary tract, and so causing infection. Cranberry and blueberry juices contained the compounds. Grapefruit, guava, mango, orange, and pineapple juices did not.

UTIs are usually caused by the bacteria E. coli. They are able to resist the "wash out effect" at urination. Two compounds in cranberry and blueberry juices prevent the E. coli bacteria from sticking to the urinary tract walls. Fructose, which is present in these juices, interferes with some bacterial adhesion. However, it is another as yet unidentified component which seems to be a more potent inhibitor.

To prevent infections, physicians recommend drinking plenty of fluids and urinating frequently, especially before and after love making. There is no evidence that cranberry and blueberry juices can kill bacteria. Drinking these juices is a preventive measure, not a treatment.

Diet

Hot spicy foods such as peppers, cayenne, chili, and curries can irritate the urinary tract. So can coffee, tea, chocolate and alcohol. Avoid foods which cause even a mild digestive reaction. It seems that diets high in refined sugars and starches such as white flour, white rice, and pastas, may affect some women. Switch to brown bread and rice. Try whole and unrefined foods.

Ascorbic acid helps to acidify urine. Supplements of Vitamin C are another route to try. Avoid taking more than the recommended daily 1,000 mg. Though excess Vitamin C is excreted in urine, it seems likely that taking megadoses can be harmful. There is some evidence that ingesting more than 1 g (1,000 mg) daily, and over a prolonged stretch of time, can increase oxalic acid levels in the kidneys and promote the growth of kidney stones.

Perfume in Products

Perfumed body soaps and cleansing liquids are obvious trouble-makers. They can irritate the skin of the vulva, and inflame the delicate mucus lining of the urethra. As hot urine passes over the sore area, a stinging, burning pain is felt. This aggravates the condition, and opens the tissues to *secondary infection*.

Check for the presence of perfume in other substances such as bubble baths, talcum powder, and decorated toilet paper. Eschew vaginal deodorants. Allergic reactions can be due to substances in laundry products such as fabric softeners, detergents, and bleaches. Is the wash cloth *really* clean? Is the bath *completely* rinsed of whatever products were used to clean it?

Sexual Disease

Sexual disease is a major source of the symptoms of UTI. Women have a particular problem with sexual disease. They can harbor infections which are *asymptomatic*; there are no symptoms. A woman may have no idea that she is infected. If there is any reason to suspect sexual disease, ask a partner to wear a condom. A condom not only prevents passing on the infection, but acts as a guard against auto-inoculation.

Always regard any change in the vagina fluids as suspicious. If there is an unusual volume, a different texture, a change in the normal color or odor, be on the alert. Again, use a condom until the suspected change can be medically investigated. Keep in mind that *sexual disease is a major source of UTI.*

- Empty the bladder before making love.
- Sit in a hot tub, or wash the entire area first.
- If appropriate, check that a partner is equally clean.
- Avoid too much direct stimulation of the clitoris.
- Make sure the vagina is well-lubricated before penetration.
- Try to reduce the amount of prolonged vigorous thrusting.
- The rear entry position puts added pressure on the bladder.
- Wash the hands and genitals after any anal contact.
- Avoid contact with the vulva or vagina until this is done.
- Empty the bladder again when love making is complete.

Birth Control

The *diaphragm* is a fairly popular method of birth control. Yet it has been implicated in some cases of UTI. This can happen when the diaphragm is too large; it exerts pressure against the neck of the bladder and partially blocks the angle at which urine flows out. This can cause urine outflow to drop. The pressure inside the bladder rises, and interferes with the wash out effect. The bladder cannot completely empty itself. A pool of static urine collects, known as *urinary retention.* Bacteria can then grow in the static urine.

There is an added problem due to the pressure of trying to get urine through a partially blocked structure. It upsets the normal, smooth rhythm of the sphincter muscles. If they tighten at the wrong time, there is backflow. The infected urine moves backwards rather than outwards and safely away from the body.

When a diaphragm is correctly fitted, it *cannot be felt.* The rim slips into the fornices of the cervix and is held there. If the rim is the wrong size, whether too large or too small, there is a constant awareness of the diaphragm's presence. Check before leaving the physician's office that there is no sensation from the diaphragm. If there is, the size is too large. If it is only felt when put in place at home, the method of insertion is incorrect. Remove the diaphragm and start again.

An ill-fitting diaphragm can actually encourage UTI. Bacteria can lodge in the bulge it causes, and so avoid being flushed out with the normal volume of urine. Several studies, including one reported in *Infectious Disease*, found that 74 percent of 150 diaphragm users with recurrent UTI had ill-fitting diaphragms. Even diaphragms which had been properly fitted were linked with recurrent UTI. If there are repeated UTI attacks, consider another method of birth control.

Women who use the Pill have a higher rate of UTI than those who use *barrier methods*. This tends to suggest that the infection is caused by a sexual disease. In non-monogamous relationships, the Pill provides no protection whatsoever. The barrier methods of sheath and diaphragm do act to some degree as protection against sexually transmitted disease.

Spermicides (sperm killers) can irritate the urethra. These include contraceptive creams, foams, tissues, and gels. Sponges can add pressure, and irritate the urethra, as can suppositories for the vagina. Sometimes, a dry condom will cause unnecessary friction; check that it is slightly damp before penetration. If lubrication is required, check that it is free of factors which cause irritation.

Menstruation

Period flow consists of mucus, sloughed off lining cells, and serum blood. These substances make an ideal breeding ground for bacteria. If previous attacks of cystitis have occurred after love making, consider what actions were involved. Are they responsible for passing a little of the menstrual flow to the urethra? If this seems likely, take greater care. The friction from thrusting can drive the flow further into the urinary tract. During the next few periods, avoid making love to determine if this is the source of the problem.

The use of sanitary napkins can increase the risk of UTI. Due to their hammock shape and their positioning across the genitals, bacteria from the flow can spread swiftly to the urethra. Change the pad frequently. Keep the area clean and fresh with baby wipes. Wash the genitals and anal area twice daily. If UTI tends to flare up after a period, one option is to use tampons for the next few months.

However, keep in mind that some women find the insertion of a tampon puts pressure on the urethra. There is also a chance that the tampon itself might be the cause of irritation. Where this is the case, stay with napkins. Take care, also, with the insertion of birth control methods such as sponges and diaphragms.

E. Coli

The most common cause of non-sexual UTI is the transmission of bacteria from the anus. The chief culprit is E. coli (Escherichia coli), which are found in the colon and rectum. When transmitted to the urethra, they can travel up the short, two-inch passage to the bladder and reproduce millions of bacteria within *24 hours*. One report found that 85 percent of *first* UTIs are caused by E. coli. This may be too high. Other estimates suggest that as many as 10 to 15 percent of *recurrent* UTIs are due to chlamydia, a sexual disease.

Though urine is sterile when first made, feces are not. There is a whole colony of bacteria living happily within the large intestine. Some of these bacteria have a useful function; they complete the final stages of certain digestion. When feces leave the body in a bowel movement, their content is highly infectious.

Auto-inoculation is self infection. After a bowel movement, the anal area is often wiped from back to front. While this may clean the anus, it drags forward and wipes across the urethra a whole potpourri of germs. Bacteria are too tiny to be seen, and the risk of auto-inoculation is sometimes ignored.

Mid-Stream Void

A diagnosis of UTI is made by testing a specimen of urine for bacteria. The urine must be mid-stream only. The test can be done at home with a self-screening kit which can be bought at the local pharmacy. These kits work best with concentrated urine, so the "first catch" in the morning is the most appropriate. Harmless organisms called flora live inside the urethra. If urine is collected in a specimen cup, these flora are flushed out at the same time. Their presence can give a false diagnosis at *urinalysis.* The following directions show how to collect a clean mid-stream void:

- Drink a large glass of water.
- Bathe the entire area thoroughly in a warm tub.

- Dry thoroughly with a fresh, clean towel.
- Start to urinate into the toilet bowl.
- The flora are flushed out after 10 to 15 ml of voiding.
- Without stopping the flow, move the cup into position.
- Collect flow until the level reaches the correct cc mark.
- Stop. Remove the cup and finish voiding in the bowl.
- Avoid holding or even touching the rim of the cup.
- Even clean hands can harbor germs, which will confuse the diagnosis.
- Test the urine according to the instructions on the kit.
- Keep in mind these kits cannot detect all the organisms.
- UTI often disappears without treatment. See the physician if the condition lasts for more than two days.

Medical Help

UTI responds to antibiotics. Pyridium is an effective urinary pain killer. Antibiotics can cause diarrhea, and yeast infections in the vagina. Plain yogurt or acidophilus help by replacing the normal bacteria destroyed by the medication. Pyridium turns urine orange, and stains underwear permanently. Its side effects can include nausea, dizziness, and more rarely, allergic reaction.

One of the most effective ways to stop UTI before it can develop is to drink plenty of fluids. This cannot be stated often enough, to avoid the misery of an infection. However, a woman with chronic UTI may flood her system with fluids at the first symptoms of infection. When she produces a urine sample for laboratory testing, the bacteria count may be less than 100,000 per milliliter. Some physicians do not consider this high enough to diagnose UTI. The woman is told to relax, take a holiday, stop worrying, practice meditation; the usual responses from a physician who considers her condition is "all in the mind", that it is psychogenic.

Because recurrent attacks of cystitis are such miserable things to endure, the woman can appear tense, angry or depressed. This is hardly surprising. Take care to avoid these pitfalls. Also, keep in mind that certain medications affect the results of urine tests. Be sure that the physician is aware of any attempt at self-care therapy. If necessary, insist on a further urine test.

If the symptoms of UTI persist after a course of antibiotics, have a *culture and sensitivity* test, known as C&S. It determines whether the bacteria are sensitive to some antibiotics, whether they have developed a resistance or not. A C&S test can be of enormous value with chronic cystitis. The medication is changed and, with luck, the condition finally clears.

In chronic cases, the germs can hide in the Skene's glands, those tiny bumps near the entrance to the urethra. There are no ITU symptoms and the woman feels fine, until an occasion of sexual activity puts pressure on the Skene's glands. The infected pus is then squeezed out. Bacteria travel up the urethra and the UTI symptoms start up again. A further and more prolonged course of antibiotics is required.

Visit the physician promptly if there is pus in the urine, or if there are chills, vomiting, fever, or backache. Pus in the urine makes it appear more frothy. The urine can be slightly pink, or with flecks or streaks of blood. A dull, aching pain may be felt over the pubic bone. If any of these symptoms occur, the infection might have spread from the bladder to the kidneys. This is *pyelonephritis*, a serious condition requiring urgent medical attention.

Cystoscopy is an X-ray of the bladder after it is filled with opaque fluid. An intravenous pyelogram involves the injection of a dye into the bloodstream. The dye collects in the kidneys, and any blockages will show up on the X-ray.

A Leakage Problem

It is estimated that up to 50 percent of women over age 50 have some degree of *incontinence*. This can be no more than a slight leakage of urine when laughing, sneezing, coughing, exercise, or standing up suddenly from a sitting position. Yet the symptoms can be more severe, with a frequent and urgent need to go to the bathroom. Neurological disease can be the cause of incontinence, but this is rare. The two common reasons in otherwise healthy women are stress or urinary incontinence.

Stress incontinence is caused by a defect in the bladder neck. This can be due to a gradual weakening over the years. Laughing, sneezing, and so on cause the diaphragm to press down, which puts extra pressure on the defect with a resultant leakage of urine. Stress incontinence is *not* due to mental stress. Some women opt for a surgical repair at the very first symptoms. They cannot tolerate even minor leakage, and wish to speedily regain control of their bladder function. Other women hope to avoid surgery, and concentrate on strengthening the bladder tone by Kegels exercises. They use panty liners to cope with minor leakage. Pads are more effective with a heavier loss.

Urgency incontinence is a condition in which the bladder walls contract spontaneously in responses to changes in pressure. These spasms can usually be linked to a long history of UTIs. A surgical repair is of no use with urgency incontinence. The two conditions were sometimes confused, and the woman underwent a repair which did not stop the leakage. A sub-specialist known as a uro-gynecologist can make sure that the two conditions do not get confused.

A *cystocele* is a small bulge of bladder which has dropped down out of place. It bulges into the vagina and can be felt as a slight lump. Most cystoceles are asymptomatic, and usually cause no problems. However, if one is large and interferes with the smooth exit of urine, there can be urgency, with only a few drops of urine passed. If urine collects in the bladder, it can become infected and cause repeated UTI and pain during urination.

A cystocele is rare in young women, because it is due to "relaxation" of the walls of the vagina. These hold the bladder and rectum in place, and only tend to relax after the stress of childbirth, or after menopause. If the urethra also drops out of place, the condition is called *cystourethrocele*. If a portion of the rectum prolapses and bulges into the vagina, the condition is a *rectocele*. Stool can "pack" in the bulge, and cause fairly severe constipation. All these conditions can be fixed by surgical repair.

Kegels Exercises

A tendency to weakening of the pelvic organs, and relaxation of the pelvic support system, increases with age. Love making is a splendid exercise, as is the act of self-pleasuring. Any exercise involving the pelvis and lower abdomen is of great value. *Kegels exercises* strengthen the muscles of the entire pelvic area. They are particularly helpful in problems of bladder control. Theirst exercise is to practice stopping the flow in mid-stream. The second exercise is to squeeze the muscles of the back passage tight. Do these two exercises in turn, and *very slowly* at first. Sudden effort can cause sudden weakening, and result in more harm than good. Start each exercise to a count of 5 to 20 squeezes, twice daily, for a week. Gradually build up to 65 squeezes each, twice daily, over the next 3 weeks. On week 4 to 6, *hold* the squeeze to a count of 3, then relax.

Avoid extra squeezes. It usually takes about 6 weeks before an improvement is noticed.

Kegels exercises can be performed anywhere, and at any time, because they are undetectable. If they are done effectively, they can put off the need for a surgical repair for many years. Women who already have a minor problem must keep in mind the following:

Avoid jogging, "Jumping Jacks," and other bouncing exercises.
Avoid lifting heavy weights the wrong way.
Learn correct lifts *before* grandchildren come to visit.

Summary

- Drink plenty of fluids, 8 tall glasses each day.
- Try to drink a glass of water every 2 to 3 hours.
- Urinate regularly, and before the urge is strong.
- Avoid trying to retain urine when the bladder is full.
- Allow sufficient time to completely empty the bladder.
- Consume a high fiber diet to avoid constipation.
- Try self-care to cure a mild attack of UTI.
- Visit the physician promptly if UTI persists.
- Practice Kegels to firm up the entire pelvic area.

CHAPTER 5

Orgasm

Erection

The clitoris is made of spongy tissue which can up fill with blood. This engorgement of tissue is *vaso-congestion*. Upon sexual arousal, extra blood from the pelvic arteries is pumped into the tissue, filling up the spongy spaces so that the clitoris swells in size. The muscles on each side contract and squeeze the only vein which runs along the top of the clitoris. This traps the extra blood inside; it cannot drain out. As more blood is pumped in, the swollen clitoris stiffens, rises, and lengthens to its maximum size. This is the process by which both the clitoris and penis become erect.

At the same time, extra blood is pumped into the vulva area, which thickens and flushes a deep red or purple. The outer labia swell to two or three times their pre-arousal size. The vagina responds with the sweating phenomenon. The walls are coated with moisture. The extensive system of connecting veins and muscles throughout the pelvis all respond to vaso-congestion. There is a feeling of fullness and heaviness, known as *pelvic congestion*. All this assists to move the woman towards the "orgasmic platform."

The nipples also contain erectile tissue. At an early stage in arousal, they begin to harden and erect. The areola swells and spreads. The entire breasts are affected; they plump up and feel more tender; they are erotically charged when touched.

71

The Big O!

The clitoris and nipples are the main organs of arousal. If one or both are erotically stimulated for long enough, excitement increases until sexual tension becomes almost overpowering. As orgasm draws near, the clitoris becomes exquisitely sensitive; it cannot tolerate any more direct stimulation. It *retracts*, pulling back and retiring beneath its hood. Less often, the nipples become equally sensitive, and require no further stimulation.

Sexual tension is built by rhythmic friction. The thrusting of the penis causes maximum friction, maximum sensation, on the outer third of the vagina walls. In the missionary position, man on top, thrusting puts rhythmic pressure on the labia, which allows stimulation of the clitoris, though to a milder degree. Sucking or stroking the nipples in rhythmic movement produces the same effect. Erotic friction can be gentle or tough, slow or rapid, depending upon the particular needs at the time. Whichever, it must be *rhythmic* and *persistent* to build maximum sexual tension. As excitement increases, the entire body is charged with waves of tense pleasure. Muscle contractions ripple throughout the system. Like a waiting sneeze which has been building up, the persistency of the "friction factor" finally becomes explosive. The orgasmic platform has arrived. Now is the point of no return.

The vagina and surrounding tissues, the uterus, and sometimes the anus muscles all contract to a rhythmic beat at 0.8 second intervals; the same beat as in male orgasm. This beat can occur from between 3 to a maximum of 15 times, the same beat as in men. The last contractions are little more than ripples or shudders, again as in men. The more intense the orgasm, the longer the contractions last. A few women (and men) can have orgasms with no erotic friction whatsoever. They do it by fantasy, by imagination alone. Other women can have orgasms simply when they are kissed; the neck, earlobes, palms of the hands, toes — any part can be an erogenous zone.

The big "O" varies. It is not always so big. There can be physical and emotional pleasure of such exquisite intensity that the feelings seem unendurable. There can be pleasing but low-key sensations which feel on a par with the satisfaction of a long-awaited sneeze. The degree of sensation at orgasm does not necessarily reflect on the woman, her partner, or the situation. They reflect on life. Orgasm is as variable as life itself.

Changes at Orgasm

The clitoris lengthens and thickens, reaching maximum size. Just before orgasm, it pulls back behind the foreskin (hood).

The vagina dilates, the inner two-thirds widen and lengthen. The walls turn deep purple and are coated with lubricating fluid.

The labia outer lips open and flatten out. The inner lips thicken and thrust forwards.

The *uterus* balloons to almost twice its size. It rises and the cervix is pulled up away from the vagina.

The *heart rate* increases from an average 60 to 80 beats per minute to between 100 and 150.

The *breathing rate* becomes fast and shallow, and can speed up to 3 times its normal resting rate.

Muscle tension: The pelvis, abdomen, back and thighs contract and are held in a state of high tension.

Body language: The face can contort into a rictus, a glaring grimace; the hands may claw, the toes curl, the feet arch.

Mind: Mental faculties appear to be "gone," so deeply are they buried under orgasm's spell.

Sex rash: A rosy, measles-like rash starts at the throat and abdomen, then spreads to the breasts in 75 percent of women.

Sneezing: Attacks of sneezing, if they occur, are due to vaso-congestion in the nose.

Perspiration: One woman in three sweats on the forehead, the top lip, and underarm. A thin film may cover the back and thighs.

The Party's Over?

Some women have multiple orgasms. When they reach the orgasmic platform, they come again... and again... and again. It is not that the first orgasm was incomplete in any way. They are able to stay at a longer, later sexual peak, and allow orgasms to roll over them. After a man ejaculates, he must wait until his store of semen is replenished. In youth, this takes a few seconds. In later life, a day or more. Some men can have so-called "multiple orgasms" by external pressure on the perineum just before the orgasmic threshold is reached; or by mind control alone.

Detumescence is the flow of extra blood out of the area. The contractions of orgasm put pressure on all the blood vessels in the swollen organs and tissues. This pressure squeezes the extra blood out of them, and decongestion is complete. The clitoris returns to its normal size within 10 to 20 seconds after orgasm. The vagina takes some 15 minutes to return to its previous state. The uterus takes longer, between 10 and 30 minutes to become decongested and return to its previous size and position.

If there is no orgasm, there are no muscle contractions to put pressure on the blood vessels. The extra blood then pools in the organs and tissues, which remain swollen for some while. Eventually, it drains away, though this takes much longer than if orgasm has occurred. With intense sexual excitement followed by consistent lack of orgasm over a long period of time, a feeling of *pelvic congestion* builds up. The sensations of this condition include vague discomfort in the pelvic area, backaches, and sometimes headaches.

Pelvic congestion is not the same as a vulva which stays swollen for a day or more after making love. In this case, the swollen sensation is due to the pounding of flesh upon flesh. From a health perspective alone, orgasm is of physical benefit to avoid pelvic congestion. It also benefits the emotional health not only of the woman, but also of her partner, and the relationship itself. Strong feelings of erotic gratification bring a closer, more profound, love.

Orgasm and Health

Orgasm is a powerful muscle relaxant. Its effects can be ten times as strong as the effects of Valium and other tranquilizers. After illness, orgasm assists on the road back to health. Some doctors believe it is the best prescription for easing *mild* back pain, and so affording a relaxed and pain-free night of sleep.

Orgasm can be excellent aerobic activity. Blood pressure, heart and breathing rate all have a thorough workout, without the bother of putting on a track suit. The benefits to psychological health can be invaluable: profound emotional release, closer partner attachment, and an increase in mutual love, support, and self-esteem.

Pain at Orgasm

Pain at orgasm can occur if the contractions of the uterus become very powerful. In a few cases, they can be as wracking as the cramps of a period. Why put up with unnecessary pain? Visit the physician promptly. The condition may be due to a hormone imbalance which can be sorted out. More often though, these powerful contractions are not experienced as pain, but as a short time of discomfort. Rest after orgasm. The pains will subside as the uterus slowly subsides and returns to its normal site.

Dyspareunia is love making which is painful or difficult. The pain is experienced at some point in the vagina. In rare cases, there can be problems of clitoral adhesions, or birth defects. There may be an allergy to some substance in the semen or sperm. More often, pain on thrusting is due to an undiagnosed yeast infection which produces no other symptoms. This pain is more a soreness, and does not begin until thrusting has continued for some time.

However, in the majority of cases, the problem is a lack of sufficient lubrication. This can be avoided by the use of external lotions such as K-Y jelly. Avoid oils and creams which contain alcohol; they irritate. Avoid vaseline, which is not water-soluble, and can upset the ecology of the vagina and urethra. Keep the lubrication at hand.

* * *

"A woman is suing her gynecologist for damages because she lost all orgasmic function, and sensation in her nipples after her hysterectomy. Had she been forewarned of this side-effect of surgery, she maintains she would not have gone ahead with the operation."

The jury is still out on whether having a hysterectomy reduces a woman's ability to be fully orgasmic. Like so many other issues of female health, lack of proper research is the problem. All that is known is that women who are pleased with their surgery report they are fully orgasmic. Among those who are not, some 30 percent report that they have lost all interest in making love.

Men and Control

If erotic stimulation of the clitoris lasts from 1 to 10 minutes, 40 percent of women will have an orgasm. If stimulation lasts for 20 minutes, 90 percent will. If the clitoris is only stimulated at penetration, and for less than 1 minute, few women climax. With thrusting time of 1 to 11 minutes, 50 percent will. Almost all women will have an orgasm after 16 minutes of non-stop erotic stimulation.

Men are biologically primed to reach orgasm and ejaculate in less than two minutes. Young boys can come in five to ten seconds. This has been called a problem of timing, but is it? A man who wishes to satisfy his beloved must work against his speedy drive. He must prepare for the long, slow feast of love rather than the short, sharp burst which is natural to him. This involves learning control of his ejaculate before the critical threshold of orgasm; not always an easy feat.

All men come too soon (premature ejaculation) or too late (retarded ejaculation) at some time. If only on the odd occasion, keep in mind that it is too soon or late for the *woman*, not for the man. Men who hold back at pre-orgasm are not being purely altruistic. Apart from the satisfaction and pride in gratifying their partner, they too want to prolong their own sensations of pleasure. If a man consistently gets his timing wrong, he has a learning problem which can be easily overcome, (see *Understanding Male Sexual Health* by the same author).

There still exist a few men who are not interested in giving pleasure, only in getting it. Others recognize that they have a problem, but refuse to try to resolve it. In either case, the man is likely to be very uncertain of his manhood. He feels too threatened to accept that he *can* learn ejaculatory control. If he knows about the boost to his manhood which comes with gaining this control, he may be more open to seeking help.

Women and Control

At a basic level, orgasm is a nervous system response which is stimulated by extreme sexual tension. The reflex which triggers orgasm is located in the spinal nerves and the unconscious brain. The ability to hold back can come from the higher conscious mind, as when a man learns to control his speedy drive. It can also come from the unconscious brain, particularly where there is fear or sexual disgust.

In non-orgasmic women there is often a conflict between these two parts of the mind: go, go, go; stop, stop, stop. One part will eventually override the other, as in the negative female response, "I shouldn't. Nice girls don't. My father will kill me. The neighbors might hear. I'm afraid of getting pregnant."

Orgasm is about *letting go*, letting go of the mind's control over the body's actions. One of the civilizing aspects of human culture is the ability to learn *not* to let go; *not* to let the body have its clamoring way over the mind's higher desires. While self-control is essential in any group, indeed our culture would break down without it, the teaching of this control can be very overdone. In the past, it was particularly harsh in the rearing of little girls, and is still harsh in some homes today.

It is hardly surprising that some women find orgasm difficult at first. "Letting go!" After all those lectures on *behaving like a lady*; sitting with legs crossed, being dainty and feminine. All those warnings about men wanting only one thing, and not having respect afterwards. All those beauty routines, having hair and nails groomed, and the body sweetly clean. And now they are supposed to dump all that unconscious and conscious learning, and lie spread-eagled on their backs, howling at the moon: mussed up, smelly, sweaty, *exposed*!

It would be strange if some women found orgasm easy, at first.

Myths

Put a check against any of the following which may have been a part of childhood learning:

- Sex is dirty and nasty.
- The act of love should end in orgasm.
- The man is the one to initiate making love.
- Women should not show that they desire sex.
- Orgasms are important for procreation only.
- Orgasms come naturally when you are in love.
- Orgasms will happen with the "right" partner.
- Orgasms are less important for women than men.
- Both people should have orgasms at the same time.
- Women over a certain age lose interest in orgasms.

A myth is a fable, a concept. A myth is defined in most dictionaries as "an idea which forms part of the belief system of a group, but *which is not founded on fact.*" In historical terms, the reality has been that female sexuality was defined by men. Women were either Madonna or Magdalene, saints or sluts. Prostitutes enjoyed sex; "nice" women (those whom men married) endured it. Women had to fulfill such male expectations if they wished to survive above subsistence level. Being economically dependent, they had little choice but to act according to the myth. Now the myth has been broken, largely thanks to the women's movement. Female sexuality can be regarded in the same light as male sexuality. Or can it? How can a woman maintain economic parity and produce babies at the same time? Many women are struggling with this difficult problem today. If they have a loving, mature partner, he can help. However, the disparity between what women need and what they must settle for seems to be growing greater, not less.

Going Solo

Problems with orgasm can be overcome by *masturbation,* or as it is now more appropriately called self pleasure. It is never too late to learn how to do this. Some women stroke or press the vulva, stimulating the entire genital area. Others prefer direct contact with the clitoris. There is no "best" way to pleasure the self. Find out what works and go with that.

Vibrators avoid the old taboo of not touching the genitals. They also ensure that orgasm *will* occur. Keep a note of the time the vibrator is held in place. At the outer limit of 20 minutes, its persistent friction on or near the clitoris *will* trigger the pleasurable contractions of orgasm. Jacuzzi jets or hand-held shower heads directly over the clitoris also work.

Erotic love is a learned skill. Like other skills, it improves with practice. If the "letting go" reflex was repressed in early childhood, practice with a vibrator until the taboo finally gone. Be aware of the pitfalls of terms like: "anxiety performance" and "*failing to achieve* orgasm." The very words "anxiety" and "performance" kill erotic desire. There is no such phenomenon as a "failed" orgasm, merely insufficient sexual tension. Nor is orgasm a goal to achieve; it happens by letting go, not by striving.

Erotic love begins with self love. Go, pleasure the self.

Partner Problems

"Dear Dr Ruth: Please help me understand what my wife has just told me. After nearly 20 years of marriage, she says I have never given her an orgasm. This was a terrible blow to me. I had always assumed she was enjoying sex since she never said otherwise. We were very young when we married, both under 20. She was a virgin, and I'd had only a minimum of sexual experience..."

"Dear Reader: No man can be positive his partner has had an orgasm. That's why it's up to the woman to let him know what she needs to reach orgasm..."

This letter and reply appeared in a national column in 1991. Both plug into that other old myth: *It is up to the man to satisfy the woman.* The man's wife says that he has never given her an orgasm. No man can *give* a woman an orgasm. A woman alone can "give" one to herself. It is tied to those other old myths: *A woman's satisfaction is independent of her actions and feelings.* And, *Sex is what men do to women, rather than sex is what men do with women."*

Some women (and men) find that once they become orgasmic on their own, the results collapse when they are with a partner. They have "partner problems." The reasons are not usually difficult to track down. A man can be the world's greatest lover, but if a woman fears or dislikes him, she may not be orgasmic. Whatever her reason for being in bed with him, her psyche warns her not to "let go" with this man. If she is there simply for fun and sexual release, and part of her mind disapproves of such behavior, her psyche takes over and refuses to trigger the reflex orgasm.

Why should a woman "let go" with a man she is less than happy with? Her psychologic makeup is protecting her from vulnerability to pain. Men have rather similar problems when the penis will not erect, no matter how hard it is coaxed. When issues of work, health, worry, and so on, are eliminated, the reason is similarly protective. The man secretly fears or dislikes the woman, and the penis sends him protective messages not to respond where he is vulnerable to pain.

Partner problems of erection and orgasm are *not* problems in themselves. The trouble is psychological. Something is amiss in the relationship, and the conscious or unconscious steps in for protection. Sometimes, a man deliberately holds back on erections to spite or punish the woman. A woman holds back at pre-orgasm to punish the man. One of the main impediments to the full enjoyment of erotic love is the "power game" either partner can inflict upon the other.

Fake It Till You Make It

The previous letter and answer highlighted the old controversy of women faking pleasure, pretending to have orgasms. Yes, women do this. Some older men do it too. The reason for faking orgasm might be to give the partner more pleasure. Can this be bad? Sometimes a woman will fake orgasm to get the tiresome business over with as quickly as possible. Again, is this of itself bad?

In philosophical terms, faking an orgasm is neither bad, nor good. It is people being people: kind, quirky, difficult, nasty; the whole human package. Yet there is one point to consider which most women know only too well. Orgasm is *not* the be-all and end-all of making love. If a woman is orgasmic when, how often, and with whom she chooses — where is the problem?

The Body as Machine

It is said that some mothers in California give vibrators to their daughters to keep them from getting sexually tense and going to bed with the nearest inappropriate man. This may unfairly malign Californian mothers; it is only a rumor, and rumors are often false. Yet it has been known for women to walk around with small vibrators tucked into their vaginas, and kept permanently switched on.

It seems that when a woman pleasures herself, she may have better orgasms than when with a partner. This does not appear to occur for men when they masturbate. They complain of an empty, desolate feeling afterwards. Perhaps women feel this too; there is insufficient research to date. If using a machine, keep in mind that no man can compete in terms of energy output with an electrically-powered gadget. A wise woman is aware of the real "threat" to male pride that a vibrator can hold.

Sexual Dysfunction

The American Psychiatric Association estimates that at least one in five adults suffers from some form of sexual dysfunction. The most common dysfunctions treated by sex therapists are:

- *Anorgasmia*: The women has never, or only rarely, reached orgasm.
- *Delayed Ejaculation*: The man can act sexually though seldom, if ever, climaxes in his partner's presence.
- *Erectile Insecurity*: Also called impotence, the condition is marked by difficulty in either getting or staying erect.
- *Inhibited Sexual Desire*: A form of sexual apathy marked by infrequent sex, and a lack of thoughts and anticipation of sex.
- *Premature Ejaculation*: The man climaxes more rapidly than he or his partner wishes, sometimes before intercourse begins.
- *Vaginismus*: The woman desires sex, but her vaginal muscles contract involuntarily, preventing penetration.
- *Inappropriate Arousal*: Being aroused by that which a culture deems inappropriate: children, animals, objects.

Most sex therapists find that when a couple finally summon the nerve to seek help, the problem is usually in an advanced stage, and can no longer be ignored, or endured. In nearly all cases, both partners need to be treated together.

The female problems, anorgasmia and vaginismus, are rare, and psychological in origin. If mild, they can be solved by the woman herself with a vibrator. If severe, visit a sex therapist without delay. Male problems of ejaculatory control respond to self therapy and professional help. An erection problem can be the first sign of pre-diabetes, and the man should be tested for this promptly. Otherwise, it is 80 percent a psychological problem under age 40, and 20 percent an organic health problem. This changes to 80 percent a health problem (often a penis blood flow disorder) at age 80, and 20 percent psychological. Both kinds can be successfully cured or managed with medical, surgical or a sex therapist's help in 90 to 95 percent of cases.

Inhibited Sexual Desire (ISD) appears to be a modern complaint amongst modern couples. Sex therapists say that it is by far the nation's most common sexual dysfunction. For what are usually complex reasons, often including a past sexual problem, one or both partners have lost all desire for erotic intimacy.

Yet ISD is a philosophical concept, not a biological one. When and how often people wish to make love is a subjective issue. At its best, erotic love is an exquisitely sensitive bloom. Even when nurtured with the utmost love and tenderness, it can wax and wane, like the cycles of the moon. "Fantasize that you are making love

81

with another person," advises one therapist. "Fantasies are wholesome; they keep the fires kindled in marital love." Be that as it may, many lovers would not appreciate knowing that the beloved is dreaming of another while murmuring sweet nothings into their ear.

It seems a very modern concept to regard the genitals as a set of engine parts which *should* be working. And that if one of these parts slows down or stops functioning, it *should* be taken to the auto body shop, and fixed. This mechanical way of perceiving what can be a most delicate interaction probably suits mechanical thinkers. It can be devastating to those who bring their hopes and their dreams, as well as their genitals, to the act of love.

Strip erotic love of its delicacy and you have an exercise in pleasure. A delicious itch which feels even more delicious when scratched. That is all you have, and many women want more. They long for the full package of love. One common complaint is that men want only the act. That is OK for Neanderthal Man (and those women whom this suits). In fact, the majority of men are very aware and sensitive. They want precisely what women want: love, trust, understanding, mutuality. They respond negatively to some imaginary level of desire.

Rape and Blame

In 1991, a young man terrorized elderly women living in a certain Florida neighborhood. First, he scouted out their comings and goings. Then, when it was safe, he broke into their homes, gagged them, stripped off their clothing, and photographed their frail, cringing bodies. He did not otherwise molest them. Yet this seems as shocking, as vicious, as inhumanely cruel as if he had actually raped them. No doubt, he went home to indulge in sex acts alone with the pictures.

Why do rape victims feel themselves partly to blame? This is another myth which women have to struggle against. It is woven so deeply into our culture's perceptions that even other women will join in the general suspicion of a rape victim's behavior. In the case above, those elderly women could not possibly have considered themselves in any way to blame. Yet when a victim of rape (or any form of sexual molestation) is young, or attractive, or scantily-dressed, or out late at night, or with a date or neighbor known to her, our culture will regard her as partly to blame.

It is important for all women to understand that men are *not* dogs at the mercy of their sex drive. They *do* have control over their sexual impulses. To consider otherwise would be a "verbal rape" of all those splendid men who love, protect, and cherish women. Except in the case of a sociopath, every man *knows* that he can stop, no matter how extreme the level of his arousal. Every woman *knows* when she has been sexually violated. The rage starts immediately. Value that rage: avoid the merest *trace* of self blame.

The Phantom Orgasm?

Sadly in life, horrendous things do happen. Women can become paralyzed in their pelvic region from road accidents, disease and so on. They can lose all sensation in their pelvic area. Yet many paralyzed women continue to be orgasmic. However, our culture tends to perceive people with such disabilities as non-sexual. Indeed, medical textbooks refer to these orgasms as "phantom orgasms." This is a phantom of medical folklore.

When men were asked what stimulated their desire, some said that 95 percent of the time desire arose in the higher conscious mind. Others strongly disagreed. They insisted that 95 percent was too low. Desire was 99 percent triggered by the conscious mind. Be that as it may, it is critical to understand:

A woman can have an orgasm without penetration.
A woman can have an orgasm without a penis.

A man can have an orgasm without an erection.
A man can have an orgasm without a penis.

In fact, some women (and men) have orgasms merely by willing them. They do not require foreplay, nor thrusting, to raise sexual tension first. This is rare, but it can and does happen. Keep in mind that people are individuals, and have very different levels of sexual drive.

The human spirit is a wonderful phenomenon. It can withstand the most appalling vicissitudes and still respond with courage and resourcefulness. Women are said to be more stoical than men. They are able to endure more pain, both mental and physical. One extraordinary finding from the concentration camps of World War 11 showed that women succumbed to gruesome torture much later than did men.

Loss of sensation is a savage assault on female primacy. A woman's first response can be equally savage and destructive. If she responds with a seemingly quiet and depressive state, this is as damaging emotionally as a raging and bitter response. Keep in mind that the healing process can be speeded up by orgasm, if so desired. Use a vibrator, erotica, anything which works.

In a loving relationship, the partner can take control. Seduce her out of her angry or passive state. Shock her out of grief and pain by relighting her sexual fires. Turn her emotional energies away from her broken body and back to where happiness awaits.

Avoid over-concern with her feelings. She is a woman still, a *real* woman, and will find your particular brand of "medication" irresistable. Tell her that she is desirable. Continue to enchant her until she has an orgasm. Then tell her she is so desirable that she must be prepared for another love making session soon.

What Is Nyphomania?

A *nymphomaniac* is "a promiscuous woman. One with excessive and uncontrollable desires, whose sexual appetites cannot be sated." *Promiscuous* means "having indiscriminate sexual relations without regard to the restrictions of marriage and cohabitation."

Can a woman be a nymphomaniac? Who decides how much sex is excessive? Physicians? Sex therapists? John and Mary Doe? Nymphomania, like inhibited sexual desire, is a philosophical concept. Some women do have more sexual passion than others. Whether they become promiscuous or not often depends upon their moral choices. When a man regards female desire as excessive or insatiable, that is his subjective *opinion* only.

There is no precise synonym for excessive desire in men. A *satyr* is "a lascivious man, one who is fond of wine, riotous merriment, and lechery." The word comes from Greek mythology: Satyr was a minor god, represented as part man and part goat, with horns on his head, a hairy body, and the feet and tail of a goat. A species of butterfly and orangutan also bear this name. The word *satyriasis* is far less often used about men than nymphomania is used about women. *Erotomania*, which is "excessive or uncontrollable sexual passion in either gender" avoids this sexist sting.

Why does a woman become a prostitute? To earn money. However, men who use prostitutes often regard them as nyphomaniacs. Vanity must be appeased, and prostitutes are experts at faking orgasm. Not all prostitutes do this, only the successful ones who wish to build up repeat business; a regular clientele. Prostitutes are not more orgasmic than other women. Given their history, often less. Prostitution is offensive to society for all the usual, sensible reasons.

Further Comments

In a recent study, researchers found that, *for women*, orgasm was only one bond in marriage, and that the frequency of love making depended more on the quality of the relationship than on the quality of orgasm. If the marriage was happy, women were more likely to have sex; if it was unhappy, women were less likely to do so. These findings suggest that marital and sexual satisfaction for women is more closely related to the total relationship, instead of to orgasm outcome.

In response to a question which appeared in Ann Landers' column, women overwhelmingly reported that they would rather be held and cuddled than engage in sex. Some experts took this to mean that women did not enjoy making love. They could not, or would not, experience orgasm. It can be argued that women know what some experts may have forgotten: orgasms are not the be-all and end-all of love.

Barbara Amiel, a U.K. journalist, writes, "Sex is now in the open, and many people just cannot cope with the emotional wear and tear involved. We seem to think that the alchemist's stone would be to create a paradise for sex in which everyone will have everything they want at no price at all. Sexual and emotional freedom will be painless for everyone...

"We say our divorce laws are at fault. We attempt to suspend moral judgments on breeding arrangements. Our preoccupation to make sex painless is wrong. The right preoccupation is to develop character in people so that they understand realistically what their sexual pain threshold is likely to be, what price they can afford to pay, and prepare them for that price. There may always be individuals who can navigate sexual shoals and get bargains. They do not need any help. Most of us do."

— *The Sunday Times, 1991*

- Fifty-eight percent of Americans say they wish they could spend more time making love.
- Ninety-two percent report having had 10 or more lovers, with a lifetime average of 17 lovers.
- Four in 10 Americans have had more than one lover in the past year.
- One in 3 say that love was their primary reason for getting married; 1 in 10 say that sex was the reason.
- Twenty-nine percent of married Americans say that they were virgins on their wedding day.
- Fifteen percent of American adults would rather watch television than have sex.

— The Day America Told The Truth
by James Patterson and Peter Kim

Summary

- Orgasm is a powerful muscle relaxant and aerobic workout.
- Orgasm will occur after 20 minutes of erotic stimulation.
- Most women can have multiple orgasms, if they so wish.
- A penis is not necessary for orgasm to occur.
- Keep lubrication at hand if the vagina feels dry.
- Visit the physician if pain after orgasm persists.
- Visit a sex therapist if there are partner problems.
- Orgasm is as variable as life itself.

CHAPTER 6

The Uterus

Home, Sweet Home

In the *4th century BC*, Hippocrates believed that the womb went wild unless it was fed regularly with male semen. Hippocrates is honored as the "father of medicine."

In the *2nd century AD*, another doctor, Aretaeus, wrote, "In the flanks of women lies the womb...closely resembling an animal, for it is moved of itself hither and thither...it is altogether erratic...the womb is like an animal within an animal."

In the *14th century AD*, a French surgeon believed that the womb was a penis turned inside out. Furthermore: "It has in its upper parts two arms with the testicles...like the scrotum."

In the *20th century AD*, psychologists view the womb as "Home, Sweet Home" from which humankind is expelled, never to completely recover from the birth trauma.

In the *20th century AD*, Germaine Greer called the uterus, "The Wicked Womb." It became wickedly old-fashioned to call the uterus a womb. It means hysteria. A hysterectomy is the complete removal of this "hysterical" organ.

The Moving Home

The uterus is held in place by ligaments and smooth muscle. It lies over the bladder and at a *right angle* to the vagina. This is called *anteflexed*, and occurs in 80 percent of women. The other 20 percent are *retroflexed*, bent backwards. It used to be thought a retroflexed uterus caused period cramps, backache, and urine leakage, but it is normal. Unfortunately, surgery to "correct" a "tipped" uterus was fairly common in those days.

The uterus can move. It can change position if either the bladder or the rectum are full. It changes position at puberty and menopause, during the monthly cycle, and at sexual arousal. Women can feel this last, and they feel the uterus contract at orgasm. In fact, if the uterus cannot move, there are problems such as scar tissue holding down the ligaments. The *fundus* is the top of the uterus and leads to the oviducts. The *cervix* is the base, and dips down into the vagina.

The Expanding Home

In her excellent book *From Woman To Woman* Dr. Lucienne Lanson wrote, "Although the fertile valley between the Tigris and Euphrates is regarded by some historians as the cradle of civilization, we women know better. The real cradle is the uterus. Just how far do you think civilization would have come without the uterine cradle? What makes the uterus such a remarkable cradle? Stretchability to accommodate pregnancy. Without a doubt the uterus is one of the most fantastic organs in the body.

"From the size of a small pear, the uterus can blow up to bigger than a watermelon and then revert to the size of a respectable pear in short order. In the nonpregnant state the uterine cavity would barely hold a teaspoon of water, and yet nine months later, it can accommodate a 9-pound baby, a 1-pound placenta and some 3 pints of amniotic fluid."

The uterus is about the same size as its owner's clenched fist. It is shaped like an upside-down pear. The walls are made up of thick, heavy, powerful muscles. They comprise 90 percent of the uterus' size. The lining of the uterus is the endometrium, which only gets a brief rest after a period each month.

The Welcoming Door

The cervix has a front door, the *external os*. The os is tiny, about 3 millimeters across. It is known as the "mouth of the little fish" (os tincae), because its function is to open at mid-cycle and welcome in millions of sperm. After mid-cycle, it closes firmly to keep out all other objects. It opens slightly at a period to allow the flow through. In rare cases, the os can be blocked, causing *cervical stricture*, and has to be opened surgically.

The external os leads into a corridor, the *endocervical canal*. This is 3 centimeters long, and lined with over a hundred glands which produce *cervical mucus*. Cervical mucus is profuse at mid-cycle, and scant otherwise. It plays a very important role in fertility. Last comes the *internal os*, the door which leads into the uterus. The medical name for the cervix is "portico vaginalis," the portal which leads to "Home, sweet Home."

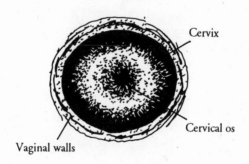

A HEALTHY CERVIX

The cervix is one-third the length of the uterus. It feels wobbly, rather like the tip of the nose. After childbirth, it is larger, one-half the length of the uterus. It feels more solid, more like the tip of the chin. Nor can the os return to its pre-birth size.

The cervix can be self-viewed with the aid of a speculum. It can be felt more easily if bending slightly forward. Check hands are clean and fingernails short. Avoid any sudden or jabbing movements. Keep in mind that the cervix responds to estrogen, and will look slightly different at different times in the monthly cycle. Avoid touching the cervix to avoid contact bleeding and the risk of germs. Some physicians consider that there is a health risk in viewing the cervix. This is an issue of personal choice.

Problems of the Cervix

A healthy cervix is pinkish in color. The lining of the canal is red. Redness on the os can mean inflammation of the canal. It is estimated 90 percent of all women will have some degree of cervical inflammation at some stage in their reproductive years. This is not suprising, considering that the cervix works non-stop at producing different amounts of mucus and monitoring the passage of sperm and menstrual flow throughout the cycle. (Not to mention supporting a fetus and dilating for childbirth.)

A *cervical cyst* is a mucus gland which is plugged up. It looks like a whitish pimple on the os. There can be one, or many. They are painless and *not* serious, often due to a healed infection or other past irritation of the cervix.

A *polyp* is a small red growth on a stalk from the canal or uterus lining. If touched, even lightly, it contact bleeds. This can happen at deep penetration, or with a douche or manual self-exam. Cervical polyps are common, particularly after age 40. They rarely become cancerous, but can look like a precancer. Have a Pap test to check that all is well.

Cervicitis is a covering name for infections and inflammations of the cervix. Some sexual diseases attack and damage the cervix; they cause erosions and weakness which look like precancer. Other STDs travel through the cervix, uterus, and out of the tubes into the lower abdomen, causing pelvic inflammatory disease (PID). *Condyloma* is a sexual disease caused by the human papilloma virus. The infection develops into genital warts. Condyloma is found in 85 percent or more of cancers of the cervix. Sexual activity before age

18, or with multiple partners, increases the risk that genital warts will become precancerous. Between 20 to 30 percent of sexually-active Americans are infected with this disease. A Pap smear can detect the presence of the human papilloma virus. Appropriate self-care for a healthy cervix is to avoid sexual risk.

Cancer of the Cervix

Cancer of the cervix is the second most common female cancer. Each year, about 45,000 non-invasive and 16,000 invasive cases are diagnosed in the United States. The rate is 1 in 100,000 for women aged 20 to 24. It rises to 50 in 100,000 at ages 45 to 65. Cervical cancer used to be an older women's disease. Today, it is showing up more frequently in young women. In the 1960s, 9 percent of cervical cancers were found in women under age 35. In 1992, 25 percent of the cancers are found in women under age 35.

Dysplasia is a change in the size, shape, or number of cells in the cervix. It is *not* cancer, though the cells look abnormal. Dysplasia is classified as mild, moderate, or severe, depending upon how abnormal the cells look. It is more common at ages 25 to 35, but can occur in other age groups.

Carcinoma in situ is very early cervical cancer. Only the top layers of cells are affected. The deeper layers may not be invaded for many months, perhaps years. It is more common at ages 30 to 40, but can occur in other age groups.

Invasive cervical cancer is cancer which has spread into the cervix. It may have invaded nearby tissues and organs. The most usual ages are between 40 and 60.

A *Pap smear* can detect the presence of abnormal-looking cells. A colposcope allows a magnified view of the cervix, so the physician can see the suspect areas. The cervix is bathed in a vinegar-like solution which outlines the shape and structure of the cells. A colposcopy is 95 percent accurate in detecting abnormalities.

Mild dysplasia requires only a "watch and wait" management program. Moderate dysplasia can be removed by the new Loop Electrosurgical Excision Procedure, LEEP, which cuts out the abnormal cells in a small plug in one pass, and blocks bleeding at the same time. Moderate dysplasia can also be removed by *cryosurgery, cauterization* or *laser ablation*. Severe dysplasia and very early cancer respond to *conization*. A cone-shaped section is cut out of the cervix and canal. In 85 percent of cases, all the abnormal tissue is taken and the dysplasia does not return. Cone biopsy is not a minor procedure. It requires general anesthesia. In some cases, there can be profuse bleeding.

Physicians have a saying: "Real cancer requires real treatment." Invasive cancer of the cervix must be treated aggressively. This means hysterectomy to remove the cervix, uterus, and ovaries. The nearby lymph nodes are removed to stop cancer spread. New therapies to try to avoid hysterectomy include radiotherapy, hormone drugs, and combinations of radiation and chemotherapy.

Dysplasia and early cervical cancer rarely cause symptoms. *They are only detected by a pelvic exam and Pap smear*. Symptoms do not generally appear until the cancer has become invasive. The most common symptom is abnormal bleeding. Abnormal bleeding can be due to many factors which do *not* signify cancer. Nevertheless, visit the physician promptly if:

- Bleeding starts and stops between regular periods.
- The flow lasts longer and is heavier than usual.
- There is bleeding after making love, or douching.

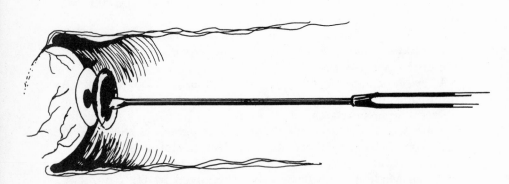

THE LEEP TECHNIQUE An electrfied loop excises abnormal cells in a small plug in one pass and blocks bleeding at the same time.

The National Cancer Institute reports: "The outlook for women with dysplasia and very early cancer of the cervix is *excellent*. Nearly all women with these conditions can be cured."

A Pap Smear

Avoid douching or making love before a Pap test and pelvic exam. Choose any non-period time. A spatula is put into the os to collect a layer of cells. Another collects cells from the canal. The test is not normally painful. If it does hurt, ask the doctor to use a lighter touch. There can be mild spotting afterwards. It is rare to get cramps.

An abnormal Pap result does not mean cancer or precancer. It can show a cervicitis, a chronic yeast infection, or a sexual disease. Have another Pap smear once the condition is cleared. After age 18, all sexually-active women should have annual Pap smears. When these have been normal for 3 years, they can be done less often. Ask the physician's advice on this, as some women have an increased risk of cancer and need more frequent screening. If the results do show cancer or precancer, a biopsy will be performed.

A Swedish study found Pap tests every 3 years reduced the rate of noninvasive cancer to 1 to 5 per 100,000 in the older age group. Women who had no Pap tests had 2 to 4 times the rate of those who were regularly screened. *Most cases of invasive cervical cancer could have been prevented if all women had pelvic exams and Pap smears regularly.*

Support for the Home

The pelvic cavity is lined with a tough weave of ligaments, muscles, and other tissues which make up a supportive sling. Any weakness or sagging in this sling is called "relaxation of pelvic supports." Where the sling sags, the uterus (or other organs) slip down, causing a bulge in the usually taut vagina wall. Think of a prolapse as a hernia, a bulge of tissue which protrudes into the vagina.

Prolapse is due to normal wear and tear, especially in mothers. Lifting heavy weights incorrectly puts great strain on the pelvic supports. Consider how often a mother dives to save her infant, or scoops up a child who is in immediate need of a hug. She doesn't have time to think of correct lifts. Young women can be taught these lifts so that they become automatic. If it is already too late, regard a prolapse as a "symbol of honor."

The first sign is "stress" or "urinary incontinence," a slight leak of urine when coughing, sneezing or laughing. The diaphragm presses down at these actions; it is *not* due to mental stress. It is rare to leak when lying down, and not at night. There can be a heavy sensation, or an aching feeling that something has "fallen out."

If the leakage is slight and panty liners can cope, some women prefer not to seek medical help. But if the uterus has fallen some way down the vagina, or if the leakage is bothersome, others want the problem surgically fixed. A surgical procedure called a "suspension operation" can be done through the vagina walls. The uterus is sewn back in place, the slack ligaments are shortened and tightened, and the pelvic lining repaired.

A *pessary* avoids surgery. It is a plastic or rubber device fitted around the cervix to prop up the uterus. There can be problems in getting an exact fit, and having to remove and clean the pessary frequently with a risk of infection or irritation. At love making, it limits the depth of penile penetration. But if there is strong anti-surgery motivation, a woman will be just as strongly motivated to make sure a pessary works.

Self-care of the uterus involves a daily set of exercises to tone up the muscles and keep them firm. Love making is also great exercise for all the pelvic supports.

A Home Extension?

A *fibroid* is a benign growth (non-cancer lump) of gland tissue which develops inside the uterus wall. Average fibroid size is 2 to 2 1/2 inches in diameter. They are more common, and grow earlier and more quickly in black women; it is not known why. Usually, a fibroid is asymptomatic and is only found at a pelvic exam.

It is estimated that 20 to 50 percent of all women develop fibroids by age 35. They grow more quickly with estrogen, either from the Pill, or from estrogen supplements at menopause. When estrogen levels drop after menopause, the fibroid shrinks. Many women with no symptoms avoid surgery. They prefer to live with fibroids, and wait for them to shrink after menopause. A "watch and wait" management program includes regular checks to ensure that they are not growing rapidly.

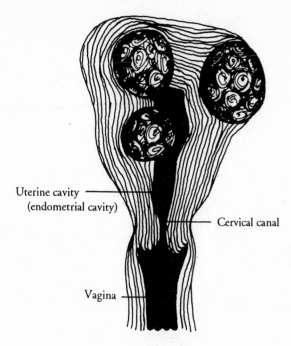

Uterine cavity
(endometrial cavity)

Cervical canal

Vagina

VERY LARGE FIBROIDS

Large fibroids can over-stretch the uterus wall, causing heavy bleeding and/or severe period pain. Watch out for anemia; check iron content in the diet. *Myomectomy* is a procedure which scoops out the fibroids and leaves the lining intact. After pregnancy, delivery is usually by Caesarian section. New hormone therapy to shrink fibroids is in the clinical trial stage.

There is less than a 0.3 percent chance of fibroids becoming malignant. If they grow rapidly, especially after menopause, a biopsy is necessary to check. If the growth is benign, laparoscopy and laser surgery are procedures with a high success rate. They avoid a large scar, and cost far less than an hysterectomy. With malignancy, it may not be possible to avoid an hysterectomy.

Fibroids grow only in the uterus. They do not increase the risk of *breast fibroadenomas*, as some women fear. The same kind of fibroid growths occur in men at about the same age. BPH is a benign hyperplasia (overgrowth) of the prostate gland which starts in mid-life men.

Endometriosis

"Normal tissue in an abnormal location" is the definition of endometriosis.

It is a mystery why cells can sometimes detach from the endometrium, find their way to other body parts and attach there. Various theories exist. Perhaps they are bits of menstrual flow which back up through the fallopian tubes and enter the pelvic cavity. Douching may force some fragments out of place. Strong menstrual cramps might do the same. Love making during a period is suspect, as is scarring from previous surgery. They could be scraps of prenatal tissue which develop into endometriosis under the influence of estrogen.

Each time the uterus responds to estrogen, these bits of cells do the same. They swell at mid-cycle and bleed during a period. The menstrual debris cannot leave the body; it irritates nearby tissue. This, in turn, tries to protect itself with adhesions and scar tissue. At pregnancy and menopause, when there are no periods, the growths shrink and the pain goes. However, the scar tissue remains and can continue to cause pain.

Like fibroids, endometriosis can be slight and asymptomatic. It is estimated that 15 percent of all women have some degree of endometrial growth before menopause. The most common symptoms are pain before and during a period; heavy or irregular bleeding; pain when making love. In serious cases, scar tissue on the ovary and/or oviduct blocks the release of the egg or its passage through the tube. This is a common problem of infertility. Oddly enough, the degree of pain is not related to the extent of the growth. Some women with many growths have no pain, while others with minimal endometriosis have severe pain.

Hormone Therapy: Because hormones control the monthly cycle, controlling their output can be very effective therapy. The Pill, progestens, and danazol (a male hormone derivative) are all used in different ways. When taken for six months, the endometriosis shrinks and the pain stops. After hormone therapy, when periods start again, there is a chance that the endometriosis will not return.

Hormone therapy supresses, but does not cure. There are side effects from each of the hormones. A new drug option is GnRH Analogs. When taken for six months, they stop estrogen production. The fragments shrink, giving relief from pain. GnRH Analogs avoid the masculinizing side effects of danazol. But they produce some symptoms of menopause, such as hot flashes and vagina dryness. These are reversible when drug therapy stops. The major advantage of GnRH Analogs is for a woman wanting a child.

Surgical Options: Conservative surgery removes individual areas of endometriosis. Surface growths are cut out, or destroyed by electric current or laser beam. It is a critical option in the child-bearing years, because the uterus lining is left intact. Radical surgery includes total *hysterectomy*, which is removal of the cervix and uterus, and *bilateral salpingo-oophorectomy*, which is removal of the ovaries and oviducts. Both conservative and radical surgery are considered last-ditch options to relieve severe pain after all other methods have failed.

State-of-the Art

Hysteroscopy: a hysteroscope is a fiberoptic scope used for viewing the uterus. The scope is on an ultra-thin rod which is inserted through the cervix. A fluid or carbon dioxide gas is put in the uterus to stretch it and make viewing easier. This splendid new procedure avoids cuts through the abdomen wall. The side effects are minor; there may be some cramping and bleeding after. Normal activities can be resumed in a few days. If surgery is required for polyps or fibroids, the uterus can be re-entered this way. The growths are removed by a sharp instrument, a *rescotoscope*. A biopsy sample of endometrial tissue is taken and sent to the laboratory for investigation. Any suspect tumor sites can be detected.

Laparoscopy: a laporoscope allows the same view, only the scope is put into the uterus through a small cut above the navel. Other small cuts are needed to remove a sample of tissue, and even more surgery can take place this way.

Laser surgery: (Light Amplification by Stimulated Emission of Radiation). This converts energy from an intense, sharply focused beam of light into heat energy, which is used to cut, coagulate, and vaporize the uterus lining. This procedure is *endometrial ablation*. It is more appropriate for mature women as it destroys the lining and removes any further chance of pregnancy. A *laser hysteroscopy* or *laser laparoscopy* simply means both are used for the procedure.

Transvaginal ultrasound (sonogram): this allows the uterus, tubes, and ovaries to be viewed from the vagina. A plastic probe is put into the vagina, and moved around to show each of these structures on a television screen. It can be used with the above procedures.

It all seems magical compared with *dilation and curettage* (D&C). Surgeons can *see* what they are doing. At D&C, the surgeon works "blind." The os is stretched open with a series of larger dilating instruments until a curette can be put in the uterus. This is a spoon-shaped instrument used for scraping the endometrium, working across the lining in a clockwise fashion. D&Cs were mostly done for abnormal bleeding and taking biopsy tissue. Many women gained relief from their symptoms, but studies show some that results were "hit and miss." The surgeon could only guess if the entire lining had been scraped.

The new hi-tech procedures take more time because the work is far more delicate and precise. They require the skills of an experienced surgeon, and the facilities of a modern hospital. Yet the only way for surgeons to acquire these skills is by practice, and some hospitals cannot afford the new equipment. Avoid losing faith in the old D&C. A highly experienced D&C surgeon may be preferable to one who wields a laser beam for the first time!

Polyps, fibroids, and endometriosis used to be cured by hysterectomy. The new advances in both medical technology and hormone drug therapy make it possible to avoid hysterectomy for most non-life-threatening conditions. However, a prolapse can be too severe for repair, not all fibroids respond to drug therapy, and so on. The decision to opt for hysterectomy depends upon many factors: the severity of the problem, the woman's general health, her reproductive life stage, and so on.

Cancer of the Uterus

Endometrial cancer and uterine cancer are the same thing. It is a mid-life disease, the peak ages being from 50 to 64. The rate is 0.1 per 100,000 women aged 20-24. It rises to 12 per 100,000 aged 40-44. Uterine cancer is easy to detect with the new methods of endometrial sampling. The warning symptoms include: irregular bleeding and/or spotting between periods; bleeding after making love. *Any* bleeding after menopause. Early detection saves lives. If these symptoms appear, visit the physician promptly.

The risk factors associated with uterine cancer include:

- Advancing age.
- Family history of this cancer.
- History of breast or colon cancer.
- Nulliparous: never pregnant.
- Late first pregnancy, after age 35.
- Late menopause, after age 55.
- Obesity, being seriously overweight.
- Polycystic ovary disease.
- Diabetes.
- High blood pressure.
- Hormone replacement therapy after menopause.

Long-term use of the Pill might reduce the risk, and repeated pregnancies seem to protect against it. A sample of the uterus lining is taken by hysteroscopy or D&C, and cells from the site are sent to the laboratory for investigation. If cancer is found, therapy can be hysterectomy and radiation and/or chemotherapy. Synthetic progesten is now being tried in order to treat this cancer. It seems to act on the endometrial cells in the same way as normal progesterone acts after mid-cycle, changing an endometrium which is growing and dividing into one which is nondividing and specialized. Hormone therapy is in the clinical trial stage. Keep up-to-date on the latest findings.

Hysterectomy

Hysterectomies in the United States: 1965 to 1984

Diagnosis	Number
Prolapse	2,375,000
Fibroids	3,112,000
Endometriosis	1,586,000
Cancer	1,220,000
Other conditions	2,933,000
Total	11,226,000

Of the above, half the women were age 45 and over. Only 20 percent had life-threatening conditions. In recent years, gynecologists have been taken to task over performing unnecessary hysterectomies. These were called "numerectomies"; a regular and highly paid source of income. However, some conditions do require hysterectomy. It is clearly appropriate, in fact *life-saving*, in some cases of invasive cancer of the uterus, cervix, vagina, oviducts, or ovaries; in serious conditions which do not respond to other therapies; and in dangerous complications of childbirth.

A vaginal hysterectomy involves reaching through the vagina to the uterus. This procedure heals faster, leaves no visible scar, and does not damage the muscles. It is appropriate for prolapse and other non-tumor conditions which affect the uterus but not the ovaries. However, the procedure does require a very skilled surgeon, and is not appropriate for cancer.

Love after Hysterectomy

Sexual desire abides in the head. Sexual urges and libido come from the central nervous system. If the clitoris is stimulated for long enough, orgasm will occur. Hysterectomy affects none of these, but it can affect a woman's image of herself. The results can be positive or negative, depending upon certain factors.

If past problems with the uterus caused pain at love making, there is now freedom from fear and misery. The release of tension can cause an increase in libido. There are no uterus contractions at orgasm. For some women, these were too strong and hurt, so it is an added benefit. The vagina may be shorter and tighter, which enhances the gripping effect. Once the pain and recovery time are over, the positive side of hysterectomy can be a brand new attitude to sexual desire.

On the negative side, surgery and/or radiation therapy can change the size of the vagina too much. If scar tissue builds up, the vagina is too tight or too short. Penetration and prolonged thrusting hurts. If the cervix was removed, lack of mucus causes problems of lubrication. Estogen creams reduce the discomfort of a dryish vagina. The female superior position gives more control over movement and so can help to avoid some pain.

The American Cancer Society was founded in 1913 by a group of physicians and volunteers. Its goals are to find the causes of cancer and help relieve the suffering of cancer patients. Today, it is a vast organization, with 2.5 million volunteers. Its work includes sponsoring, supporting, and operating educational and advocacy programs to prevent, detect, treat, and cure cancer. ACS provides cancer patients and their families with free services and rehabilitation programs. To find the nearest ACS chapter or Reach to Recovery contact, call the national hotline: 1-800-ACS-2345. The address is: American Cancer Society National Office, 1599 Clifton Road, N.E., Atlanta, Georgia 30329

The National Cancer Institute is part of the National Institutes of Health and is funded by the U.S. government. It funds research into the causes and treatment of cancer and offers a variety of informational services. To ask questions, request NCI publications, or information on certified radiologists, call the Cancer Information Service hotline: 1-800-4-CANCER. Or write to: The National Cancer Institute, Bethesda, Maryland 20205.

The Hereditary Cancer Institute is a nonprofit organization dedicated to research into hereditary cancers. It disseminates information on cancer genetics and research, and evaluates families to identify hereditary cancer. Call: 1-800-648-8133 or write to: The Hereditary Cancer Institute, Creighton University, P.O.Box 3266, Omaha, Nebraska 68103.

The National Coalition for Cancer Survivorship is a network of independent groups and individuals offering support to cancer survivors and their loved ones. It provides information and resources on support and life after a cancer diagnosis. Write to: The National Coalition for Cancer Survivorship, 323 Eighth Street, S.W., Albuquerque, New Mexico, 87102

Home, Sweet Home

The following is a list of the most common gynecological complaints. Some are discussed in this chapter, others in other parts of the book.

- Menorrhagia (heavy bleeding).
- Amenorrhea (no periods).
- Pelvic pain (PID).
- Vaginal discharge.
- Lump or mass in abdomen.
- Prolapse from vagina.
- Urinary leakage.
- Hot flashes.
- Infertility.
- Painful sexual intercourse.

For a few women, the uterus can seem to be a source of never-ending problems. Keep in mind that growths such as fibroids, polyps, and endometriosis occur because the lining is specially created to support growth, to support life itself. No mention has been made of the primary function of the uterus; childbirth is outside the parameters of this book. However, this is the upside of a troublesome uterus; to be the first cradle of the world's children.

Summary

- Have a Pap smear at a regular pelvic exam.
- Certain sexual diseases can cause cancer of the cervix.
- Health of the cervix involves a healthy partner.
- If at risk, have a check to make sure all is well.
- Report heavy or irregular flow, or spotting between periods.
- A change in periods does not necessarily mean precancer.
- Prolapse can be cured by suspension vaginal surgery.
- Many fibroids and endometriosis shrink at menopause.
- Endometriosis pain can be relieved by new drug therapies.
- Early detection is of major importance in cancer therapy.
- Have regular Pap smears and pelvic exams.

CHAPTER 7

The Ovaries

Ovulation

At birth, there are about 500,000 eggs in each ovary. They remain dormant in sacs called *follicles* until puberty. By this time, only 125,000 eggs per ovary are left; it is not known why. Of these, only 200 per ovary will make it to *ovulation*, calculated roughly on months from puberty to menopause. Each month, three or four eggs are "chosen" to be ripened. Of these, only one is "chosen" to be released at ovulation, except in the case of twins, triplets, and so on. The others shrivel and become re-absorbed. It is not known why certain eggs are chosen rather than others; nor why one ripened egg is chosen for ovulation, rather than the others.

The follicle of a "chosen" egg fills with estrogen-rich fluid. It bulges like a blister on the surface of the ovary, over a quarter of an inch across. The egg inside is being prepared for fertilization; the chromosomes must be reduced from 46 to 23. It grows from a tiny 20 microns to 140 microns (1/1,000 of an inch to 1/200 of an inch). By ovulation, it is visible to the naked eye, about the size of the period at the end of this sentence. When enough LH has been produced, the follicle ruptures. The egg, which was attached to the follicle by a little stalk, then breaks free.

The release of the egg can be sudden and dramatic, or slow and take several hours. The body temperature rises slightly at this time. Some women know when they ovulate. They have pain in the lower abdomen and/or mild blood spotting. This is *mittelschmertz*, German for middle pain. (Some physicians deny the phenomenon of mittelschmertz, believing that the pain is due to gas). For women who do not feel this, other ways to check for ovulation include changes in the thickness of cervical mucus, body temperature changes, and the use of home ovulation kits.

If one ovary is diseased, or has been removed, the other will double up to produce an egg each month. The ovaries, like the testicles, are *gonads*. They produce the very seeds of life itself. So important is their function, that there are two as a fail-safe. Each one alone can, and sometimes does, carry on the full and complete work of two.

As the egg is released into the pelvic cavity, a trace of blood-tinged fluid exudes from the rupture. The empty follicle turns into a temporary gland, the *corpus luteum* (Latin for yellow body; it is bright yellow). The corpus luteum produces both female hormones. Progesterone softens the uterus lining, making it thick and lush for the arrival of a fertilized egg. If there is no pregnancy, the corpus luteum degenerates. If an egg is fertilized, it continues to produce both hormones until the placenta can take over the work.

The Oviducts

The *oviducts* (or Fallopian tubes) are two narrow, pliant tubes. They are specially designed to transport the egg on its journey to the uterus. The outer walls are made of smooth muscle which propel the egg forward. Inside, it is no wider than a single bristle on a hairbrush. The walls are thickly fringed with *cilia*, tiny little hairs which wave towards the uterus in an endless beat. This movement is at its strongest at ovulation time. Cells on the inner lining secrete nourishing fluids for the egg.

The ends of the oviducts are fringed, *fimbria*, rather like the fringed edges of a daffodil. They act as delicate fingery scoops to catch the newly released egg. The tubes are movable; they turn at ovulation to bring their fimbria close to the egg. Once contact has been made, it is rather like touching a sea anemone with a pencil. The fimbria immediately close tightly over the egg. All this takes only about 20 seconds.

It seems strange that the egg is set adrift from the ovary, after the complex work of ripening it for fertilization. One theory suggests that it is Nature's way of making sure that every precious egg counts. Because if a woman has only one ovary working on one side, and only one oviduct which is unblocked on the other side, she can still become pregnant. Somehow or other, the egg is wafted right across the pelvic cavity until it reaches the other oviduct.

External scarring of the oviducts can restrict their ability to move towards the egg. The scars can be from an infection which damaged the tubes, or abdominal surgery such as appendicitis. Keep in mind scar tissue is tough and fibrous, with no give. It can tie down the tubes and prevent all movement. External scars are more usually called *adhesions*. Scarring from endometriosis can also tie down the tubes.

If a colored dye is introduced into the uterus and pumped onwards, it can be seen traveling clear through the oviducts and flowing out through the fringed ends of the fimbria. But if there has been an infection or scarring from surgery, the fringed ends tend to heal by closing in on themselves. The thickened scars do not allow fluid to pass out, and the tube swells up with retained fluid. This is called *hydrosalpingitis*. It is a common cause of female infertility. The mucus lining inside the tubes becomes very damaged when the ends are blocked. (The open tubes show why a severe infection causes such devastation. The germs pass straight out into the abdomen, causing havoc as they go. The result is pelvic inflammatory disease, PID.)

Once the egg is safely caught, the tiny fringe-like cilia take over its transport. They move now to a very fast and muscular beat; wafting forward and forward in the direction of the uterus. The egg is rolled rapidly onwards until it reaches a wider little part of the tube, the *ampulla*. Here it remains, waiting to be fertilized. This is where it will meet with sperm, or not.

A Short Shelf Life

The egg is held in the ampulla for up to 24 hours. After this, if sperm do not arrive, it is overripe and dies. The timing is critical. If the estrogen level is too high, the egg is moved too quickly and the endometrium is not ready, lush and soft, when it arrives. If the lining of the oviduct is damaged, the egg cannot be transported to the ampulla.

The vagina is an acid environment to help protect against infection. Semen, which contains sperm, is alkaline. So the vagina presents a fairly hostile environment to sperm. Some 20 percent of sperm die immediately. For couples trying to conceive, the man should ejaculate deep within the vagina, as close to the cervix as possible. This increases the chance of fertilization by reducing the distance that sperm have to swim in their struggle along the unfriendly vagina.

The cervix is welcoming. At mid-cycle, stimulated by estrogen, the output of mucus increases ten-fold. It becomes watery and streams out of the open os. It forms tiny liquid channels, less than one-hundredth of one-millionth of an inch thick. Many sperm fail to find the entrances to the channels. The lucky ones stream through in an endless line.

Sperm have a short shelf life. The upper limit of sperm survival seems to be about 48 hours. Moving sperm have been found in cervical mucus as long as six to eight days after love making. The fact that they are moving does not mean that they still have the power to fertilize. The life span of the egg is even shorter, perhaps little more than 24 hours.

Once inside the vagina, average times for sperm survival rate have been estimated as follows:

- Vagina 2.5 hours
- Cervix 48.0 hours
- Uterus 24.0 hours
- Oviduct 48.0 hours

In fact, sperm with good swimming skills, *and* a keen sense of direction, can travel through the vagina at a speedy rate. They arrive at the cervix a few moments after ejaculation. Smooth muscles in the uterus and oviducts contract in waves. These contractions move the sperm more rapidly than they could swim by themselves.

The vast majority of sperm do not make it. Of those 3 to 5 hundred million in an average ejaculate, only about 50 actually reach the egg. The majority fall at the first hurdle, the cervix. Many do not make it as far as this. Some get sidetracked in nooks and crannies. Others swim round and round in circles, or backwards. Still others frantically try to fertilize any round bump or cell they meet on the way.

Fertilization

Once through the cervix and uterus, the surviving sperm must then find their way to the oviduct. During their travels, sperm go through a process known as capacitation. The covering which protects their heads drops off, and internal changes prime them to break through the egg's tough outer coats. After capacitation, their life span is even shorter. They are at the point of no return. They must reach the egg, or die.

Once through the cervix and uterus, sperm hone swiftly in on their target. It is a race against time; a race for life itself. They crowd around the egg, frenziedly battering their tiny frames against the hard outer walls. Though only one sperm can fertilize the egg, it requires the relentless pressure from a hundred or more to break down that outer protective coat.

As soon as a tiny crack appears in the wall, a few sperm immediately wriggle through. These might be the strongest, the sturdiest, but this is not known. The remaining sperm outside begin to die off. The outer wall of the egg promptly seals itself shut. The tails of the sperm inside drop off. Now, there is only one wall left. Only one sperm can get through.

As the one victorious sperm moves towards the nucleus of the egg, its head and body fall away, leaving only its nucleus. At last, the two nucleii meet and fuse together. The two become one.

Implantation

The fertilized egg begins to divide rapidly into two cells, then four, eight, sixteen, and so on. Each division is a replica of the first, though the process becomes more complex. The egg does not grow in size during this time. While in the ampulla, it is nourished by secretions from the lining of the oviduct, and rolled swiftly along and down into the uterus.

Again, the timing is critical. The egg must reach the uterus within two to three days of fertilization. Once it arrives there, it nestles against one of the walls, often near the fundus, the top of the uterus. Tiny, delicate fronds gradually emerge from the uterus wall to meet the tiny, delicate fronds which are gradually emerging from the fertilized egg. When the fronds meet and hold, then implantation is complete.

Ectopic Pregnancy

A fertilized egg does not always arrive safely in the uterus. It can

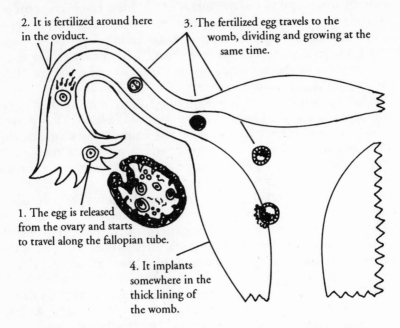

2. It is fertilized around here in the oviduct.

3. The fertilized egg travels to the womb, dividing and growing at the same time.

1. The egg is released from the ovary and starts to travel along the fallopian tube.

4. It implants somewhere in the thick lining of the womb.

A STYLIZED VIEW OF FERTILIZATION AND IMPLANTATION

become implanted elsewhere, usually in the ampulla of the tube where it was fertilized. It then begins to grow, and bulges against the walls of the oviduct. When the pressure becomes too great, the oviduct ruptures, often with heavy internal bleeding. In rare cases, the fertilized egg backs out of the oviduct and attaches itself to any nourishing tissue.

The symptoms of ectopic pregnancy are the same as for normal pregnancy: swelling breasts, itchy nipples, missed period, nausea, and fatigue. There can be blood spotting. It is often only when the pain gets fairly severe that the woman goes to the physician for investigation. A mistaken diagnosis of normal pregnancy can further delay treatment. Meanwhile, the internal bleeding could be causing more damage within the pelvis.

Treatment is urgently required; it is a surgical emergency. The pregnancy is removed and the surgeon repairs the oviduct. If this is not possible, the entire tube may have to be removed. If the pregnancy was advanced, there can be extensive adhesions, fibrous bands of scar tissue which tie the tubes, ovaries, or uterus down and prevent movement. A skilled surgeon tries to reduce the extent of the damage. After one ectopic pregnancy, there is an increased chance of a second. The less damage, the greater the chance for a normal pregnancy.

In recent years, the number of ectopic pregnancies has risen. This may be due to the rising numbers of scarred tubes from infection, IUD use, or previous surgery. An ectopic pregnancy can be mistaken for: appendicitis, salpingitis, urinary tract infection, an ovary cyst, or the start of a miscarriage. If there is *any* reason to suspect a pregnancy, and there is pelvic or abdomen pain, avoid a "watch and wait" approach. Visit the physician promptly. An ultrasound can show fetal tissue in the uterus, and a blood test can check for pregnancy. Regard bleeding or spotting with sudden pain 6 to 8 weeks after a missed period as an emergency. Get to hospital at once.

Pelvic Inflammatory Disease

PID is a generic name for any infection of the uterus, tubes, and ovaries. These are normally germ-free. Their position keeps them safe from infection, with added protection from the cervix, and its mildly antiseptic mucus. An infection is very dangerous once it reaches the cervix, because PID often starts with a cervical infection which travels to the uterus lining, then to the uterus muscle, the tubes (salpingitis), ovaries (oophoritis), and out into the pelvic cavity (peritonitis).

Once an infection reaches these normally germ-free areas, organs and tissues are now *inflammed*, swollen with pus and disease. Symptoms include: fever, chills, lower abdomen pain, irregular bleeding, spotting, pus-filled discharge from the vagina, and pain during or after intercourse. The more severe the infection, the worse the pain and symptoms. About 100,000 women each year become infertile as a result of PID.

Visit the physician promptly. Therapy is urgently required to reduce the extent of damage. Hospitalization is necessary for the first PID attack, so that antibiotics can be given intravenously (IV). If the infection is widespread, PID may not respond to antibiotics. Surgery is required to drain an abscess or pus-filled cavity, or to remove infected tissue. Hysterectomy used to be an option, but is now regarded as a final choice. One attack of PID gives no immunity against further attacks.

Other causes of PID include miscarriage and abortion. Surgery is required to remove any fetal or placental tissue still in the uterus. The infection is associated with intrauterine devices, and the IUD should be removed. Birthing and endometrial biopsy also open the cervix and increase the risk of PID. Some women are more vulnerable after a period. In others, the risk seems higher after sexual intercourse. It is thought that germs on sperm proteins could be carried up through the uterus and out to the pelvic cavity via the tubes, but this is not proven.

Salpingitis

The 14th century doctor, Gabriele Fallopio, described the oviduct as a tuba or curved trumpet. Hence, the name fallopian tubes for the oviducts. In fact, they look more like straight tubes with a trumpet opening at one end. The oviduct is also called "salpinx," which is Greek for "tube." Hence:

- *Salpingitis* is an infection of the oviduct.
- *Salpingectomy* is removal of one or both oviducts.
- *Salping-oophorectomy* is removal of the same-side tube and ovary, or both sides.
- *Oophorectomy* is removal of one or both ovaries. It used to be performed at the same time as a hysterectomy. This no longer happens because it is now known that the ovaries produce *androgens* into old age, even though at menopause they shrivel and stop most of their estrogen production. Other studies find that the risk of developing ovarian cancer after hysterectomy is too small (1 in 100) to justify removing these important organs.

Loss of the ovaries is not the same as loss of the uterus. If the uterus has been troublesome, a woman may be glad to be free from further worry. Having the ovaries removed is very different. It is castration, and a woman may react to the idea as negatively as a man reacts to loss of his testicles. It is naive to think a mature woman does not mind this surgery as much as a younger one.

Cysts

"A nine-and-one-half-hour operation to remove a 180 pound ovarian cyst was an ordeal both for the patient and a surgical team from John Hopkins Hospital. The 40-year-old woman can look forward to a full recovery although potential dangers lie ahead. She was listed in a stable condition.

The woman, who weighed 708 pounds before the operation, now weighs about 400 pounds."

The ovaries work very hard. From puberty to menopause, they produce estrogen, ripen eggs, spring them from the follicle, and then turn that same follicle into a hormone producing cyst. This constant activity makes them prey to certain disorders. Sometimes the egg is not sprung; it continues to grow and the ovary over-produces estrogen. In rarer cases, once the egg is sprung, the follicle goes on growing with over-production of progesterone. This causes a late or very long period, or one coming every two weeks for a month or more. There is pain if the enlarged cyst presses on the follicle walls.

Both these conditions are self-healing. The egg is released, or the fluid reabsorbed, usually within two months. Many women are not aware that they have a cyst while it develops and disappears. A cyst is often only detected at a pelvic exam. However, some cysts do cause symptoms; an unexplained swelling of the abdomen, pain during intercourse, an upset in the menstrual cycle, or sudden pain at either side of the abdomen.

Ovarian cysts used to be removed as soon as they gave trouble. Nowadays, if an enlarged cyst is found during a pelvic exam, the therapy program during the next two monthly cycles is to "watch and wait" for it to disappear. However, if an enlarged cyst starts to bleed, or cause acute pain, surgery is needed to repair the ovary. There are other types of cysts which also involve a "watch and wait" program. In women under age 30, some 90 percent of ovarian growths are benign cysts.

Ultrasound is used to examine the cyst and the general condition of the ovary. Factors which help decide whether surgery is required include: size of cyst, how long it has been present, and whether part of the cyst is solid or not. The problem is in trying to decide if the solid part might be a sign of cancer. If the cyst is becoming smaller in a woman of reproductive age, it is likely to be benign. After menopause, the risk of it becoming malignant increases. Surgery may then be advised.

Heart Disease

Estrogen output drops at menopause, and women then become as susceptible to heart disease as men. Researchers have found that a condition in about 20 percent of the U.K. female population is an accurate indicator of susceptibility to heart disease. By screening all women, and then counseling the high-risk groups, it is hoped that many thousands of lives can be saved each year.

The condition is known as *polycystic ovarian syndrome*, PCOS. It not only threatens women's fertility, it also interferes with the finely tuned hormone balance that gives women far more protection against heart disease than men. The screening test, using an ultra-sound scan, identifies polycystic ovaries, a symptomless condition which provides an early warning signal for heart disease.

The same high-risk factors for heart disease, including smoking, lack of exercise, weight gain, and high sugar intake, activate the benign cysts, making them flare up into full-blown PCOS. Thus, in watching the progress of one disease, physicians now have a useful early indicator for the biggest killer of modern times, heart disease.

Cancer of the Ovary

Ovarian cancer occurs in 1 to 1.5 percent of women. Like other cancers, it is not known what causes the tumor to start growing in the first place. The peak ages for ovarian cancer are between 50 and 59; the disease is diagnosed in about 2 per 100,000 U.S. women aged 15-24 each year. At these ages, it is the most common reproductive cancer. It can be difficult to treat if it is not detected very early. Many cases are advanced before they are found. Have regular pelvic exams to avoid this risk.

Ovarian cancer is hard to detect because if the cancer cells stay in the ovary, they rarely cause symptoms. A tumor in the ovary can grow for some time before it causes pressure, pain, or other problems. Even when symptoms appear, they can be vague and are often ignored. Report any *sudden* weight increase around the waist or abdomen. The tumor can grow very large; a 180-pound one was recently removed from a woman in San Francisco.

In 1989, 12,000 women in the U.S. died of ovarian cancer. There is an urgent need for early detection. The ultrasound probe gives a detailed picture of the ovaries. However, normal ovaries have cysts which look like tumors, and exploratory surgery is required to tell the difference. All surgery carries a risk, and this can be high when many of these tumors are cancer-free.

The Iowa Study

Nearly 100 women who were newly diagnosed with ovarian cancer took part in a unique Iowa study. In one-third, the cancer was confined to the ovaries; in the other two-thirds, it had spread. The women were questioned closely about any physical changes that may have occurred in the months before diagnosis. The results are now accepted as serious warning signs:

- Swelling or bloating
- A loss of appetite
- A feeling of fullness, even after a light meal
- Indigestion, weight loss, or nausea
- Fatigue, feeling tired for no obvious reason
- Discomfort in the lower abdomen
- Constipation, due to pressure from the tumor
- Urination problems (frequency, difficulty, or discomfort)
- Irregular bleeding
- Bleeding after menopause

Almost 80 percent of those with early disease had one or more of these symptoms. Yet the majority of women had delayed seeking medical help *because they did not know that these symptoms could mean cancer.* In fact, fewer than one-fifth felt concerned, and then not enough to see a physician.

If any of the above symptoms last for a week, especially if there is more than one, with no other health reason, avoid delay. Visit the physician promptly. The tests for cancer include:

- An ultrasound can distinguish between healthy cysts, fluid-filled cysts, and tumors. They all produce different echoes.
- A Cat scan is an X-ray procedure which gives a detailed picture of cross sections of the abdomen. The pictures are created by a computer.
- A lower GI (gastro-intestinal) series or a barium enema is a series of X-rays of the lower bowel. The barium highlights the bowel on an X-ray and may show abnormal areas caused by ovarian cancer.

- An intravenous pyleogram (IVP) is a test in which X-rays are taken of the kidneys, ureters, and bladder after an injection of a dye which highlights these organs. (Ureters are the tubes which take urine from the kidneys to the bladder).

Cancer Management

According to the National Cancer Institute, a *tissue biopsy* is the only sure way to detect the presence of cancer cells. To obtain the tissue, the surgeon removes the entire ovary. This may seem drastic, but if cancer is present, cutting through the outer layer will spill out the malignant cells and the disease will quickly spread to other sites.

If cancer is found, the surgeon nearly always removes the second ovary, the uterus, and the fallopian tubes (oviducts). Biopsy samples are also taken of nearby lymph nodes, the diaphragm, and fluid from the abdomen, to find out whether the cancer has spread. This process is called "staging." Careful surgical staging is needed to tell the extent of the cancer so that follow-up treatment can be planned.

Ovarian cancer can be treated by surgery, by chemotherapy, or by radiation therapy. Only one of these may be used, or they are combined. Before starting therapy, ask for a second opinion or contact one of the cancer agencies mentioned in Chapter 6.

Surgery in a mature woman involves hysterectomy and bilateral salpingo-oophorectomy. In a younger woman who wishes to have a child, only the diseased ovary may be removed. For this, however, the tumor has to be detected at a very early stage, and it has to be slow-growing. If the cancer has spread to other organs, the surgeon will try to remove as much of it as possible. This leaves a smaller area to be treated by chemotherapy and/or radiation therapy. If the cancer cells have spread to organs where surgery is contraindicated, radiation therapy and/or chemotherapy are used. Chemotherapy for ovarian cancer uses a combination of several *cytotoxic* drugs. They are usually given in cycles: a treatment session followed by a rest time, then another session, rest time, and so on. Chemotherapy can be given on an outpatient basis, at the doctor's office, or at home. It depends upon the mixture of drugs and how they are administered; if through a vein in the arm, a hospital stay is required.

Radiation therapy uses high-energy waves to damage cancer

cells and stop them from growing. Like surgery, radiation therapy is *local*; it affects only the cells in the treated area. Treatments are usually given 5 days a week for 5 to 6 weeks. Another type is *intraperitoneal* therapy. Radioactive liquid is placed directly in the abdomen, as near as possible to the cancer. A short hospital stay is usually required for this. Sometimes, both types of radiation therapy are used.

Physicians are also studying intraperitoneal chemotherapy. This new approach places the cytotoxic drugs directly into the abdomen through a tube. It is hoped that, by this method, more of the drugs will reach the cancer directly.

Another new type of treatment is *biological therapy*. This cancer treatment uses natural and laboratory-made substances to stimulate the body's immune system so it can fight the disease more effectively. The treatment is being studied in women with recurrent or advanced ovarian cancer to find if it is effective against the disease.

* * *

Birth control pills protect strongly against ovarian cancer. Women who have ever used the Pill have a 40 percent lower risk than women who have never used it. Women who have been pregnant are half as likely to develop the disease as never-pregnant women. The more pregnancies, the lower the risk. The disease may be related to high fat diets. A family history of ovarian cancer adds to the risk. There may be added risk if there was PMS, heavy periods, a tendency towards spontaneous abortion, or infertility. There is twice the risk with breast cancer.

Researchers are trying to improve the ultrasound probe, using it to check blood flow to the ovaries, because blood flow might increase if there is a tumor. They are also trying to identify certain chemicals in the blood which might warn of cancer developing in women who are tumor-free. Blood tests are another route. Researchers have found 80 percent of women with ovarian cancer have raised levels of a protein called CA-125 in their blood. However, this protein can be elevated in other conditions which are benign.

Ovarian cancer is the fourth leading cause of women's cancer deaths, coming after breast, lung, and colon cancer. It kills more women than cervical and uterine cancer combined. The hope lies in new early screening methods, in much the same way that mammograms screen for breast cancer. Ninety-five percent of the women with small tumors confined to the ovary can be cured. The number plummets for women when the disease is in its later stages.

To date, there is no one screening for ovarian cancer which is recommended for all women. Exciting new research in molecular genetics may help identify women who are most at risk. Scientists have found a link between certain chromosomal abnormalities and certain cancers, e.g. defects on chromosome 17 have been linked to breast cancer. These tests could help physicians determine which women should be intensively screened. Women with a family history of cancer who do not carry the mutation can then be free from fear.

Summary

- Some women are aware when they ovulate.
- Fertilization of the egg occurs in the oviducts.
- The fertilized egg travels to the uterus for implantation.
- If it remains in the oviduct, ectopic pregnancy can occur.
- Be aware of the symptoms of ectopic pregnancy.
- Salpingitis is an acute infection of the oviducts.
- Salpingitis can block the oviducts and cause infertility.
- PID can be due to an untreated infection of the cervix.
- Have regular check-ups if there is reason to suspect STD.
- The ovaries are prone to develop benign cysts.
- Many cysts respond to "watch and wait," or drug therapy.
- Be aware of the warning signals of cancer of the ovaries.
- Regular pelvic exams will check the health of the ovaries.

CHAPTER 8

The Breasts

Breast Shape

Is it round like an apple?
Is it smooth like a pear?
The average breast is shaped like a tear.

Many a tear has been shed over the average breast — tears of pride and pleasure, tears of panic and pain. It is not difficult to understand the tears of pride and pleasure. But what of the panic? And wherefore the pain?

For some women, breasts are the most anxiety-provoking area of the body. This is partly due to their prominent position. They cannot be kept entirely hidden from view, like the vagina or penis. Breasts are out there in the open, the unmistakable statement of a woman's sexuality.

It seems likely that it is this exposure which makes a growing girl feel so vulnerable about her breasts. She believes:

- They are too big.
- They are too small.
- They are too low.
- They are uneven.
- The nipples are all wrong.
- Everyone, but everyone, is aware of these defects.

From these early anxieties can start a lifetime of breast-worry.

Why do my breasts ache? Why are they lumpy? Should I wear a bra? Why do I dislike the idea of breast-feeding? What are my chances of avoiding breast cancer? It is hard to love any structure which causes so much anxiety.

Yet breasts are to love, and to celebrate: By a partner, by a baby, by the owner of them.

Mammals

A male physician wrote in a woman's magazine: "The breast is a mammary gland which is specially shaped and situated in a convenient location for both mother and child." Though this definition is not incorrect, as a description of the breasts it could only have been written by a man. A woman rarely, if ever, thinks of her breasts as "mammary glands." Nor does she regard them as "specially shaped and situated in a convenient location," making them sound rather like a council bus stop.

The dictionary definition of a gland is, "An organ or group of cells which is specialized for synthesizing and secreting certain fluids, either for use in the body or for excretion." In the case of the breasts, producing milk for a baby. Now, this is such a valued ability that all living creatures which can do it are classified as *mammals*. Even the duck-billed platypus, which has wings and a beak and lays eggs, is a mammal, *because* it has mammary glands and can suckle its young. (The milk flows along its downy chest and the baby happily licks the fur.)

Of all the different species, mammals are considered the most highly evolved. Top of the list are humans, distinguished from other mammals by their greater mental development, their power of meaningful speech, and their upright posture. It could be argued that top amongst humans are women. For it is women who possess the power not only to grow breasts (as some men do), but to suckle their young (as no man is able to).

Breast Size

There reigns in our culture a tyranny over the size of the sexual organs. In particular, breasts must appear large, the fuller the figure the better. It seems that it is *quantity* which matters, not *quality*; the popularity of breast implants clearly demonstrates this. Yet implants can be felt; they are a means of "show and tell."

118

This tyranny over sexual size does not only affect women. Men suffer from it too, and often more painfully. Studies suggest that men are even more worried over penis size than women are over breast size. The following is from a questionnaire into male problems of body image: *All the male respondents, with the exception of the most extraordinarily endowed, expressed doubts about their sexuality based on their penile size.*

Yet size and sexuality are in no way equated. Such muddled perceptions are very sad. No man or woman should "express doubts about their sexuality based on sexual organ size." Women with smaller breasts may perceive that they are less attractive to a certain type of man, but that is not the same as *doubting one's sexuality*.

It is thought that breast size is programed on the genes, though this is not proven. Small, pert breasts or large, heavy ones, each have their benefits and their drawbacks. Some women do have extremely large breasts, far too heavy for their general body size. *Breast reduction* surgery can bring relief. Other women seek *breast augmentation* to increase their size. More than 2 million women in America have received breast implants. It is estimated that about 150,000 of the devices are now implanted annually. Some 80 percent of these are for cosmetic purposes; the rest are for *breast reconstruction* after a mastectomy or other injury.

Breast implants contain pads of silicone gel encased in a polyurethane foam shell. They are surgically implanted, generally under the pectoral muscles of the chest. There has always been a risk of some problems with implants: infection, pain, hardening of the surrounding breast tissue, false mammography results. Added to these is now the risk that the encasing shell can break down, allowing silicone to leak into the body, with a potential for long-term risks like immune reactions and cancer.

The FDA advises women to hold off buying new implants. *At the same time*, it reassures all women who already have implants that the risk of surgical removal far outweighs that of cancer from the implant. "If the implant breaks down in the body as it does in the lab, the chances are one in a million that a woman will get cancer," according to Dr. Elizabeth Jackson at the FDA's center for devices and radiological health. Keep up to date on the latest information on which types of silicon gel implants might involve a health risk. An industry survey found that most women were very satisfied with their implants.

Breasts, like other body parts, are not perfectly symmetrical. Each has its individual shape and structure. Almost invariably, one breast is smaller than the other, the right one usually being a little smaller than the left. In 80 percent of cases, asymmetry is so slight that it is not noticeable. Bra cups fit well enough on both sides. However, in 20 percent of women, the difference in size can be anything up to 10 percent, and it is noticeable. The condition runs in families. Some women enjoy their quirky, unequal state. Others are embarrassed by it. Asymmetrical breasts can be adjusted by plastic surgery, if so desired.

"Getting to know you
Getting to know *all* about you..."

Run the fingers down the center of the chest. Feel the hard *sternum* (breastbone), and the ribs attached to it. Breast tissue is present from the sternum and right into the armpit. Feel the ribs under breast tissue. The chest muscles, the major and minor *pectorals*, cannot be felt. They lie underneath breast tissue. In some female bodybuilders, the "pecs" can be almost as developed as those of a man.

There is no voluntary muscle (muscle which can be worked) in breast tissue, so exercise cannot develop the breasts. Yet it does develop the pectorals, and helps keep them firm. Pectorals which have been effectively exercised give a slightly raised pad beneath the breasts, and this can make breasts of all sizes more noticeable.

However, no exercise can increase the size of the breast. *Any advertisement which promises this promises zero, zip, zilch.* In much the same way, creams and lotions for massaging into the breasts which promise to increase their size also promise zilch.

Breast tissue is soft, pliant, and naturally droopy. Support is provided by a covering of strong, elastic tissue, which lies just under the skin of the breasts. This support is an extension of the tissue which covers the pectoral muscles of the chest wall. The firmness of this covering gives the young breast its high, pert look. When the elastic weakens and relaxes with age, or is stretched after many pregnancies, the breast drops.

The Areola

An areola is any colored part around a central focus (like the iris of the eye around the pupil). In breasts, the areola is an extension of the nipple, from which it spreads out in a radius of one to two cm. The areola and nipple are both heavily pigmented. As they are both part of the same system, they are sometimes called the areola-nipple complex.

The skin covering the breasts is smoother, thinner and more translucent than skin over the rest of the body. Areola skin is particularly thin. At puberty, the areola and nipple darken. In sexually-active Caucasian women, the color can be a grape-red, a royal purple, or a sepia-tinted brown. Eurasian and dark-skinned women have nipples which run the entire palette of lovely creams, cafe-au-lait, brown-as-a-berry, black.

Montgomery's Glands

Look for the little bumps sprinkled over the areola. These are *sebaceous glands*. They are called Montgomery's glands because that is the name of the physician who first described them. Sebaceous glands produce *sebum*, an oily, waxy fluid which is secreted in small amounts. Sebum keeps the skin soft and supple, and the hair shafts glossy and clean.

The sebaceous glands of the areola do not start producing sebum until puberty, when they are stimulated by estrogen. It is not unusual for the pore of a gland to become blocked. The trapped sebum dries, hardens, and forms a waxy, yellow plug. To avoid this, towel rub the areola-nipple complex after a bath or shower to remove any oily deposits and keep the pores open. The waxy plug can be removed by gently popping it out, and applying a *very* mild antiseptic; it can be left to surface on its own, and get rubbed away naturally in the normal course of events.

Nipple Shape

Is it long and prominent, a wise Roman nose?
Is it cute and cheerful, a small rosy button?
Or is it inverted, a shy bashful maiden?
Why are nipples so appealing to men?
Find the openings at the center of the nipple. This is where the milk ducts come together inside the breasts. From puberty onwards, a trace of milky fluid is exuded from the nipples. If not washed off, it can dry and form a tiny crust. Nipple skin is wrinkled

and has elastic properties, so it can be lengthened. If a woman wishes for more prominent nipples, she can pull gently to stretch them. They will become longer, though this takes a fairly long time.

An *inverted* nipple is usually the result of a minor birth defect. For some unknown reason, scar tissue inside the nipple has built up. Scar tissue is inelastic, with no give or stretch. The milk ducts cannot grow down to the tip. The tough scar tissue acts like a bow-string, pulling the nipple inwards, and tethering it in place.

Some women are not bothered by inverted nipples. Others feel great distress. There is often an inability to breast feed. One option is to have the condition reversed by *nipple extraversion*. The tough, restraining tissue is cut away, freeing the nipple, which is then sewn down so that it stays in place. However, the procedure does not always work; surgery can leave external lumpy scars, and the inversion can return of its own accord. If opting for surgery, discuss these factors with the surgeon.

In most cases, inverted nipples are no cause for concern, *if* they have been inverted since puberty. However, if either nipple *starts* to turn inwards at any age after puberty, particularly after age 35, visit the physician promptly. It could be a serious symptom.

The nipple is an *orifice*; it has openings into the body. Like other body orifices, germs can get in. Infection is the most common of all nipple problems. Keep in mind that the breasts exude a milky fluid which can dry and become encrusted. A *mild* towel rub will remove any crusts of fluid at the tiny duct openings. Avoid harshness on this delicate skin, while making sure that the nipples are really clean.

Nipple Erection

When breasts start to develop, they gain a special degree of sensitivity. This special sensitivity is even stronger in the areola-nipple complex. Before a period, some women find the entire breast area feels exquisitely tender. In a few cases, she cannot bear to have her breasts touched; even her bra can cause a feeling of irritation. This extra degree of sensitivity subsides once the period flow starts. All this is perfectly normal.

Upon sexual arousal, extra blood flows to the breasts. It causes the nipples to swell, harden, and become erect. This is known as *spontaneous* erection; it is not under the control of the conscious will. The woman cannot stop it, even if she tries to. However, the nipples also spontaneously erect at non-erotic forms of stimulation: cold, fear, tension, or other non-erotic touch. The mechanism of erection is discussed in Chapter 5.

Men are acutely aware of nipple response. A woman who dresses so that her nipples show through her clothing creates a magnet for male eyes. It does not matter that the nipple is erecting in non-erotic response, e.g., in response to a chilly wind. It is the fact that the nipple is *seen to erect* which is fascinating to men.

From puberty onwards, men must learn to cope with spontaneous erections of the penis. It takes a while before these can be got (almost) under control. Men can feel very vulnerable when unwanted bulges show through their pants. Perhaps part of the pleasure they get at viewing women's nipples is linked to their own vulnerable state. In an erotic situation, it is not only exciting but immensely reassuring for the man to know that his partner is responding to desire.

The excitement men get from nipple erection is one of the main reasons why breast size is far less important than some women, (and a few men) think. Breast *action* is what men value, a nipple which responds and erects eagerly for love.

More Than Two?

Seven percent of baby girls are born with *polymastia*. This means "many breasts," having one or more extra nipples. The most usual site is directly under one breast, but they can be anywhere in a line down the abdomen. A woman with polymastia has a one in five chance that it will occur in her daughter. Baby boys are also born with this condition, though it is more rare. The reason for polymastia is still a mystery.

In a few cases, an extra nipple is not noticed. More often, it is mistaken for a freckle or a mole (especially in men with hairy chests). Polymastia causes no health problems in most cases, though the nipple can be stimulated by childbirth and start to produce milk. Like uneven breast size, some women enjoy their extra nipple; others do not. In the latter case, one option is surgical removal. Another is to mask it with heavy makeup.

Areola Hair

After puberty, hair follicles in the areola start to produce a few wispy hairs. The nipples themselves are hairless. (This can be more clearly seen in men with non-hairy chests.) As time passes, a few more hairs can appear. It is thought that the birth control pill might stimulate the growth, but this is not proven. Breast hairs tend to be fine and hardly noticeable. The following options are for women with a heavier growth, or those who wish to remove them anyway:

Tweezers: Tweezing is quick, easy, and cost-free. But the hair can grow back under the skin, parallel to the breast. If this occurs, sterilize a needle and tweak the tip free. Avoid tweezing again until the small area of skin has healed.

Depilatories and Waxing: There is no sting with a depilatory cream; waxing can hurt. Breast skin is soft and delicate; tugging to pull away hair may seem like a harsh option. Make sure neither product gets anywhere near the nipple openings.

Shaving: Contrary to myth, shaving does not make the hair grow back more thickly. But it does grow back stubbly, which can look unattractive and feel unappealing.

Electrolysis: This is permanent removal of unwanted hair. A fine needle, with an electric current running through it, is inserted into the hair follicle and destroys the root so the hair does not grow again. That is the theory. In practice, the healing process can be over-helpful. It can rush to repair the damaged follicle, which then starts to sprout another hair. Swelling, inflammation, infection or scarring are rare, but do happen. It depends upon factors such as: skin type and its healing properties, general body resistance to infection, and whether the skin type is easily scarred or not. It also depends upon the hygiene standards of the operator. Check these very carefully. In the era of AIDS, take extra precautions over any procedure which involves the use of needles. Electrolysis is not only costly but, as only a few hairs can be treated at one visit, it is also time-consuming. Both these considerations put the procedure in the luxury class for many women.

Keep in mind that none of the above methods can be recommended because none have yet been researched for negative side effects.

The Anatomy of the Breasts

The various structures which make up breast tissue are listed as follows:

- Arteries, which branch into tiny arterioles, bring fresh blood rich in oxygen and nutrients.
- Veins, which are closer to the surface, remove the used blood and waste products of metabolism.
- Nerves, which branch into tiny nerve endings, increase the sensitivity, especially in the nipples.
- Lobules, which are part of the mammary gland tissue, produce milk.
- Ducts, which are the other part of mammary gland tissue, bring milk to the nipples.
- Muscle fibers, which line the lobules and ducts, squeeze out the milk.
- Connective tissue, which is woven throughout the breasts, make up the support system.
- Fat, which plumps up the breasts, is woven throughout the mesh of connective tissue.
- Erectile fibers, which are in the areola-nipple complex, respond to erotic stimulation.
- Lymph channels, which are part of the immune system, drain breast tissue of extra fluid.

The Squeeze Syndrome

In one study, women of varying ages had breast pumps attached to their nipples. When the breasts were gently squeezed for a sufficiently long time, 83 percent of the women produced some milky fluid, whether they were young, old, mothers, previously pregnant, or never pregnant. Squeezing sends a message to the *pituitary* gland in the brain, which translates this into a call for *prolactin*. Prolactin is the hormone which stimulates the breasts of a nursing mother to produce more milk. The more her baby sucks at her breasts, the more milk is produced. Milk is synthesized, not from blood, but from the nutrients carried by blood.

During nursing, the breasts will start leaking if the mother only *thinks* of her baby. She cannot stop this; she can only try to stop thinking of her child. The fibers lining the milk ducts are *smooth* muscle, like the fibers for nipple erection. They are not under the

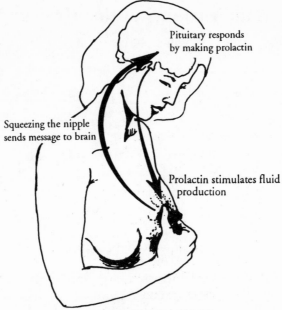

Pituitary responds
by making prolactin

Squeezing the nipple
sends message to brain

Prolactin stimulates fluid
production

THE SQUEEZE PHENOMENON

control of the conscious will. These two kinds of muscle are the *only* ones in the breasts.

Keep in mind that if the nipples are squeezed for long enough, they *will* produce fluid.

The Mature Breast

According to the distinguished breast specialist, Dr. Susan Love, "In a technical sense, breasts are not fully mature until after a birth and the body has begun to produce milk. The breasts of women who do not give birth remain in the earlier stage of development until menopause. The breast does not reach its full potential until after a full-term pregnancy."

Now what can a woman with a D cup bra make of this?

At puberty: The duct tissue grows and branches out like the twigs of a young tree, forming lobule buds. The connective tissue grows and spreads in a network, and fat builds up within the mesh. The breasts feel *dense*, very firm and packed with lobules and ducts.

At pregnancy: The breasts grow rapidly. Breasts which were almost flat will also grow to a very large size. The areola-nipple complex darkens, and the nipples become more erect. The blood supply increases, and the veins become more noticeable.

After childbirth: Breast tissue returns to its pre-pregnancy state. But the areola-nipple complex stays larger, and the darker pigment remains. The veins also remain noticeable, a delicate bluish tracery running lightly across the breasts.

At menopause: The gland tissue shrinks to nearly its pre-puberty state. In under-weight women, the breast size can shrink considerably. In women who put on weight, though the breasts increase in size, the contents are mainly fat tissue.

At each stage of a woman's reproductive life, the breasts respond to estrogen output. They also respond each month after mid-cycle, when there is breast swelling and tenderness before a period.

To Bra or Not to Bra?

The average weight of each breast is between 150 and 200 g. This increases to 400 to 500 g during nursing. The *combined* breast weight of the average C-cup bust is 8 to 16 pounds. With the average D-cup, the weight is 15 to 23 pounds. With a DD-cup, it can be 30 pounds. Women who are full-figured appreciate the comfort and support of a well-fitting bra, as do nursing mothers. The debate is for women with neat pert breasts, for younger women, for all-size women who cannot find a bra which really fits without pinching or riding up, or without the straps digging into the shoulders and underarms.

* * *

According to Dr Miriam Stoppard in her book *Being a Well Woman*, "The height and shape of your breasts depends on a rather weak suspensory system — bands of fine ligaments called the *ligaments of crupa*, which are continuous with the deep coverings of the chest muscles, weave between the fat and lobules of the breast, and are attached to the skin.

"Ligaments are inelastic. Once they are stretched they can never return to their previous short size and shape. It follows, therefore, that if you allow the ligaments of crupa to become stretched, your breasts will sag. This is why the fashion of going bra-less is deleterious to the shape of any breast except the smallest and lightest, and why it is absolutely necessary to wear a bra when you are pregnant and when you are lactating."

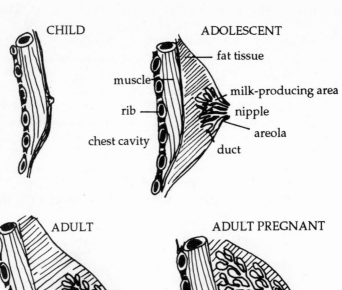

CHILD

ADOLESCENT

fat tissue

muscle

milk-producing area

rib

nipple

areola

chest cavity

duct

ADULT

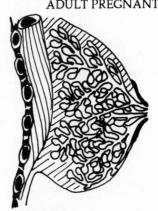

ADULT PREGNANT

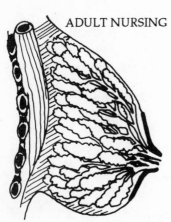

ADULT NURSING

ADULT AFTER MENOPAUSE

According to Dr. Susan Love's *Breast Book*, "A mistaken popular belief maintains that wearing a bra strengthens your breasts and prevents their eventual sagging. But you sag because of the proportion of fat and tissue in your breasts, and no bra changes that. The only time when I would recommend a bra for medical reasons is after any kind of surgery on the breasts. Then *the pull from a hanging breast* can cause more pain, slow the healing of the wound, and create larger scars.

"Otherwise, if you enjoy a bra for esthetic, sexual or comfort reasons, by all means wear one. If you don't enjoy it, and job or social pressures don't force you into it, don't bother. Medically, it's all the same." (Emphasis added.)

* * *

Some smaller breasts, even when supported by a bra, drop early in life. Some larger breasts remain high and pert with no bra support. It seems to be the luck of the genes. The majority of women wear bras; they accept that the force of gravity could have some effect on their breasts. "The *pull* from a hanging breast..."

Some suggestions for wearing a bra include: if the breasts weigh over a pound each, if the lower part dips to touch the chest wall, when taking exercise, during pregnancy, and while nursing.

The findings from one study suggest that 7 out of 10 women have fitting problems with bras. The general recommendation is to have cup size measured by a bra-fitting specialist every few years. Though the body weight can stay the same, the distribution of breast tissue changes. The following tips might be useful when considering buying a new brassiere:

- A bra should feel comfortable when fastened on the middle hook.
- The breasts should be separated and completely contained within each cup.
- The cups should fit snugly over the breasts, with no pleating or creasing.
- The straps should be wide enough to protect against shoulder strain.
- Once the straps are adjusted, they should neither slip off the shoulders, nor dig into them.
- The bust line should rest midway between the shoulders and elbows.

- The band should fit snugly under the bust line, and not cause a midriff bulge.
- The elastic should provide enough "give" to allow for easy movement without digging or cutting.

Breast Skin

Study the skin of the breasts. Become familiar with the size, shape, texture, and color of any moles, freckles, or lumps. In teen girls, these are few. As time passes, most skins tend to get a little freckly, and more moles appear. Bras and moles together make a hazardous conjunction. This is because a bra, no matter how well-fitting, can rub the mole if it is at the shoulders, and cause friction if it is under the breasts or across the back.

- Regular friction is an irritant.
- Irritants can be carcinogens (cancer-causing substances).
- Carcinogens are serious hazards in areas of constant friction.

Check to make sure there is no mole along any of the bra strap lines. Some physicians consider it is a preventive health measure to remove any mole which is on the line of a bra strap *before* it can give trouble. This is an issue of personal choice. If deciding against removal, avoid anxiety with the decision. Forget the mole. Simply check at regular intervals for the following:

- Any change in the shape, size, or thickness of the mole.
- Any alteration in its color or texture.
- Any redness surrounding the area.
- Any inflammation near or actually on the mole.
- Any new mole or other growth which suddenly appears.

Consult the physician promptly if any of the above occur.

Pimples and spots on breast skin are fairly rare. But they can occur at the cleavage, and in the skin creases under the breasts. Take care that these areas do not become sites of infection. Check out personal hygiene. Daily washing with soap and warm water may not be enough. Increase this to twice a day.
Pimples and spots on breast skin can be treated like spots on the face, or left to heal by themselves.

Lumpy Breasts?

Smooth as satin?
Just a bit nodular?
A purseful of marbles?
Why are my breasts full of lumps?

At a microscopic level, breast tissue is wonderfully neat. Inside the mammary area are bubbly, balloony lobules connected like twigs on a bush to their ducts. The lobules can be closely packed together or spaced far apart. Woven in and out and surrounding them are fat and connective tissue. No wonder breasts can feel like very lumpy structures.

- Breasts can be lumpy, smooth, or any texture in between.
- Some lumps can be at the armpits, and not at the top.
- Other lumps can be at the top, and none near the armpit.
- Some lumps are in the same place on one or both breasts.
- Other lumps are in different places on one or both breasts.

Keep in mind that healthy breasts can feel very lumpy.

Tender Breasts

Each month, *the breasts are prepared for a possible pregnancy.* This phenomenon begins when the egg is released at mid-cycle. The tiny lobules swell up with fluid, and the breasts feel larger. In the week before the menstrual flow starts, even smooth breasts can feel lumpy, or grainy, or full of tiny bumps. There is a general feeling of heaviness and tenderness, the nipples tingle or itch. It has been estimated that this *cyclic swelling* causes discomfort in 50 percent of all women.

If no pregnancy occurs, the flow begins. The fluid in the lobules then drains away. The swelling, lumpiness, tenderness, and itching stop. The breasts return to their pre-period size, but they do not shrink back completely. Each month, there is a tiny increase in mammary development. This continues until about age 35. By then, it seems that the lobules and ducts have grown to their maximum (pre-pregnancy) size.

Keep in mind that breast tissue changes during each month.

Gynecomastia

Gynecomastia means "female-like breasts" in men. It happens to

131

some degree in 50 percent of all boys at puberty, and is due to the surges of female as well as male hormones at this time. This type of gynecomastia is harmless, and disappears within two years. However, the swellings can become large in boys who are overweight, and cause acute embarrassment. Gynecomastia can also occur in overweight men. Reduction in diet is the appropriate answer. Cosmetic surgery is another option.

A few men with no weight problems develop breasts as they age. This is due to a drop in testosterone production, so the effects of estrogen can show through. Gynecomastia can also be caused by a rare disorder, by certain medications, and by marijuana use. Men under age 50 who are not overweight should seek the advice of their physician.

Bountiful Breasts

Not much which was uplifting came out of the concentration camps from World War Two. Yet there is one heart-warming tale from the end of that conflict. A group of young mothers, starving to death themselves, were unable to provide enough milk for their babies. Older women, many of them grandmothers, were moved beyond endurance by their plight. They took the starving infants and put them to their own breasts. The babies sucked urgently until the grandmotherly breasts finally produced milk. Though this tale is apocryphal, it shows the power of human love. It also shows the bounty and resourcefulness of breasts.

Summary

- Become familiar with the smooth skin of the breasts.
- Know the site, size, and texture of any moles or freckles.
- Learn the appearance of the nipples when warm and erect.
- Learn also how they appear when cold and puckered.
- Note if one or the other nipple naturally turns inwards.
- Learn any other differences in the areola and breasts.
- Know the monthly swelling patterns of the breasts.
- Feel for an indent under the nipple, where the ducts meet.
- Squeezing the breasts will often produce a harmless fluid.
- Most women have some breast discomfort now and then.
- Most women are conscious of lumpiness from time to time.
- Most women are aware when their breasts feel more tender.
- No exercise or lotion will increase the size of breasts.

CHAPTER 9

Care of the Breasts

Breast Injury

The most common form of breast injury is a *bruise*. This is hardly surprising. The breasts, like the penis and testicles, are outside the body. They are not protected from injury in the way that the internal organs are. In fact, the breasts are more at risk of external injury than the male genitals because the latter gain some protection from the pelvis and thighs.

A blow to the breast can cause a *hematoma*, pooling of blood in the tissues under the skin. (A hematoma can also occur after breast surgery.) Blood and blood fluids escape and leak into the nearby tissues. These swell into a bruise, and the area feels tender. As the blood starts to clot, it shows through the skin as the familiar black-and-blue coloring of a bruise.

A bruise on the breast is self-healing. It can take a week or more for the leaked blood to be reabsorbed. From its dark hue, the bruise turns through a mottled range of colors until it becomes faint and finally disappears. The color changes are due to the escaped blood being reabsorbed into the body.

A blow to the breast is usually accidental. Without realizing it, a baby or toddler can jab the breast hard, causing a nasty bruise. Some women fear that a blow to the breast can trigger cancer. *To date, no bruise has yet been known to cause breast cancer.* (A woman whose breasts are intentionally hit by a partner should visit the physician promptly; the evidence of bruising may keep her safe from further domestic violence.)

For self-care of a bruise, apply a cold compress to the area. Cold constricts the tiny blood vessels, which reduces the volume of leakage, and so reduces the amount of swelling. If required, a mild pain relief such as aspirin or ibuprofen can be taken. A visit to the physician is not usually necessary, but will bring peace of mind.

* * *

According to Dr. Strax, a pioneer in breast cancer screening:

Most, if not all, women have suffcient breast symptoms at one time or another to cause anxiety and warrant a visit to the physician. Such examinations are important and should be sought for the slightest reason. The reassurance of a normal examination is often vital to the well-being of a woman. Considering that there are so many normal variations, it is difficult to spell out what breast conditions warrant special observations. Apart from obvious things, such as infection or abscess, one would say that a normal breast is one that does not have a cancer.

— *Make Sure That You Do Not Have Breast Cancer*

Breast Infection

A *boil* can develop on the breast, just as on any other skin part. The germs of staph bacteria enter through a hair follicle, or a break in the skin. The immune system is activated and sends out white blood cells, which fight the germs and destroy them. *Pus* is formed during the fight; pus is a mixture of white cells, serum fluids, and dead or dying bacteria. The boil slowly rises to a head, and eventually bursts. It begins to heal as soon as the pus is able to drain away.

A boil remains local because it forms a tough inner coat to prevent the germs going further into the body. If this coat breaks down, the invading germs enter into the blood stream, and cause widespread infection. Visit the physician if a boil occurs, or any other type of breast infection. Antibiotics destroy the bacteria. Take the whole course. Keep in mind that it is the toughest germs which are the last to be killed.

An *abscess* can form under the skin of the areola. Bacteria enter the tiny pores of the sebaceous glands, and the sebum is filled with

134

pus. The trapped pus forms an abscess which needs to be incised (cut) to allow the pus drain away. A few women suffer repeated staph infections, such as boils and abscesses. These can be a symptom of a pre-diabetes condition. Visit the physician.

Underarm Infection

The *axillary sweat glands* are those under the arm. The tiny ducts which bring the sweat to the surface can get blocked. Any underarm infection takes longer to heal, due to the dampness of the area and the constant rubbing from arm movements. The infection spreads easily, and it can recur. In persistent cases, there can be an underskin tunneling and local scarring.

A persistent boil which grows and festers underarm is known as *hidradenitis suppurativa.* It can be very painful. Antibiotics destroy the infection, and antibiotic lotions can be of help. In stubborn cases, a cortisone injection may be effective. Some physicians use isotretinoin, the anti-acne drug, but this must not be used during pregnancy because of potential damage to the fetus. If there is scarring, surgery or even skin grafting may be necessary.

However, most underarm infections only produce mild irritation. Avoid roll-on deodorants which tend to spread the germs each time they are used. During the infection, avoid shaving or otherwise removing axillary hair, because this can cause tiny nicks in the skin. Hidradenitis suppurativa also occurs in the genital area if the sweat ducts get blocked. Visit the physician for professional help.

Itchy Breasts

Itchy breasts are fairly common. A natural tingling can occur, with an urge to scratch, once the skin is no longer confined in a bra. Breast swelling after mid-cycle is another common cause of itching. Check for any allergic substances which could be the cause. Common allergens include: metals in bra fasteners, washing powders and rinses, perfumed soaps, lotions, and talcs, synthetic fibers in underwear, and so on. Track down and remove any allergy-causing substance. Check to make certain that breast skin is really well-rinsed after using soaps. Apply a non-perfumed lotion if the skin feels dry.

At times the nipples can itch maddeningly. It is not known why this happens, though the condition is fairly common. Make sure

that the nipple openings are free of encrusted fluid, and the sebaceous glands unblocked. Rub the areola-nipple complex fairly
briskly to avoid this. Visit the physician if no allergy or other cause
of itching is found.

Avoid scratching itchy breasts. Friction brings blood to the skin's
surface, and produces heat. Heat increases the itching. A cool
shower will bring relief, and reduce skin temperature. Apply cala-
mine lotion to soothe. (Showering the breasts with cold water is
purported to increase their natural tension and support).

If the itching is in both breasts, there is usually no cause for
concern. If it is only in one breast, visit the physician. In rare cases,
itchy breasts can be a signal that something serious is amiss.

Nipple Discharge

In medical terms, any fluid from the breasts is a *discharge*. A tiny
volume of milky discharge from *both* breasts is normal. After childbirth, milk can continue to be produced for years. Only a very slight
squeezing of the breasts will set it off. The Pill and certain anti-de-
pressants can be responsible for breast fluid. Marijuana use has also
been implicated. In some cases, it is due to something as simple as
chafing of the breasts from clothing.

Consider the following points before checking breast fluid:

- Some 80 percent of all newborns produce nipple fluid.
- At puberty, there can be a time of fluid production.
- At menopause, there is often an increase in nipple fluid.
- These are life stages of great change in hormone production.
- Keep in mind that fluid from the nipples is hormone induced.
- The more breasts are squeezed, the more fluid they produce.

Now check the following:

- Are the breasts squeezed or sucked during love making?
- Does self-pleasure include strong breast squeezing?
- Has there always been a tendency to produce breast fluid?
- Is the fluid a continuation of milk long after childbirth?
- Does the fluid come from both breasts?

The following are warning signals that something is amiss:

- Spontaneous: fluid appears without squeezing the breast.
- Persistent: fluid continues to appear.
- Unilateral: fluid comes from one breast only.
- Color: fluid is clear, watery or pale yellow.
- Texture: fluid feels tacky or sticky.
- Blood: fluid has streaks or flecks of blood in it.

If any one of these warning signals occur, visit the physician promptly. Changes in the nipple also need speedy investigation; if it pulls to one side, or begins to invert. If none of the warning signals is present, have breast fluid checked at the next visit.

Mastalgia

"Mast" is Latin for breast and "algia" for pain. *Mastalgia* is breast pain, and most cases occur at the same time each month. This is *cyclic mastalgia*, and is usually due to changes in the levels of female hormones. Cyclic pain can be controlled by taking male hormones. This is only advisable for intense pain, because male hormone therapy has masculinizing side effects, and it cannot be taken for long stretches of time.

It is not known what causes *non-cyclic mastalgia*, breast pain which is not linked to specific times in the month. Therefore, there is no conventional medical therapy to relieve the pain. Self-care methods often work: warm, soothing baths; very gentle massage; regular exercise; an improved diet; vitamin and mineral supplements; or over-the-counter pain-killers.

Other Breast Pain

Dear Dr. Joan: I have been diagnosed with *costochondritis*. At first, I thought it was breast cancer, and was worried until I saw the doctor last week. Now I am thinking of having a cortisone injection. Do you recommend this?

Dear Ms. G.: Costochondritis is a type of arthritis, a painful rib-cartilage inflammation ("costo" means rib, "chondro" is cartilage). It usually subsides on its own, but the process can be helped with anti-inflammatory medicines such as aspirin, indomethacin, or ibuprofen. A cortisone injection is considered a big gun in anti-inflammation therapy. The shot is put into the inflammation around the cartilage just under the skin.

You are not alone in mistaking the pain of costochondritis for breast pain. When men have this condition, they can mistake it for the pain of a heart problem. Other breast pain can come from arthritis in the neck. The swollen area pinches a nerve, and the pain spreads to the breast. With any pain in the chest area, see your doctor. Do not stay at home and "invent" your own diagnosis.

Breast Self-Examination (BSE)

Study after study shows that American women do not practice breast self-examination regularly, although many have tried to and almost all women believe they should. Women who do begin the routine usually discontinue it after a few months. Those who learn the technique from a doctor or other medical personnel are more likely to continue it than those who learn it from another source.

The authors of this chapter found that no one in our group of seven regularly examined her breasts (although two of us have had mastectomies and are at high risk for breast cancer). Extending our informal survey, we found that almost no one we knew examined her breasts regularly. Most had tried to develop the habit and many were actively involved in women's health issues.

— *Our Bodies, Ourselves. The Boston Women's Collective*

This extract was written in 1980. It is hoped that more women now do BSE. One recommended place is in the bath or shower. The flat of the hand moves more easily over softened, soapy skin. Some physicians suggest that a general awareness of the need to check for lumps is more appropriate than trying to follow a slavish routine. This avoids obsessive worry over the health of the breasts. The majority of lumps which are found on breast self-examination are *benign*.

Lumps

A *cyst* is the most common cause of a lump from ages 30 to 50; some 30 percent of women have them. A cyst feels like a small water blister, smooth on the outside with fluid inside. It swells before a period, and shrinks afterwards. About 50 percent of all breast surgery is done to determine if a cyst is a harmless lump. A large cyst

Using the flat of the fingers gently but firmly feel the breast for any lump or unusual thickening. Start at the inner side and feel towards the nipple.

In the same way, examine the lower, inner part. Examine the area all around the nipple too.

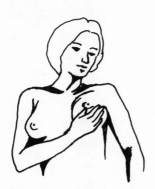

Feel the upper, outer part until you have come full circle. There is a little extra section of breast tissue between the upper outer part and the armpit so examine across the top of the breast towards the armpit.

Bring your left arm down to your side as you start to examine the lower, outer part.

BREAST SELF-EXAMINATION

can be treated by *needle aspiration*; the fluid is drawn off through a syringe and the walls then collapse. However, the cyst can fill up again at some future date. Needle aspiration can be an office procedure. A novocaine shot to numb the area gives a short but burning sensation. Some women find this shot as painful as the aspirating needle, so the physician may choose to do without it. Each woman has her own pain threshold *and* not all physicians are equally adroit. Ask for a shot if this appears to be necessary.

- A lump found in the 30 to 50 age group is probably a cyst.
- A lump that changes size with a period is probably a cyst.

A *fibroadenoma* is a lump of fibrous tissue which feels round, smooth, and hard; it moves easily when pushed. There may be one or more, in one or both breasts. They tend to develop in the teens and twenties, and can last a lifetime. Some will shrink at menopause. Fibroadenomas are *benign*, and rarely become cancerous.

5 mm   Size of tumor seen on mammography but cannot be felt

1 cm   Size of tumor first felt by breast self-examination

5 cm or larger   If the tumor is this size or larger, 50% will have spread to other areas of the body (metastases)

Nobody knows why they grow. They could be related to a high-fat diet, but this is not proven. The problem with benign cysts and fibroadenomas is that they can be confused with a more serious growth. Many physicians want to remove a lump and have it checked to make certain that it is harmless. A clear diagnosis brings that wonderful medication — peace of mind.

- A lump found in the teens and twenties is most likely to be a fibroadenoma. (They are rare over age 30).
- A lump that does not change size with a period is most likely to be a fibroadenoma.

Lumps can appear in the breast which are neither fibroadenomas nor cysts. In fact, they are not lumps at all, in that they are not growths of tissue. They can be due to a rib pushing upwards, making the area above feel compact and hard. They can be a patch of hardened scar tissue, or "fat necrosis" from a previous biopsy or some other surgery.

Keep in mind that a cancer lump is usually:

- Irregular in shape.
- Harder to the touch.
- Less easy to move around.
- Identified for certain only by a biopsy.
- Cancer is very rare in younger women with lumps.

Biopsy

Fine-needle biopsy uses breast X-rays to pinpoint the exact site of the lump. A needle is then inserted to remove several cells, which are examined to determine if they are malignant. No incision is made, and only a few cells are removed. Fine-needle biopsy can be performed without delay, and the results can be available the same day. It is relatively pain-free. There is some pressure during the X-ray, followed by a slight needle prick. It leaves less of a scar, is less time-consuming, and costs far less than a surgical biopsy.

Surgical biopsy is done under local or general anesthesia. A wedge of tissue is taken, or the entire lump excised (cut out). There is usually a wait of a few weeks while the biopsy is scheduled, and these can be filled with anxiety. Because a small portion of the breast is removed, it is potentially disfiguring. There is a slight yet increased risk of scar tissue building up.

Fine-needle biopsy would seem preferable to a surgical one. The problem is that a few lumps are part cancer and part benign. With fine-needle biopsy, there is a slight risk that only benign tissue is removed. The cancer could be in the unbiopsied part, and remain undetected. The choice of which type of biopsy is not easy, and can depend upon the site of the suspect lump.

The Cruel Statistics

- Every 6 minutes, breast cancer is diagnosed in the United States and every 12 minutes a woman dies of the disease.

- One of every 4 cancers in women is in the breast, making this organ the most common of all cancer sites.

- Breast cancer is the most common cause of death in women aged 39 to 44.

- The chances of developing the disease increase throughout a woman's life, the rate of development being much greater at age 70 than it is at 40.

- Despite our surgical, radiotherapeutic, and chemotherapeutic techniques, we are probably curing only about 25 percent of women who present themselves to their physicians with this disease — and all because most breast cancer seen by the medical community is *late cancer."*
  — *Make Sure You Do Not Have Breast Cancer* by Dr. Strax.

What Is Late Cancer?

Late cancer is cancer which has spread beyond the breast. The spread is known as *metastases*. When cancer cells leave the tumor, they are trapped by the lymph nodes in the armpits (axillary) and chest wall. Lymph nodes are bean-shaped filters made up of white blood cells which play a major role in immunity. The lymphocytes fight to defeat the cancer, until they are overcome. Cancer cells then pass directly into the blood, traveling until they set up home in any susceptible organ.

Previously, when cancer reached the lymph nodes, surgery used to be a *radical mastectomy*. The breast, chest wall, and underarm glands were removed. This mutilating operation left a horror in

142

women's minds. It may be the reason why many still avoid breast exams. Yet therapy for breast cancer no longer involves an immediate decision to remove the entire breast.

Most breast cancers are found by women themselves. If a woman does find a lump, this is what occurs: "Only half of the patients saw a doctor within one week of discovering a lump. 20 percent waited 3 months or longer, and some took 6 months to a year before seeking medical advice. Small wonder that in many of these patients, the cancer had spread outside the local area of the breast and in some, throughout the body."

This is similar to the findings for men who detect a suspect lump in the testicle and put off visiting the physician. It seems a very human trait not to go looking for trouble, particularly for trouble of such magnitude. Yet the American Cancer Society reports in one of its pamphlets, "over half a million women alive have survived breast cancer. Survival rates have increased even more dramatically in recent years due to breast self-examination and mammography. It is becoming evident to everyone that breast cancer often is curable *if diagnosed and treated early*. In fact, the cure rate for breast cancer that has *not spread* is very high, the data vary from 85 to 100 percent."

The Early Bird

When a cancer cell divides, it produces two daughter cells which are also defective. As cell division continues, there is a growing malignancy which continues to multiply. The smallest tumor which can be felt by hand is 1 cubic centimeter (1/30 oz). A tumor that small already contains millions of cancer cells. By the time a lump is large enough to be felt, it can be deadly with tumor cells spreading from the breast into the body.

A mammogram can detect a pinhead.

Some cancers are fast-growing; others are slow. Many have been present for 6 to 8 years before they show on a mammogram. According to the Federal Centers for Disease Control: "Of the 40,000 deaths from breast cancer yearly, *almost 1 in 5 deaths could have been prevented with mammography*. In spite of which, 35 percent of women over age 40 have never had a mammogram. And only 30 percent of women in high-risk groups have mammograms done with any regularity." The question is, why?

143

Radiation Scare

A mammogram is an X-ray of the breast. X-rays are a form of radiation which damages human tissue. In 1976, the media reported that mammography actually increased the risk of breast cancer due to the effects of radiation. This made physicians cautious, and unnecessary X-rays were stopped. It frightened many women, and some who would have benefited from early screening refused to have a mammogram.

Today, advances in X-ray techniques have reduced the amount of radiation, and so the risk of cancer from mammography has been reduced. This risk is highest in young women, and decreases with the passing years. Nevertheless, there is a carcinogenic potential from mammograms. The American College of Radiology has a certification program to help women choose a safe and competent radiologist. Call the federal government's Cancer Information Service at 1-800-4-CANCER for a list of approved local facilities, or call the American Cancer Society at 1-800-ACS-2345 and ask where a reliable mammogram can be done.

Who's For Mammography?

Average Risk of Breast Cancer in a Year in White Women

Age	Risk Per Year
30	1 in 5,900
35	1 in 2,300
40	1 in 1,200
50	1 in 590
60	1 in 420
70	1 in 330
80	1 in 290

At age 40, there is a 1 in a 1,000 chance or 0.1 percent risk
At age 50, there is a 1 in 500 chance or 0.2 percent risk

The much-quoted figure of breast cancer occuring in 1 woman in 9 is very confusing. It is not incorrect; it is a valid statistic based on average life span to *110 years*. What is incorrect is for a woman age 30 to believe that she has a 1 in 9 chance of getting cancer in any given year. She has not, and the table clearly demonstrates this.

144

The National Cancer Institute recommends breast screening:

<u>By Physician</u>
Women 20 to 40, every 3 years
Women over 40, annually

<u>By Mammogram</u>
Women 35 to 39, once
Women 40 to 49, every 1 or 2 years
Women 50 and older, annually

The mammogram at age 35 to 39 acts as a baseline for future detection. If lumps are found at a later time, a comparison can be made with the healthy breasts. About 52 million women fall under the NCI screening guidelines. By 1991, the number of women having regular mammograms rose to 18 million. This was 8 million more than in 1987. Yet this number was still just over a third of those for whom annual screening is recommended. The rest, some 34 million women, stayed away. About 4 million of these are expected to contract breast cancer at some later stage.

Unfortunately, mammograms can miss a few malignancies. Not all breast tissue near the underarm and up by the clavicle (front shoulder bone) can be X-rayed. Laser beams are the hope for the future. A camera-like machine can detect objects in breast tissue which measure 3 to 5 millimeters in thickness. Researchers are now working to improve the beam so that it can probe deeper into the breast.

Risk Factors

Though rare in youth, breast cancer can occur at any age. The peak ages are from 50 to 60. Factors such as benign lumps, number of pregnancies, and obesity have not been shown to *significantly* increase the rate. Breast cancer in a sister or mother, especially before menopause, increases the risk by 3 to 4 times. Early pregnancy, before age 18, may have some protective effect.

Environment: Women in cities have a higher breast cancer rate than in rural areas. Affluent women are at greater risk. High fat diets have been implicated as a risk factor for breast cancer. For example, Japanese women have a low incidence, while Japanese women in the U.S. who eat a high fat diet have a significantly higher rate of breast cancer. Perhaps the pollution in cities also plays a role. Breasts, like testicles, are external. They lack the protection of internal organs, making them more vulnerable to the effects of pollutants. Cancer of the penis is extremely rare, but the penis is not made of glandular tissue.

Hormone Medication: The Pill, hormone replacement therapy (ERT), and estrogen diethylstilbestrol (DES) have all been implicated with a slightly increased risk of breast cancer. These hormones have to be taken long-term before this risk occurs. For many women, the benefits of the Pill or ERT far outweigh the increased risk. The Pill carries a protective factor against cancer of the uterus and of the ovaries.

Previous Surgery: In the 1960s and 1970s, most breast lumps were immediately biopsied. All surgery creates scar tissue which is fibrous, inelastic, and tough, with no bounce or give. Though it is not known whether scar tissue is carcinogenic in some way — it might irritate the nearby cells — scar tissue in the breast is known to slightly add to the risk of cancer.

Stress: Stress factors are found in many cancer patients. Stress which is painful can lower the immune system. There is growing evidence that resistance to cancer is linked to a robust immune system. This is an area of great excitement, not only to immunologists, but to all those who are interested in health. Learning how to boost the immune system by natural methods includes special diets, vitamin and mineral supplements, acupuncture, homeopathic medicines, visualization, and so on.

The excitement turns sour when it includes psycho-babble which can make a woman who is already dreadfully ill feel worse. For psycho-babble can suggest that women get breast cancer if they allow their lives to become too stressful, or ignore their own needs while playing a caretaker role for others.

The following are stress co-factors in many cancer patients:

- Depression before the cancer developed.
- Problems over sexual matters.
- Poor ability to express hostile feelings.
- Unresolved tension concerning a family member.

These findings can suggest self-blame for cancer, even though its cause is unknown. For example, visualization suggests that a "good" lifestyle and "positive" thoughts can help cure cancer. It follows by extension that a "bad" lifestyle and "negative" thoughts caused it in the first place. This psycho-babble is not only deeply cruel but highly offensive, parceling out cancer to women with "the wrong attitude."

Consider those stress co-factors: depression appears to be endemic in modern society; everyone has a sexual "problem" at some time in life; the ability to cope with hostile emotions is a hallmark of maturity; unresolved tensions over a family member are common, not rare.

On average, women lead stressful lives, period. Much of this stress is related to their reproductive health, period. Until medical research concentrates more on female issues and offers positive preventive measures, it is an impertinence to accuse women with breast cancer of not leading stress-free lives.

"If every woman in the world were to have a baby before age 25, 17 percent of the world's breast cancer would be eliminated."

Yes, but is this the best that preventive medicine can do?

* * *

Japanese women have the longest life expectancy in the world. It is 82.5 years compared with 78.6 years for American women. Nobody knows why breast cancer is on the increase, nor why it is much higher in North America and Europe than in Asia and Africa. Nor does anybody know its cause. Risk factors are just a *chance* of an increased risk. Keep in mind that in over 75 percent of cases of breast cancer, there are *no* known risk factors.

Take Daily!

People who eat the highest amounts of fresh vegetables and fruit have the lowest death rates from many cancers, including cancer of the lung, breast, and prostate. The diets which are now recommended by the National Cancer Institute and the Department of Agriculture include at least five half-cup servings a day of nutrient-rich fruit and vegetables. Therefore, take daily:

- Two servings of fresh fruit
- Three servings of fresh vegetables

One serving equals one half-cup of a vegetable or one medium piece of raw fruit. Six ounces of juice makes up one serving. It is now recognized that fresh juice, though useful as part of the daily diet, is not as beneficial as eating the whole fruit.

One survey found that only 9 percent of Americans consumed this amount of fruit and vegetables in the previous 24 hours. Although more people now *buy* more fresh fruit and vegetables, these foods often stay wrapped in their plastic, and are left to rot in the refrigerator.

Is this because preparing fresh fruit and vegetables can be a fussy business? Who has time for food preparation; that washing and peeling and scraping and cutting? Women who say these things are often the same women who spent hours and ruined their hands and broke their nails by washing and scraping and peeling fresh fruit and vegetables for their babies. Keep in mind that breasts are like babies in that they flourish best with lots of TLC.

- Go scrape a carrot!
- Go take a shower and do BSE!
- Go for a breast exam and mammogram!

Cancer Management

The most common type of early breast cancer is a small tumor which has invaded breast tissue, but has not advanced to the lymph nodes. These early tumors accounted for 80,000 cases in 1990, up from 35,000 cases in 1975. In 1990, the National Cancer Institute stated that most of these cases can be treated with a *lumpectomy*, (removal of the lump and nearby tissue only), followed by *radiation therapy*. Physicians are still unsure which of these cases also require *chemotherapy*, cytotoxic drugs taken for at least 6 months afterwards to mop up any cancer cells which might have spread to distant parts of the body.

An even earlier type of breast cancer, *carcinoma in situ*, is a self-contained cluster of malignant cells which have not yet invaded nearby tissue. Ten years ago, only 3 percent of cancers were detected at this stage. Today, some studies show that this figure ranges from 20 to 30 percent. Physicians are not sure whether a lumpectomy or *mastectomy* (removal of entire breast) is the safer route to take. Eventually, the answers to these very difficult quandaries will be known. In the meantime, some women learn all they can before agreeing to one form of therapy. Others prefer to leave the decisions with their physicians.

Surgery involves removal of some, or all, breast tissue. It differs most in the amount of underlying tissue, muscle, and lymph glands also removed. Neither surgery nor radiotherapy can stop tumor cells which are already circulating in the blood or lymph, nor those which have reached the liver, lung, bone, or brain. Once metastasis has occurred, chemotherapy is necessary to track down and destroy the cancer cells. Chemotherapy is known as *systemic* therapy because the powerful drugs affect the whole body, the entire system.

Hormone therapy is an exciting new addition to the list of powerful therapies to fight cancer. The latest drug is *tamoxifen*, a synthetic hormone which blocks the action of estrogen in the breasts, and so deprives many cancers of the fuel which feeds them. The National Cancer Institute is mounting a five-year study to investigate the benefits and drawbacks of tamoxifen. If the hormone prevents cancer, women at high risk could be advised to take it for the rest of their lives. It is also thought that tamoxifen might protect against heart disease and osteoporosis in women after menopause.

Stop Press

Scientists have identified a new chemical compound in the body which triggers the rapid multiplication of breast cancer cells and could one day play a role in treating breast cancer. The new growth factor, P75, attaches itself to a special site on highly aggressive breast cancer cells, triggering a series of events which leads to rapid cell division. The site, called the erb b-2 receptor, is not present in normal cells.

While low levels of P75 stimulate rapid cell division, large doses of the compound defeat growth, leading to a possibility that it could prove useful as a drug to inhibit tumor formation.

Note the phrases: "one day," "there is a possibility." Avoid despair. There is always, *always* hope.

Male Breast Cancer

Cancer can develop in male breast tissue, though this is rare. The incidence is less than one percent of all male cancers. It is not until after age 60 that this disease usually strikes. Even then, a lump in the breast is often overlooked until the cancer is advanced. All senior men are advised to do regular breast exams. If a malignancy is found, the therapies are the same as for female breast cancer.

However, in almost all cases, when a lump is found in male breast tissue, there is no cancer risk. A lump in one breast only is known as unilateral (one-sided) gynecomastia, and can be due to obesity, medications for hypertension or heart disease, or from smoking marijuana.

Summary

- The best person to know the breasts is the owner of them.
- Self-care involves a monthly breast self-examination.
- Self-care involves an annual exam by the physician.
- Self-care includes a mammogram, if in the age range.
- The odds are strongly against cancer, but be on guard.
- Report any change in the breasts or nipples promptly.
- Only a physician can make an informed diagnosis.
- Alert women friends to the value of early screening.
- Cancer *can* be healed if caught while still in the breast.
- Cancer is a mortal foe, but powerful therapy can fight it.
- Keep in mind that most breast conditions are harmless.
- Keep in mind that "breasts flourish best with TLC."

CHAPTER 10

Fertility Control

And she shall bring forth
in sorrow and labor —

When Queen Victoria insisted on anesthetics for childbirth, there was a great uproar in parliament. Her refusal to suffer unnecessary pain caused shock and outrage. The fight against pain relief at birthing was on. Queen Victoria was said to be "flying in the face of nature, going against a woman's natural role." The sensible lady overrode her (male) government's objections. All women at birthing have had reason to bless her since.

The fight to stop women from controlling their own fertility was almost as difficult. The advent of the Pill brought it rapidly to a halt. With the exception of certain religions, most people regard birth control as a blessing and boon. It not only reduces the potential number of infants in an already over-populated world; it protects women from the ravages of constant birthing.

Now, at the end of the 20th century, comes another step forward. The concept is simple. Women no longer *have* to reproduce to *prove* that they are feminine. It is acceptable to put off pregnancy for years, or not to want children at all. For on the bottom line:

- It is safer never to be pregnant than to give birth.
- It is safer to use contraceptives than to risk pregnancy.

Opposing these two factors, however, keep in mind that never-

151

pregnant women have a slightly higher risk of breast cancer, and cancer of the reproductive organs.

According to a 1991 report from the Alan Guttmacher Institute, "Women who use birth control devices, *no matter what type,* are preventing more than pregnancy."

- The Pill reduces the chance of reproductive cancers.
- Barrier methods protect against sexual disease.
- All methods are less likely to result in ectopic pregnancy.
- All methods prevent the risk of complications at pregnancy and birthing.
- Of the 6 million pregnancies in the United States each year, 57 percent are unintended, over half.
- Of the 3.5 million unintended pregnancies, slightly more are likely to end in abortion than birth, whether they are from not using contraceptives or from contraceptive failure.
- Women age 35 and over more usually choose abortion.
- Only 10 percent of women use no protection at all.
- Those using no protection account for only just over a half of the 3.5 million unintended pregnancies.
- Ten percent of planned abortions end in spontaneous abortion first.

A *spontaneous abortion* is one which occurs without medical intervention. It is known to occur in 15 percent of cases. Yet it is estimated that 50 percent of early fetal tissue spontaneously aborts before week 11 of gestation, often before a woman is aware that she is pregnant. Though tragic for would-be parents, spontaneous abortions can be a blessing in disguise. The fetus is almost always severely compromised. The fate of any 1,000 fertilized eggs has been estimated as follows:

	Number	Percent
Lost before implantation	250	25
Lost before pregnancy diagnosed	150	15
Spontaneous abortion	100	10
Normal infants born	400	40
Stillborn infants	10	1
Special care infants	90	9

You Can't Be Too Rich or Too Thin

Nor can you be just a little bit pregnant.

Fertility control is about stopping the egg and sperm getting together, or stopping the fertilized egg from implanting in the uterus. In girls, an egg is not produced until some 18 months after menarche. In older women, egg production stops at some time during menopause. These dates cannot be more specific. It is essential for those wishing to avoid pregnancy to stick to the rule of thumb:

- *A woman is fertile from her first to her last period.*
- *Sperm production continues from puberty until very old age.*

Motivation is the key factor for effective fertility control. Ambivalence will do many a couple in. Health professionals know that it takes not one, but *two*, unintended pregnancies before ambivalence dies and motivation grows keen. For couples who do control their fertility, the decision *when* to start a family can be difficult. For them, the olden days when a pregnancy "just happened" have gone. In either situation, fertility control is at the very core of female existence. It involves the most profound choices which a woman makes in her life.

There are further choices to be made concerning the different methods of contraception. None are perfect. Each has benefits and drawbacks in terms of health, effectiveness, reproductive stage, lifestyle, aesthetic appeal, and so on. No one method is carved in stone. Some couples forget this, and stay with a contraceptive they really dislike, or one which is outdated for their needs. Be prepared to change, according to particular needs.

Points of Prevention

- Egg in the ovaries: hormones by Pill, injection, implant.
- Egg in the tubes: sterilization, or hormones.
- Egg in the uterus: hormones or IUD.
- Sperm leaving testicles: sterilization by vasectomy.
- Sperm leaving penis: condom, withdrawal, periodic abstinence.
- Sperm in vagina: condom, diaphragm, cap, sponge, spermicide.

The terms birth control, contraception, planned parenthood, fertility control, all mean the same thing. Each woman can learn her fertile times, her times of high risk.

High Risk Times

Mucus from the cervix is the key to fertile times. By changing in texture and amount, it can block sperm or assist them safely through the cervix. After a period, cervical mucus is scant. The vagina is dryish. At about day 6, mucus production is rising. At ovulation, it is profuse, clear and watery. Now is the fertile time of the month. The os (door of the cervix) opens to welcome in the sperm. Cervical mucus practically *pours* out, coating the vagina with fluid. (This is not the same thing as the sweating phenomenon, which coats the vagina at sexual arousal.)

After ovulation, when progesterone is made, the os closes. Mucus production almost stops. What is left forms a mesh; thick, sticky, and opaque. It appears on underwear as creamy, crumbly lumps. Sperm cannot get through. (With fertility problems, the "cervical factor" means that the cervix is producing only thick scant mucus, and the sperm are blocked.)

Learn high risk times by checking the cervical mucus. Keep in mind that it will be watery enough to *flow* to the outside. So check it at the vulva only, or on underwear, toilet paper, or a sudden sensation of being wet. If held between the fingers, cervical mucus feels slippery; it stretches rather than breaks. (Take care also not to confuse it with the wetness from semen, spermicides, or the discharge of an infection).

Home ovulation predictor tests are a far more accurate way to find ovulation time. They measure the surge of LH hormones which appear in urine. They respond to the LH surge by changing color. The actual time of ovulation can be predicted daily, twice daily, even more, by repeated testing and charting the results. Keep in mind that there is a time lag before LH appears in urine. The kits can be bought at a local pharmacy. The instructions differ, so read them carefully.

It is considered fairly safe for unprotected intercourse in the early "dry" 5 or 6 days after a period. There *is* a slight risk of pregnancy if sperm survive into the "wet" days which follow. Avoid unprotected intercourse from the start of a rise in mucus output until at least 3 days after mucus levels peak. Unprotected intercourse is considered fairly safe again after ovulation.

It can be seen there is much caution in this advice. Though both egg and sperm have a short shelf-life, they have been known to get together after amazing lengths of time. The upper limit for sperm survival is about 48 hours. Sperm which are moving have been found in cervical mucus up to 6 to 8 days after intercourse; they may have lost the power to fertilize by then. The life span of the egg is even shorter, between 10 and 24 hours.

Never rely on douching as a method of birth control. Though some sperm will be washed out, the rest are actually pushed up and through the cervix by the flood of water entering the vagina.

Mucus production lessens as a woman nears menopause. Checking the amount and consistency is also a useful way to gain some idea if menopause is approaching.

Abstinence

Total abstinence involves complete avoidance of physical intimacy. It is, without doubt, the only method of birth control which never fails. Yet abstinence now has another meaning, known as "outer-course." It is love making with no penetration; love making with no genital contact; love making with *no vulva-penis contact at all*. This must be stressed because sperm can swim up from the vulva and into the vagina.

"Outer-course" is a centuries old tradition for partners who wish to avoid pregnancy. It is also used in the early weeks after birthing, and where there is risk of a sexually transmitted disease. It has no side effects; each partner can bring the other to orgasm to avoid pelvic congestion. It is free, simple to use, and can be reversed instantly when the couple are ready to start a family.

Withdrawal

This is another centuries old and even more popular method of birth control. It is used worldwide and by lovers of all ages. The success rate depends upon the man. He must have acquired full ejaculatory control, which is not an easy skill. The man has to learn and practice this over many years. Even then, he can lose ejaculatory control at any time, for any of a number of ordinary reasons: over-excitement, tiredness, and so on.

Most young men lack ejaculatory control. Their orgasms feel imperative, and overwhelm attempts at control. Withdrawal is not a method of contraception which works in youth. Ironically, due to its *apparent* simplicity, it is the number one choice when young couples start making love. Inform a son or daughter that those who use withdrawal are often called "parents" in nine months time.

Another disadvantage is that the man must always be on guard. He cannot relax his vigilance as he nears the orgasmic threshold. In youth, this can cause immense stress. It is thought to be one of the main reasons why control problems (premature or retarded ejaculation) develop later on.

In couples of all ages, withdrawal can fail due to the drops of fluid which appear on the penis at erection. Their function is to lubricate the glans and ease penetration. However, the fluid comes from Cowper's glands, part of the male reproductive system. It contains millions of sperm, which will be deposited inside the vagina. If using withdrawal, make sure that the tip of the penis is wiped dry first.

Nevertheless, withdrawal remains the most popular method of birth control worldwide. It has no side effects for older couples, is free, simple to use, and instantly reversible.

Withdrawal is used by 2.0 percent of American couples.

It has a failure rate of between 14.7 and 27.8 percent.

Periodic Abstinence

The movement away from conventional medicine and back to self-care has also affected choice of contraception. The "natural" methods involve abstaining from intercourse at high risk times, and is now called "periodic abstinence." It is a boon for women who cannot take the Pill for health reasons, and/or fear the side effects of its long-term use. It appeals to couples who dislike barrier methods, and/or those whose religion denies them access to birth control by any artificial device.

The *calendar method* involves guessing the ovulation date based on the woman's previous history and timing of her periods. The *basal body temperature (BBT) method* involves taking the vagina temperature and noting the rise which signifies ovulation. The *mucus method* was previously discussed. The *symptomothermal method* combines the BBT and mucus method, also noting other signs of ovulation: swelling or tender breasts, and mittelschmerz. All these methods are less reliable than the home ovulation predictor kit.

Periodic abstinence can be very effective. It requires total commitment by both partners, with no vulva-penis contact at high risk times. Motivation is critical in recording and keeping exact information on period and temperature charts, mucus changes, and physical signs. There are no side effects in older couples, and it is immediately reversible.

Periodic abstinence is used by 2.1 percent of U.S. couples.
It has a failure rate of 13.8 and 19.2 percent.

Spermicides

Spermicides are foams, creams, gels, tissues, or suppositories which dissolve in the vagina. They contain chemicals which kill sperm. They are designed to be used with a diaphragm or cap; they have a high failure rate when used on their own. Protection lasts between 6 and 8 hours, but *only* if used with the above devices to keep the spermicide in place. Otherwise, the dissolved fluid will flow out of the vagina. If using spermicide alone, insert it *very* soon before intercourse for better protection. Make sure that it is high up in the vagina, as near the cervix as possible.

Spermicides can be used for extra protection with a condom. In a few cases, the vagina or penis is allergic to their chemicals. This can be felt as a slight burning sensation. It is now thought that spermicides might encourage female urinary tract infections. One study found that the level of bacteria in the vagina was much higher in women who used them regularly than in women who did not. It is thought that the chemicals might be killing off benign bacteria, which upsets the vagina's natural ecology. This allows infectious strains to flourish, and enter the urinary tract from the vagina.

However, spermicides do provide a *slight* protection against sexual disease. Some couples dislike the extra wetness from the chemicals as they dissolve. Otherwise, there are no side effects, they are not difficult to use, and are instantly reversible.

Spermicides are used by 1.7 percent of American couples.
They have a failure rate of 21.6 and 25.6 percent.

The Condom

The condom is another centuries old, tried and true method of birth control. Also known as sheaths, rubbers, or French letters, they are made of latex rubber; five percent are from the guts of lambs. Lambskin condoms are an option for men who seek increased sensitivity, and for those who are allergic to rubber. However, "skin" condoms are natural membranes: they have larger pores than latex ones. This makes them less effective at protecting against the transmission of sexual disease.

Condoms are straight or shaped, smooth or ribbed, lubricated or dry, colored or transparent, with or without a reservoir tip at the end. The tip is fairly important. Semen, pumped out of the penis under high pressure, can more easily burst a condom without a reservoir tip. Condoms are "one size fits all," but they are packaged in different amounts, 3, 6, and so on. If the pharmacist asks "what size?", the question means "what amount?"

Condoms must be donned before *any* vulva-penis contact. Some couples use this as part of their love making. A condom must stay in place until ejaculation is completed. Then the covered penis is removed, taking care not to let any of the contents spill out. Some women dislike the sensation of condoms; others are pleased not to "leak" afterwards.

Health professionals promote the use of condoms as "safer sex." Yet a condom can be defective, and a condom can break. It may not be worn *before* vulva contact; it may not be worn until all contact ends. It is as well to know what health professionals know: "Condoms do not provide 100 percent protection against unintended pregnancy, sexual disease, AIDS, or anything else."

A few people are allergic to latex rubber. There has been only one case of a life-threatening reaction to the condom; the others were from latex gloves, anesthesia equipment, a rubber dental device, even a racquetball handle. In 1991, the FDA urged the makers of latex devices to try to remove the water-soluble rubber proteins which might be causing the allergic reactions.

Nevertheless, condoms are extremely popular. They are not costly; couples with limited means can obtain them at reduced price from health clinics. They have no side effects, are easy to use, and are instantly reversible.

Condoms are used by 13.1 percent of American couples.

They have a failure rate of between 9.8 and 18.5 percent.

Diaphragm

The diaphragm is a dome-shaped rubber cup which covers the cervix. It has a flexible rim which fits snugly in place. It is used with spermicide put inside the dome before the diaphragm is inserted. It can be inserted prior to a date, but keep in mind that spermicide effectiveness is lost after six to eight hours. When love making is completed, leave the diaphragm in place for six to eight hours. If removed before this, any sperm still alive can swim through to the uterus.

Diaphragms come in several sizes. They require a prescription, and are fitted by a health professional. The springy rim should slip easily into the fornices at the top of the vagina, and be a snug fit. When correctly in place, the woman is unaware of its presence, she *does not feel it*. If she does, then it is the wrong size, or the rim has not slipped into place. Check to make sure that there is no sensation before leaving the physician's office. If the diaphragm is only felt when inserted at home, remove it, and start again.

Diaphragms have been implicated in endometriosis, toxic shock syndrome, and urinary tract infection, though there is no proof. Nevertheless, **avoid leaving a diaphragm in place for longer than eight hours.** The *cervical cap* is smaller and cone-shaped. It blocks sperm in the same way as the diaphragm, though it only covers the cervix, being held in place by suction. It has no rim to rest in the fornices, and so avoids the problem of UTI.

Diaphragms or caps can be checked for wear and tear by filling them with water, or holding them up to the light. They last about two years. They must be changed after birthing or surgery which results in change of cervix size. They afford some protection against the transmission of sexual disease. They are easy to use, not costly, and instantly reversible.

Diaphragms and caps are used by 5.2 percent of American women.
They have a failure rate of between 12.0 and 38.9 percent.

Sponges

Blocking the cervix by putting a sponge high up in the vagina is another centuries old custom. Nowadays, commercial sponges are made of polyurethane, and filled with enough spermicide to last for 24 hours, no matter how often intercourse occurs. However, sponges have been linked to problems by blocking the menstrual flow. Therefore, it is advisable to remove sponges six to eight hours after making love. They afford some slight protection against the transmission of sexual disease. They are easy to use, have no side effects, and are instantly reversible.

Sponges are used by 1.0 percent of women.
They have a failure rate of between 16 and 51.9 percent

Return of the IUD?

An *intra uterine device*, which is placed in the uterus, stops the process of implantation. It is not known exactly how this works. Perhaps the IUD sets up irritation of the uterus lining and the fertilized egg simply cannot implant. It became unpopular over ten years ago in America. One brand, the Dalkon shield, had a design flaw. The tail string was multifilamented, which enabled bacteria to travel from the vagina into the uterus. One study concluded that the tail increased the risk of PID by 60 percent.

In many countries, the IUD never went away. It is the world's most popular contraceptive device which is reversible. It is also one of the most effective. American researchers are re-examining the evidence and, though not exonerating the Dalkon shield, consider other IUDs do not increase the risk of PID. According to a spokesperson for Planned Parenthood: "Used appropriately, the IUD is a very safe and effective method of birth control with very little risk. If the results of the new study hold up to further analysis, that will be good news for women."

An IUD is inserted by a health professional. Once in place, the woman (or partner) makes sure that it has not been expelled by regularly checking the string which hangs down in the vagina. There is a 40 in 100,000 risk of perforation of the uterus wall, but only at the time of insertion. This is not considered a large risk. IUDs last five to six years. The main problems include: pain, bleeding, partial or total expulsion of the IUD, retraction of the string so it can no longer be felt, irritation of the penis by the string.

An IUD offers no protection against sexual disease. It is more appropriate for mutually monogamous couples. Users should have no previous history of pelvic infections and at least one baby; childbirth reduces the risk that the device might be expelled. Some American physicians are hoping that the IUD will be used here again. It offers 96 percent protection against pregnancy. Once in place, there is no further fuss. Apart from checking the string, the IUD can be forgotten until it needs to be changed.

IUD devices are used by 1.8 percent of American women.
They have a failure rate of between 2.5 and 4.5 percent.

Hormone Methods

Oral contraceptives contain two synthetic hormones, estrogen and progestin. The combined Pill works by suppressing ovulation; no egg, no pregnancy risk. Some also change the composition of cervical mucus so it is difficult for sperm to swim through. They slow the passage of the egg down the tubes, and change the uterus lining to prevent implantation if fertilization occurs.

The main side effects are spotting and breakthrough bleeding. The lower the dose of estrogen, the more likely this will be. The Pill can produce symptoms of pregnancy: nausea, weight gain, breast swelling, and headaches. As the body adapts, the symptoms usually cease. In some cases, the "mask of pregnancy" appears, strange brown patches on the face or neck. Chloasma, its medical name, can last some while after coming off the Pill.

Mini-Pills contain only progestin. They prevent pregnancy by keeping the cervical mucus thick, slowing down egg transport, and stopping implantation. They suppress ovulation, but not as well as the combined Pill. The side effects include irregular periods, spotting or breakthrough bleeding, shorter and scantier flow; periods can stop altogether.

Implantation involves six match-stick sized silicon tubes being implanted, fan-shape, under the skin of the upper arm. The tubes contain progestin, which is released at a slow, steady rate over five years. They act like the mini-pill. According to a Population Council report, they are "More effective than oral contraceptives. As effective as sterilization." The American Life League reports "It's an early abortion-causing drug."

The side effects include irregular bleeding in 75 percent of users. Periods can come at odd intervals, 3 or 7 weeks apart, or one is missed altogether. The flow lasts longer, 8 days instead of 5. The manufacturers state these effects lessen after 2 years. The cost of implant and medical procedure is estimated at about $500, which puts it out of range for many young women. Yet it compares well with an average $900 for five years of the Pill.

Morning after pills are multiple and very high doses of female hormones taken as soon as possible after unprotected intercourse. They prevent pregnancy by stopping implantation, if an egg has already been fertilized. They are not FDA approved for this purpose, because they can produce severe side effects. However, some physicians and clinics will provide them. They are only to be used in extreme emergency.

Health Risks and Benefits

- Cardiovascular Disease. Estrogen in the Pill interferes with blood clotting in complex ways. Progestins cause small and subtle changes in blood pressure, blood sugar, and insulin, and larger changes in cholesterol and related lipids. The overall added risk appears very low in young women and nonsmokers who have no predisposing factors for heart disease. After the woman comes off the Pill, the effects disappear rapidly; former users seem to have no effects no matter how long they used the Pill. According to the Alan Guttmacher Institute report in 1991, "Most of the changes in blood pressure, cholesterol and blood sugar are not large. In an individual woman they may be much smaller than the beneficial changes that she herself can bring about — by maintaining a healthy diet, doing aerobic exercise regularly and avoiding obesity."

- Cancers. The Pill reduces the risk of cancer of the uterus and ovary. This benefit affects women soon after starting on the Pill, becomes stronger with longer use, and lasts for many years after use is stopped. Some studies suggest that prolonged Pill use in the teens or early 20s increases the risk of breast cancer. They also suggest that as these women become older, they may be less likely to develop breast cancer than never-users of the Pill. It can be seen that the link with breast cancer is still very unclear.

The Pill is contraindicated with the following conditions:

- Smoking.
- High blood pressure.
- Severe varicose veins.
- Surgery in the next 4 weeks.
- Hepatitis, or other liver disease.
- Cancer of the breast, or reproductive organs.
- Heart disease, stroke, or blood disorders.

The Pill provides no protection against sexual disease. It can upset the ecology of the vagina, with a risk of recurrent yeast.

Benefits of the Pill:

- Periods arrive every 28 days on the dot.
- There is a lighter, scantier flow.
- Relief from period pains and cramps.
- Relief from PMS.
- Relief from irregular, or heavy bleeding.
- Relief from acne in some women.
- Relief from fear of pregnancy.
- Reduced risk of cancer of the ovary and uterus.
- No clear information on cancer of the breast.

Hormone methods are used by 27.7 percent of American women.
They have a failure rate of between 3.8 and 8.7.

Tubal Sterilization

This is a surgical procedure which cuts and seals off part of each oviduct. The egg cannot be transported to meet the sperm. *Tubal ligation* is done under local anesthesia, on an outpatient basis, with a few hours spent in the recovery room. There is no interference with natural hormone production, and the couple are free of fears of pregnancy as it is extremely effective. It is appropriate only for those who have completed their families, as it is a permanent method of contraception. The tubes can be unblocked and sewn together, but reversal is a difficult, costly, and not always successful operation.

Tubal ligation is used by 24.8 percent of American women.
It has a failure rate of 0.5 percent.

Vasectomy

In male sterilization, the sperm-carrying tubes leading from the testicles are cut and sealed off. The sensations at orgasm remain the same, the only difference being that no sperm are present in the ejaculate. Vasectomy is a simple procedure, far more so than tubal ligation. The side effects are minor and temporary: swelling, bruising, and discomfort. Vasectomy should be regarded as irreversible. Though reversal is possible, it is costly and not always successful.

Once again, vasectomy is being linked to a slight increase in prostate cancer. The link is considered *very* slight. One study involved 1,697 men who were hospital patients. Of the 220 with prostate cancer, 10 percent had vasectomies. Of the 960 men with other cancers, 3.3 percent had vasectomies. Of the 517 men without cancer, 2.4 percent had vasectomies. A second study compared 614 patients with prostate cancer against 2,588 male patients with other cancer. About 5 percent of men with prostate cancer had vasectomies, compared with about 4 percent of the other patients. While these results are unlikely to be due to chance, it cannot be entirely ruled out.

Vasectomy is the choice for 10.5 percent of American men.
It has a failure rate of 0.2 percent.

The Male Pill

A new contraceptive Pill for men now undergoing clinical trials could be the first reversible method since the condom. Worldwide, 250 couples are participating in the trials. The men receive shots of synthetic testosterone enanthate (TE). When sufficient TE is injected, the brain senses it, and signals the testicles to suppress further sperm production. It works like the Pill in that the shots control the man's hormone production.

The problem with finding a male contraceptive to date has been the unacceptable lowering of a man's libido (sex drive). This new approach may overcome it. If the TE trials are proven safe and effective, the shots should be available in about six years. Men will then have a reversible option to vasectomy. Women will be freed from some of the burden of fertility control.

RU-486

RU-486 contains Mifepristone, a drug which induces miscarriage during the first seven weeks of pregnancy. It is used as an alternative to surgical abortion in France. Thousands of women in Britain and Scandinavia are taking part in RU-46 *protocols*. These are clinical trials for testing the effectiveness and potential problems of new drugs.

RU-486 blocks progesterone. Three pills are taken followed by an injection of synthetic prostaglandin, which makes the uterus contract. RU-486 has been effective in inducing abortions in 96 percent of those who used it. Close monitoring with 4 visits to the physician's office are essential: before, during, and after drug administration. One death is linked with RU-486. A 31 year old woman in her 13th pregnancy and a heavy smoker had a fatal heart attack after the prostaglandin shot. Since her death, the French government has banned its use in women over 35, and those who are smokers. The FDA has banned RU-486 in America for safety reasons.

The ethics of abortion are not at issue here. The concerns of this book are female reproductive health. Paradoxically, there is a life-saving aspect to the drug; it can slow down certain tumors which need the hormone to grow. It has been used in Cushing's disease, and advanced breast cancer. RU-486 also blocks the stress hormones which act on almost every cell in the body and can lower immune function. For this reason, it may have sweeping powers against a variety of ailments as yet unknown.

The Future

Birth control is not a new concept. Barriers such as sponges have been used for centuries, as have "outer-course" and withdrawal. Nor is the sheath a new device. What is new is the huge advances made by medical researchers in finding other methods to protect against pregnancy. Usually, the more complex the advance, the more protection it offers, and the greater the risk of side effects.

Other methods of fertility control are being studied. They include: a hormone-releasing IUD, a hormone badge taped to the arm which releases a contraceptive through the skin, a hormone-emitting vaginal ring which the woman can insert and remove at will, and a female condom. Some of these new methods may reduce contraceptive failure, and the high rate of unintended pregnancy.

Summary

- Withdrawal is rarely safe for couples under age 25.
- Outer-course provides a sometime method of birth control.
- Spermicides on their own do not give effective protection.
- Barrier methods reduce the risk of sexual disease.
- Barrier methods protect the cervix, and reduce the risk of cervical cancer.
- The longer a barrier method is used, the lower the risk of cancer.
- Barrier devices and spermicides can cause allergic response.
- Avoid the diaphragm and cap if suffering from recurrent UTI.
- Avoid the IUD if there have been tubal infections.

- The risk of side effects with IUDs decrease with age.
- Hormone protection is the top choice of American women.
- More women are staying on the Pill into their 40s.
- The risks of the Pill are now reduced with lower doses.
- Smoking increases the risk of heart disease on the Pill.
- Regard sterilization as a permanent method of contraception.

CHAPTER 11

Fertility Problems

Fertility Data

In 1965, 18.4 percent of women age 30 and over were infertile.
In 1982, 24.6 percent of women age 30 and over were infertile.
In 1965, 3.6 percent of women aged 20 to 24 were infertile.
In 1982, 10.5 percent of women aged 20 to 24 were infertile.
— *The National Center for Health Statistics*

A 1988 survey of women aged 15-44 found that 6 percent reported that they or their partner were unable to have a child; an estimated 3.5 million women. Male fertility is also on the decline; the data for this are not entirely satisfactory. One study found that the average sperm count was 40 million higher in 1950 than in 1988. The reasons for these declines in fertility are not understood. One cause is thought to be the rise in sexual diseases which cause *tubal obstruction* (blockage of the egg and sperm-carrying tubes). Yet it is estimated that tubal obstruction accounts for only 10 percent of infertility in each gender.

Twenty-five percent of couples in their 30s are infertile. Only 1 percent of teenagers are. There is a worldwide, emotionally wrenching epidemic of infertility, making it our nation's number one public health problem. Even in a country like India with severe overpopulation, the most common reason for a visit to the doctor is infertility. From our teen years (when the last thing we really want is a child) to our mid-thirties when we finally feel emotionally and financially secure enough to start our family, there is a seventy-five fold decline in our ability to get pregnant.

—Dr. Sherman Silber,
distinguished microsurgeon in reproduction medicine.
How to Get Pregnant With the New Technology.

Problem Areas

Some women get pregnant very very easily. Others believe it is a miracle when they finally conceive. Fertility problems are now regarded as "couple problems," yet the breakdown between the genders is interesting.

Infertility can result from:

- Male problems: 25 percent of couples
- Female problems: 35 percent of couples
- Female and male: 24 percent of couples
- No known cause:16 percent of couples

Factors to be investigated include:

- Man: Is the quality of sperm poor or good? (testicles)
- Woman: Is a viable egg produced at midcycle? (ovaries)
- Man: Are the sperm tubes unblocked? (epididymis & vas)
- Woman: Are the egg tubes unblocked? (oviducts)
- Woman: Is the uterus lining well-prepared? (endometrium)
- Both: Are the sex hormones produced in proper balance?

However, many fertility problems are not really problems, and can be resolved by the couples themselves. The first factors to consider do not involve medical intervention.

Frequency

Ninety-two percent of couples can expect pregnancy to occur within 18 months of intercourse without contraception. If under age 25, some fertility experts recommend waiting between 18 months and a full two years. It is recommended that couples over age 25 visit a fertility clinic after unprotected intercourse for one full year.

Consider the following data from a study of fertile couples:

- Of those who make love 3 times a week, 51 percent conceive within 6 months of trying.
- Of those making love twice a week, 40 percent conceive within the first 6 months.
- Of those who make love once a week, 32 percent conceive within the first 6 months.
- Of those who make love less than once a week, only 16 percent conceive within the first 6 months.

Be sure that infrequent love making is not the problem.

Body Weight

Overweight in women. Fat cells absorb and release the female hormone estrogen. In women who are overweight, estrogen is not only produced by the ovaries, but also from the extra fat cells in other parts of the body. This release of extra estrogen from extra fat cells upsets the fine balance of the feedback system between the pituitary hormones and estrogen. If the problem can be detected on the bathroom scales, reduce weight to within the normal range for age.

Overweight in men. Heat damages sperm production. In men who are overweight, an excess of flesh at the buttocks, inner thighs, and lower abdomen not only keeps the groin hot, it raises the temperature in the testicles. This reduces their ability to produce vigorous sperm. The testicles should be a few degrees below body heat; hence their cooler position outside the body. Wear loose cotton shorts, and reduce weight to within the normal range for age.

Underweight in women. Being underweight can also upset the feedback system between the hormones. A certain level of fat cells is necessary for hormone production. If body weight drops too low, ovulation can be suppressed. Some women athletes and long-distance runners have scanty or absent periods. Avoid crash diets. Avoid any slimming or exercise program which promises a sudden weight loss, or one which drops the body weight below the minimum normal range. Increase carbohydrate consumption. Aim for an even body weight within the normal range for age.

The Biological Clock

The ovaries have a lifetime supply of egg follicles from birth. These ripen into eggs, which can be fertilized to produce pregnancy. By age 30, the eggs have been present for some time. In problems of fertility, the *quality* of the egg is critical. Therefore, the woman's age becomes a very important factor.

Age co-factors also include: less frequent ovulation and less regular periods by the late 30s and 40s. The older the woman, the greater the risk of exposure to tubal obstruction. If pregnancy occurs, there is a higher risk of spontaneous abortion. It can be seen that a woman's reproductive life has a limited time span.

A 65-year-old pregnant Chilean woman was recently included in the Guinness Book of Records. She claims to be the mother of 64 children, though only 55 births have been documented. Some of her offspring were twins and triplets. It is not known why her menopause has not arrived. Her fecundity is a medical mystery. It was previously thought that the maximum age for pregnancy was 52. Keep in mind that fertility data are averages only. No woman can consider that she is too old to conceive until her menopause is complete.

The risk of birth defects rises with increasing years. Down's Syndrome, a chromosome disorder which affects the mental and physical abilites of the baby, is the most common female age-related defect. It occurs:

- 1 out of 365 births at age 35
- 1 out of 109 births at age 40
- 1 out of 32 births at age 45
- 1 out of 12 births at age 49

In 1985, the risk of men age 40 plus passing on birth defects was estimated at 3 per 1,000. Recent findings seem to suggest that it could be higher. Researchers now understand that sperm in men of all ages are more likely to cause birth defects than was previously thought. For example, a male sex-linked defect called fragile-X retardation occurs about 1 per 1,250 men. Often undiagnosed, it accounts for between 5 and 10 percent of the nation's cases of mental retardation.

Irregular Periods

When a fertilized egg arrives in the uterus, the lining must be precisely prepared to receive it. If the egg is released too soon or too late, the uterus lining will be either too immature or too ripe for implantation. The fertilized egg cannot survive unless it becomes implanted in the uterus, and will be shed. It can be seen that the *timing* of ovulation is a critical factor for successful implantation.

One early warning signal that ovulation might be occurring too early or too late is irregular periods. Another warning signal is a lack of copious and watery mucus at mid-cycle. Anovulation, no egg production, is an obvious cause of infertility. This can also show as very irregular periods. Painful cramps during a period are not implicated in early or late ovulation, nor has PMS been found to be involved. If any of the warning signals are present, visit the fertility clinic without delay. Fertility drugs can be effective in the management of irregular periods.

The Timing Factor

Timing for the optimum chance of fertilization is critical. Once the egg is in the oviduct, it only remains viable for the next 12 to 24 hours. It must be fertilized during this time. Sperm only remain viable for a maximum of 48 hours. It is essential to know the precise date of ovulation to maximize the optimum chance of fertilization.

Ovulation predictor tests are commercial kits which can be obtained from a local pharmacy. They are inexpensive, simple to use, and accurate. They measure the surge of LH hormones which trigger ovulation. By frequent testing of urine samples and charting the results, the actual time of ovulation can be worked out.

Transvaginal ultrasound is the new high-tech method to detect the time of ovulation. The probe is placed in the vagina, and shows the ovaries with their developing follicles on a monitoring screen. Ultrasound to detect ovulation is costly. Older women may choose this method if the sands of time are running against them. By comparison, charting the vagina temperature, the cervical mucus, and so on, come a poor third. *Ovulation* is a major factor in female fertility. Know the time of ovulation.

Self-Help

The following are suggestions which can be helpful during the time of waiting for pregnancy to occur:

- Know the time of ovulation, and the entire fertile period.
- Check that love making is sufficiently frequent.
- Avoid the "female superior" position; it allows the male ejaculate to spill out of the vagina.
- The missionary position, man on top, is the most appropriate for fertility needs.
- Avoid moving after ejaculation to allow the semen to pool in the fornix areas around the cervix.
- Remain on the back for at least half an hour with the knees drawn up and a pillow under the hips.
- Eschew the douche. The fluid can upset the ecology of the vagina and hence upset the motility of the sperm.
- If lubrication is required, avoid the use of water-soluble jellies which can be spermicidal.
- Eat a balanced diet, with fresh vegetables and fruits, low-fat proteins and unrefined grains.
- Maintain a normal body weight. Avoid all crash diets and slimming programs.
- Exercise in moderation. Exercise abuse upsets ovulation and causes irregular periods.
- Avoid alcohol and marijuana. Both reduce sperm production and can affect the female reproductive system.
- Avoid cigarettes. Couples who smoke have a significantly lower fertility rate than couples who do not.
- Hot baths and jacuzzis affect sperm production. Avoid tight-fitting pants and jockey-type underwear. Keep the groin cool.
- Relax. Stress is a factor in fertility problems.

Male Factor Infertility

The first and simplest fertility test involves a specimen of the male ejaculate. An average ejaculate contains one-half to one full teaspoon of semen. The average ejaculate volume after 3 days of abstinence is 3 to 5 cc. Sperm make up only about 3 percent of the average ejaculate. The other 97 percent consists of fluids made in the *prostate gland* and the *seminal vesicles*.

Sperm Count (millions per cc)	Pregnancy Rate (percent)
5 - 10	27.8
10 - 20	52.9
20 - 40	57.1
40 - 60	60.0
60 - 100	62.5
Over 100	70.0

100 million sperm per cc is very high; 15 million is very low. The lower the count, the higher the risk of infertility. There is no general agreement on the lower limit; some specialists believe that even a very low sperm count does not rule out the chance of fertilization, *providing* the sperm are well-formed and have good swimming skills.

In an average ejaculate, there will always be defective sperm. About 20 percent will lack proper structure or motility. They can have three tails but no head, a head but no tail, and so on. They can lack all sense of direction, clump together, swim feebly, or not swim at all. To reach the oviducts, sperm must move forward, and at fairly high speed.

Sperm Washing: When sperm are deposited at the top of the vagina, they have great distances to travel before they reach the oviducts. This allows time for "capacitation", the enzymes in the head become activated to help sperm enter the tube and penetrate the wall of the egg. Sperm washing is a high-tech procedure which allows capacitation for poor quality sperm. It can be used in combination with in vitro fertilization.

Hormone drugs can stimulate under-active testicles, and raise the sperm count. If the problem is found to be that the man produces antibodies to his own sperm, steroids can suppress this immune reaction. When planning for intercourse at specific ovulation dates, keep in mind that it takes 72 days altogether for sperm to mature in the testicles and epididymes, before they are ready to be ejaculated.

A recent study found that men who were not under stress to "perform" produced higher sperm counts than those who were. Many women can sympathize with this. It is much the same "performance pressure" as feeling "obliged" to always have an orgasm. Keep a partner from feeling such pressure at specific ovulation dates. One way could be by more frequent intercourse. Studies on college athletes showed that abstinence appears to have little effect on sperm quality.

Fertility Drugs

There are different kinds of fertility drugs to stimulate the ovaries. Each has advantages and disadvantages in terms of time, neagtive side effects, cost, and so on. Some are taken orally, others require shots. Still others are delivered via a pump which is worn at the waist with a dripfeed entering a vein in the arm; this allows for small doses to be slowly and steadily absorbed.

Fertility drugs work in various ways, usually on the pituitary and/or hypothalamus. They stimulate the ovaries in the early part of the cycle to produce more and better follicles. They are very effective; 80 to 90 percent of women will ovulate regularly on the 13th or 14th day. Where the only cause of infertility is poor ovulation, there is a very good chance of pregnancy.

In fact, fertility drugs stimulate the ovaries so successfully that more than one egg is produced. This results in the problem of *multiple births*. There is a 10 to 25 percent chance of twins and triplets; with higher numbers, some of the embryos die, and/or are severely retarded. Though fertility drugs do involve multiple births, further research may soon reduce this risk.

Female Tubal Obstruction

Adhesions are scars which form on the outside of the oviducts. They tie down the tube; it cannot move at ovulation to scoop up the free-floating egg. Adhesions can be due to previous pelvic infections, or surgery. If the scarring is widespread, the open ends of the fimbria may be completely blocked. When liquid is passed through the tubes, it cannot flow out. This is known as *hydrosalpinx*.

Corrective surgery to free the tubes from external adhesions has a success rate of 60 to 70 percent. However, this high rate only applies if the mucus linings *inside* the tubes have not been damaged by the scarring. Yet, when the fimbria are blocked, this internal lining is almost always severely damaged. The pregnancy rate then drops to between 5 and 20 percent. Keep in mind that there is always the risk that an operation to unblock the tubes can produce even more scar tissue. In these cases, one choice is in vitro fertilization.

Male Tubal Obstruction

The *epididymes* can be felt by gently rolling the testicles between the fingers and thumb. They are small comma-shaped lumps on top of the testicles; "epididymes" is Greek for "upon the twins." They are, in fact, tightly coiled tubes which, if stretched out, would measure 20 feet. After baby sperm leave the testicles, they mature in the epididymes, and develop swimming skills. If the epididymes tubes are blocked, the result is *tubal obstruction*. In rare cases, blocked tubes are the result of a birth defect. The vas tubes which carry the mature sperm to the penis can also be blocked.

Blocked tubes are a common problem in male infertility. They occur for the same reasons as in women; scars from previous infections or surgery. Surgery to repair defective tubes can be successful if the blockage is mild. However, if the degree of scarring is great, the outcome for unblocked tubes is low. One option in these cases is in vitro fertilization.

Looking Inside

A *laparoscopy* is a surgical procedure to examine the internal structures. A colored solution is introduced into the uterus via the vagina and cervix. The laparoscope is inserted though a small cut in the abdomen wall. When the tubes are open, the colored fluid can be seen to flow through them, and out into the pelvic cavity. If some fluid pools in little pockets, there may be scarring. The egg can get trapped in the pocket, and die. The pelvic cavity, ovaries, and uterus are also examined to see if endometriosis, inflammation, or some birth defect could be causing the problem. Where appropriate, surgical procedures to relieve a minor problem will be done at the same time.

A *hysteroscopy* is a procedure performed through the vagina. A fluid or carbon dioxide gas is introduced into the uterus via the vagina and cervix to expand the area and allow a better view. The mucus-secreting glands of the cervix are examined to see if they are working properly. The cervical canal and uterus lining are checked for structures which might add to the problem: polyps, fibroids, or bands of scar tissue. Some minor surgical procedures can be done at the same time, if appropriate.

A *hysterosalpingogram* (HSG) is an internal X-ray of the uterus and tubes. A radio-opaque dye is injected into the uterus through the vagina and cervix, and the X-ray is taken. HSG is a painful procedure. Cramps and spasm can give a false-positive result; there appears to be a blockage where, in fact, none exists. The iodine solution in the dye can cause an allergic reaction. HSG has become less popular in recent years.

Other Fertility Tests

There are many different tests to find the cause of fertility problems. They include:

- Evaluation of cervical mucus. This involves an examination of mucus production, which may be scanty and blocking the sperm.
- Postcoital tests. These occur after intercourse to evaulate the progress of sperm inside the vagina.
- Basal body temperature charting. This test checks the timing of ovulation dates.
- Hamster test. Sperm are evaluated to find out whether or not they can penetrate hamster eggs.
- Hormone assay tests. These check the sex hormone levels of the partners.

One major problem with these tests is that they all take time. If the woman is no longer young, it may be suggested that she bypass all tests and goes straight for in vitro fertilization. However, most tests are covered by many medical insurances, and in vitro fertilization often is not.

It is only natural to want to know the cause of infertility. If either partner has tubal obstruction, *and* corrective surgery works, the problem is cured. If the problem is with the egg or sperm, hormone therapy is highly effective. The couple can then have as many children as they wish. With in vitro fertilization, an entire new program must be undertaken each time for each new baby. No single program can guarantee success.

Research from in vitro programs shows that time is a critical factor in choice. In one program, 35 women over age 40 had their eggs fertilized outside the uterus. When the fertilized eggs were returned to the uterus, only 5 women achieved pregnancy and *none carried the fetus to term.* Yet when these same women received eggs donated by women under age 35, 20 got pregnant and 15 delivered babies.

In Vitro Fertilization

IUI is an acronym for IntraUterine Insertion. Sperm are put into the uterus via the cervix. They travel to the tubes, where fertilization takes place. Poor quality sperm can bypass the journey through the vagina and avoid the cervical mucus, which may be hostile. IUI can be combined with IVF.

IVF is an acronym for In Vitro Fertilization. The eggs are retrieved (withdrawn) from the ovary via a needle put into the abdominal wall. The man provides sperm which is mixed with the egg in a test tube (culture dish), and put in an incubator. After fertilization occurs, the resultant embryos are injected into the woman's uterus. IVF bypasses the tubes, and is appropriate in cases of tubal obstruction.

GIFT is an acronym for Gamete IntraFallopian Tube Transfer. The egg and sperm are collected as above, then injected directly into the woman's oviduct. They are not fertilized in a culture dish. Fertilization occurs naturally within the tube, and the egg then travels down to the uterus. GIFT involves the tubes, and is appropriate only if they are healthy.

ZIFT is an acronym for Zygote In Vitro Fertilization, (a zygote is an embryo). ZIFT is a variation of both GIFT and IVF. Sperm are "washed", then mixed with the egg in a culture dish, where fertilization takes place. The resultant embryo is injected into the oviducts instead of the uterus. ZIFT involves the tubes, and is only appropriate if they are healthy.

PZD is an acronym for Partial Zona Dissection. It is a new technique to help feeble sperm get through the egg's outer wall. The egg is retrieved and pierced in two places to create a tiny passageway. The sperm can then get in easily. PZD has led to 7 pregnancies so far, and could raise the odds for infertile men.

The implantation rate with GIFT and ZIFT is higher than IVF. It seems that transferring the 2-day-old embryo to the uterus might act like an IUD; it might set up an irritation factor which interferes with implantation. Multiple births occur with in vitro fertilization because the more embryos in the uterus, the better the chance of one implanting. Selective selection involves removing the weaker embryos to give the others a better chance. For some parents-to-be and physicians, selective selection can be a difficult problem involving issues of ethical and moral choice.

Seeking Donation

Sperm Donation: If the man cannot provide sperm, the couple can use a sperm bank. The sperm are put into the vagina via a catheter, and make their way up to the oviducts. The donor, often a medical student, is anonymous. This method is called Artificial Insemination by a Donor (AID).

Egg Donation: If the woman cannot provide eggs, the couple can seek an egg donated by a third person. This person may be a close friend of the couple, or a stranger. Her retrieved egg is placed in a culture dish, and there fertilized by the partner's sperm. The embryo is then put into the woman's uterus or tubes.

Embryo Donation: If neither egg nor sperm can be provided, the couple can seek help from a third woman and man. The woman donates her egg, and the man his sperm. These are retrieved and fertilized in a culture dish, and the embryo is transplanted into the woman.

Uterus Donation: A mother "loaned" her uterus to her daughter and became the first grandmother to bear her own children. The daughter had been born without a uterus, but she could provide an egg. This was retrieved and fertilized by sperm from the daughter's husband in a culture dish. The resultant embryo was implanted in the mother who successfully gave birth to twins.

Surrogacy: If a woman has lost her uterus, another woman can provide hers for pregnancy and childbirth. This is somewhat different from the previous example, because the partner usually has intercourse with the other woman in order to impregnate her, and money is involved. The custody of some infants of surrogacy birth has been bitterly fought over in the law courts. Perhaps only in very close and loving families does surrogacy not prove to be a very tricky area of human choice.

A Cautionary Note

Only a relatively small percentage of in vitro fertilization procedures result in live births. For most women, the result can feel rather like paying up to $10,000 for each miscarriage. Be aware that in vitro programs carry a very high physical *and* emotional cost. The timing for each stage of the program, and then waiting for the results can be exhausting. Keep up to date with the latest advances in surgical and hormone therapy, as well as in vitro procedures. They are all advancing at such a rapid rate that the decision to opt for one particular therapy may become easier than it now appears.

There is big money for the operators of fertility clinics, for all the various kinds of therapy. Couples in desperate search for a solution to their problems are very vulnerable to exploitation. A few fertility clinics are little more than rip-off ventures, cashing in on the couple's anguish. To avoid such unscrupulous operators, ask the family physician or gynecologist for a clinic which can be recommended.

Summary

- Allow sufficient time for pregnancy to occur.
- Try the various self-help methods during this time.
- A sperm examination is the first fertility test.
- Fertility drugs may help stimulate under-active testicles.
- Poor quality sperm can be helped by "sperm washing" or PZD.
- Poor ovulation can be treated with fertility drugs.
- Minor tubal obstruction can respond to surgery.
- Surgery for severe adhesions has a poor success rate.
- GIFT and ZIFT have about the same success rate.
- The success rate for IVF is about three times less.
- Zift is appropriate for poor quality sperm.
- GIFT and ZIFT are not possible if the tubes are damaged.
- IVF is appropriate if the tubes are blocked.
- Egg or sperm donation is another route to consider for help.

CHAPTER 12

The Baby

Fetal Life

At fertilization, the egg is programed to be either male or female. This is not apparent in the first embryonic weeks. The tiny buds of the genitals have the basic structure to become either female or male. There is a genital ridge which can become the clitoris or penis. There are raised folds which can develop into labia or scrotum. By nine weeks, the beginnings of a primitive vagina appear, (the penile tube grows longer). At eleven weeks, the external female genitals take shape (the edges of the penile tube fuse).

Both genders develop internal duct systems. Special tissues on the ducts are pre-gonads. They can become the female ovaries or the male testicles. During weeks 5 to 11, the ovaries develop and the ducts fuse to form into the oviducts, uterus and vagina. Once the ovaries and testicles produce their female or male hormones, further development for the female reproductive organs progresses smoothly. In males, however, by about week 15, male hormones must suppress the female-making tissue because all embryos are originally programed female. If something goes amiss, if the testicles are malformed or produce insufficient hormones, the fetus will develop into a female. As far as nature is concerned, Eve came first.

By the fifth month, there are about 10 million primitive egg cells (follicle tissue) developing in the tiny nubs of ovaries. From the seventh month, hundreds and thousands of these would-be eggs do not mature; they regress. By birth, the total number of eggs is reduced to about 1 million. Nor does this regression stop at birth. By puberty, there are a quarter of a million eggs left in both ovaries. This phenomenon of regression of cells destined to become eggs is not understood. However, a quarter of a million eggs at birth is more than enough.

The sexual systems of a man and woman are very different. Yet it is thought the budding tissue in early embryo life show some parallels in structure. These are perceived as:

Female	Male
Outer lips	Scrotum
Inner lips	Underside of penis
Glans of clitoris	Glans of penis
Shaft of clitoris	Shaft of penis
Foreskin (hood)	Foreskin
Ovaries	Testicles
Uterus	Epididymes
Oviducts	Vas deferens
Bartholin's glands	Cowper's Glands
Skene's glands	Prostate glands

Breast Tissue

Breast tissue starts developing in early fetal life. It grows in two lines from the level of the underarm down to the groin. These lines are called "milk ridges"; they can be seen down the abdomen of a female family pet. In humans, the milk ridges stop development before 12 weeks. There is the same kind of regression which occurs in primitive eggs. Breast tissue usually remains only in the chest area.

Seven percent of baby girls are born with *polymastia*, "many breasts having one or more extra nipples." Polymastia occurs in baby boys, though the condition is less common. The most usual site for an extra nipple is on the milk ridge line directly under one breast. However, they can be anywhere on the trunk, appearing on the line of the milk ridge. Between one and five percent of daughters born to mothers with the condition will also have polymastia. Nobody knows what causes this condition. In adult men with hairy chests, it is often mistaken for a freckle or mole.

A rare defect is breast tissue somewhere along the milk ridge, but no nipple. Breasts do not begin to develop until puberty, so the condition may not be noticed until then. At puberty, the tissue begins to grow like a breast in the normal position. Visit the physician to check that all is well.

A very rare defect is breast tissue in the usual place, and no nipple. It is often linked to other problems of chest development which can include sternum and rib deformities, curvature of the spine (scoliosis), or sparse muscle development.

Baby Secretions

At birth, the genitals of a baby girl are swollen and puffy. It is fairly common for white discharge to exude from the vagina. In some cases, the discharge is thick and creamy; it can be flecked with blood. There is no cause for concern. This is the result of the mother's hormones still circulating in the baby's blood, and stimulating this female response. Within a week or so, the maternal hormones are flushed out as the baby's system no longer receives them.

A baby girl's genitals appear loose and saggy. The labia seem far more noticeable than on a toddler; in some cases, they protrude. The openings of the vagina, anus and urethra are wider than parents expect. Again, this is perfectly normal. It is due to the later development of the pelvic supports. Once the baby stands up, the internal mesh of muscles and ligaments which make up the pelvic support system start to strengthen and tighten. The internal and external organs are drawn up into place, and the lips meet to close over the vulva. Soon after this, the little girl can control her bladder and, somewhat later, the muscles of the rectum.

The majority of babies are born with tiny swollen breasts. A whitish fluid can ooze from them. This used to be called "witch's milk," and was thought to have magical properties. Avoid any squeezing of the breasts to remove the fluid. It has the opposite effect; it stimulates the milk flow. Both milk and breasts will disappear within the first few weeks.

Foreskin Facts

A baby girl is born with her clitoris and foreskin (hood) as one single structure. During fetal life, they develop from a single bud. At birth, neither is fully formed. They are still developing and continue to do so until they are ready to separate of their own accord. In boys, this happens naturally at some time before puberty, usually by the child's second to fifth birthday. The time for girls is not noted; it is likely to be the same.

During the first years, a child cannot control her excretory functions. The genitals are frequently swamped with urine or feces. Diaper rash is common, and the skin of the entire area can become sore and raw. It would seem a clever design of Nature to keep the protective foreskin firmly attached to the glans while there is a high risk of infection. Later, when the child has learned full control of her excretory functions, the foreskin and glans are sufficiently developed to separate.

There is no need for extra cleansing of the genitals. The daily bath and wipes in between are usually enough. If diaper rash develops, protect the area with baby cream. Try to leave off diapers whenever appropriate. The urinary tract can become infected; check that the vulva area does not look sore. If a baby girl screams when urinating, the hot liquid could be stinging a sore place. Take her to the physician to check all is well.

In very rare cases, the foreskin and glans do not separate. The condition is called *clitoral adhesions*, and is not usually detected in childhood. It is thought to be one reason for lack of orgasm. The sensitive glans is not exposed at the first stage of arousal, and there is no sensation of mounting sexual tension. The adhesions can be removed, and the foreskin freed to retract or cover the glans as appropriate.

In an adult, the hood maintains its protective function. At the early stage of sexual arousal, it rolls back to allow greater stimulus of the clitoris. When this is sufficient, it rolls forward again to prevent further stimulus. Otherwise, it remains as a cover for the delicate and highly sensitive tissues, keeping them safe from harm within its protective sheath.

Circumcision is the surgical removal of the foreskin. It is pulled forward and away from the glans, or clamped in a ring, and then cut off. The process is an issue of *culture* rather than health. Male circumcision is a religious rite in Jewish and Muslim families. It is a popular custom in America and Britain among the more affluent social groups; other Europeans do not approve. Female circumcision, which can include removal of the entire clitoris, is generally considered barbaric today. Perhaps male circumcision will soon be perceived in the same light.

Birth Defects

In the last century, horror stories were told of young women who suddenly discovered that they had no vagina. This was only realized after puberty, when the absence of periods alerted parents that something was wrong. In other cases, it was as late as pre-marriage, when intercourse could not take place. Absence of a vagina is very rare; such birth defects are called *congenital anomalies*. One in 5,000 baby girls is born without a uterus; a few baby girls have only one functioning ovary. In even more rare cases, there can be two uteri and two vaginas, which are the result of an incomplete split of the fetal tissue.

Nowadays, these congenital anomalies are discovered early at the post-birth checks on an infant. The presence of a vagina is checked, and if there is any cause for doubt concerning the other internal reproductive organs, an ultrasound scan can detect if they are present. There are successful surgical procedures for constructing a functional vagina. Skillful plastic surgeons can sort out the problems of a malformed uterus and/or vagina. Hormone therapy assists in problems of non-functioning ovaries.

Perhaps the main reason why these anomalies were only found after puberty was the sexual stigma left over from the Victorian era. Gynecologists have always been under particular public scrutiny, and know that their behavior must be above reproach. In 1893, one medical writer tried to stop pelvic exams. He called them the "reckless habit of investigating the sexual organs of young women." It was, he said, "a species of rape." If an exam of the sexual organs were necessary, he strongly believed that "it should be done in the hospital under a general anesthetic."

Turner Syndrome

A baby girl born with Turner Sndrome has either no ovaries or small streaks which do not function. This condition occurs in about 1 in 3,000 live births. It is 40 times more common in spontaneous abortions. Usually, there are other defects which give the physician warning signals that something is wrong. In obvious cases, the neck is very short with a web of skin from the ears to the shoulders. In other cases, the neck is not webbed and the other signs are not so obvious, so an early diagnosis of Turner Syndrome is not always made. The girl's IQ is usually normal; in some cases, there is trouble with space perception and numbers.

At puberty, the girl does not grow tall. If short stature runs in the family, the condition is only detected late in puberty. The absence of breast development, periods and so on, alerts parents that something may be amiss. The girl is put on estrogen therapy, and all the signs of puberty begin. Though she cannot have children, she can function sexually as other women. However, some women with Turner Syndrome have had successful pregnancies with donor eggs and in vitro fertilization.

The Hospital

Nurse researchers are in a unique position for studying the behaviors of children in the hospital. They are coming up with findings which run counter to popular belief and common practice. One ongoing study in Nashville has shown not all children benefit from being told what to expect during their hospital stay.

It appears there are three separate types of coping behavior which children may exhibit. Some appear to be "avoiders"; they feel more in control if they have very little information. Others are "vigilants"; they cope by seeking as much information as they can; the more they know the more confident they feel. The third group are "combiners"; they want to know the details of surgery but nothing about possible risks or post-operative complications.

Parents learn a baby's needs by observation. *This is the basis of all effective early parenting.* Tiny mouths pucker and little foreheads crease at the first pang of hunger. The parent responds with food before the baby breaks down into open distress, and yells. Crying upsets both parent and baby; each may need equal amounts of soothing. Yet the parent must wait until the baby is soothed, and fed, and changed, and played with, and rocked back to sleep, before being able to release her distress. In most cases, the ability to relieve a baby's distress gives the parent relief from her own distress.

In the same way, parents can observe the degree of information to give even a very young toddler who requires hospitalization by observation. Being separated from a parent is always acutely distressing. Basic trust can be seriously undermined. Try to stay with a child if possible. If not, check whether hospitalization is essential. Nowadays, many procedures can be done on an outpatient basis.

Self-esteem

It seems desirable for most cultures to help children develop a solid sense of self-esteem. This is defined as "a favorable impression of the self; self-respect; self-worth." Apart from loving the child, the bedrock of self-esteem lies in being honest and honorable, in not breaking promises, and in the satisfaction which comes from personal achievement. If a child watches these values in parental action, and can achieve them (for some of the time) by about age seven, it develops a deep and lasting sense of self-worth.

Most parents nowadays understand the value of fostering self-esteem in their children. Yet some parents are unsure how to manage this effectively. They wish to praise, encourage, and respect their little girl's identity and achievements, yet fear that they might be raising a querulous, demanding, persistently disobedient child. Minor infringements are to be expected (and secretly applauded); a child who is too compliant may be living in terror of parental wrath, or of withdrawal of parental love.

The "Me Generation" was high on material achievement and worldly success, even if this involved telling lies, breaking one's word, cheating at work, acting with honor *only* where there was risk of dishonorable deeds being found out. White collar crime soared, and the results of high-level financial cheating still reverberate throughout the nation. It can be argued that it is not only in parental self-interest, but in the interests of the culture as a whole, to develop self-esteem in children.

The virtues of antiquity were honor, stoicism, and courage in the face of adversity. Little boys are taught to admire these virtues; they try very hard to acquire them. Little girls try as well, *if* they are encouraged to do so; *if* they perceive their adult roles as strong and effective achievers. This is not to "masculinize" girls. It is no accident that strong, effective heroines such as Scarlett O'Hara and the tough-cookie roles portrayed by Bette Davis, Barbara Stanwyck, and others, have a lasting appeal to female audiences.

The Scouts and similar organizations foster these qualities. Children are taught to believe in themselves, to trust their own abilities. Moral training is important for all children, but particularly for girls. The social model they must fight as they grow up is still one where women often have to manipulate men to gain self-esteem. Many women say that they do not feel worth much when on their own. They only feel good about themselves *when in the company of men*. Not only does this distort the male ego, it leaves women very vulnerable to male approval. In extreme cases, any man's approval is better than none, even if it involves violence, *providing that she is told she is wanted and needed after the blows*. On the basis of female health and safety alone, it is essential that all little girls are encouraged to build self-esteem.

Lack of self-esteem drives people crazy. The different genders tend to respond in different ways. A man who lacks self-esteem may respond by fighting or drinking, whatever makes him feel that he is somebody or can achieve something. Because of the social model for women, there can develop a desperate need to acquire a man, any man, *because this is unconsciously perceived as achieving*. If the man leaves at some later date, there is more than the natural grief of loss. There is the double whammy of loss of self-esteem.

The point to understand about self-esteem is that it cannot be acquired through others. It can only be gained through a satisfactory opinion of the self.

"Lay up not treasures on this earth," could well be translated into "Lay up not self-esteem in others, especially in male approval," for the raising of little girls.

Nature or Nurture?

One intriguing concept about self-esteem is that, in general, the female ego appears to be more fragile than the male. One study found that girls and boys as young as two years old responded to success and failure very differently. When boys succeeded at a difficult task, they showed more pride in their achievement than girls. When girls failed, even at a simple task, they reacted with more shame than boys. Girls who did poorly on a test were more likely than boys to permit that single performance to affect the way they felt about themselves, their schoolwork, and their whole potential.

Much of this difference probably stems from the different ways that little girls and boys are treated by adults. Yet there remains a crucial question: do inherent gender differences play a role? Some psychiatrists believe so. For example, most infants ages 9 to 18 months cannot tolerate being left on their own, and a study of infants ages 11 to 12 months found that when the mother left the room or put the baby to bed, the girls became withdrawn; they seemed sad. The boys became hyperactive, thrashing around. Obviously, this did not happen in all cases.

At 17 to 18 months, another difference becomes apparent: girls display greater facility with language. At 18 months, most girls can put two words together; this occurs 2 months later in boys. Girls accumulate a vocabulary and make complete sentences earlier than boys. Boys develop a better perception of space. If children are left in an ambiguous situation with ambiguous markers, the boys' chance to find the direction out is better as early as 2 years to 30 months.

It is not yet possible to answer the nature/nurture question. Parent/child relationships are very subtle. Birth order is likely to affect gender responses too. A discussion of inborn femaleness or maleness requires a definition of terms, and no such terms have yet been satisfactorily defined. While researching for this chapter, one factor arose over and over again. Little girls have, or seem to have, more pressure put on their behavior at home than boys.

The Female Form

In America, there exists a false concept of the female form which is demonstrated in thousands of subtle ways. One not-so-subtle way is the popular Barbie doll, and others of her ilk. Assuming a bust measurement of 36 inches, Barbie's proportions work out at a 36-inch bust, an 18-inch waist, and 33-inch hips. This is an unattainable ideal for the average little girl, who will develop into the average round or pear-shaped woman, who wears a size 12, weighs 144 lbs and is 5 feet 4 inches tall.

Whither went the dolls of yesteryear? What happened to the limp raggedy Anns, and other cuddly dolls with their asexual bodies? When did these sexually non-threatening toys lose their appeal, if they did? More to the point, who first put breasts on dolls, and gave them unattainable body shapes? The shape of dolls affects girls in the home. There are thousands of similar messages they absorb from the external world.

It is a tragic fact that little girls in America start dieting as early as age 8 or 9. Eighty percent of fourth graders have already been on their first diets. At some later stage, 2 percent become anorexic, and 15 percent become bulimic. A recent study found that 70 percent of girls consider themselves fat.

An eating disorder is *an abnormal drive for thinness*. There are now more than 2,000 therapists in the U.S. who specialize in eating disorders. According to one therapist, "Millions of people go from false concepts of the female form to a struggle with eating disorders, which can be extremely dangerous, cause unbelievable suffering for their families, and in the worst case scenarios, death."

The Cult of Thinness

"Mothers linked to daughters' eating disorders." In late 1991, these headlines were blazoned in newspapers and magazines. They came from the findings of a study into female attitudes towards food and beauty. The study examined pairs of mothers and daughters, with half the girls having eating disorders and half not. "It appears some of the mother's own dieting and eating behavior, and especially her concerns about her daughter's weight and appearance, pose a significant risk that a daughter will be disordered in her eating." In choosing a control group, the researchers had to exclude the lowest 10 percent on an eating disorder inventory because dieting is so pervasive that this group was not typical! These girls were in their teens; attitudes to eating are formed in early life.

A new documentary, *The Famine Within*, shows American women's collective obsession with body weight. Katherine Gilday's 1991 documentary makes a real case for the larger importance of this issue. Every era has its own idea of perfect virtue for women. The current ideal demands the triumph of denial over normal, healthy appetite. Faith in weight loss has taken on the power of religious conviction. Yet the standard to which so many women aspire "really has less to do with beauty than with the deep cultural meaning of body type."

Are the virtues of stoicism, fortitude, and courage in the face of adversity now focused solely on cookie-avoidance? It would be funny, were it not so sad. Anorexics literally starve themselves through dieting. Bulimics gorge on food, then force themselves to throw up and/or purge themselves with laxatives. Both are psychological conditions involving an abnormal fear of obesity. Both demand the virtues of stoicism, fortitude, and courage.

"In many respects, it's a critical brain drain we have. Female energy and intelligence are trapped in concern over weight loss," according to one expert. The film's point is that women, struggling to balance careers and families, are desperate to gain control over their lives. This leads them to avoid the feminine aspects of soft, round contours, and emphasize the lean, masculine ideal. By constant dieting, "we are reassuring the culture that it still has the upper hand over us and over nature."

What sorry kind of achievement is this?

"All You Need Is Love..."

A pre-anorexic personality is described as well-behaved, a highly achieving, pleasant, well-adjusted, compliant, perfectionist, rigid. The last three are the key words. Eating disorders are an issue of *control*. Their roots start in early childhood, when life feels very unsafe, and the child is not made to feel safe in ways which really matter. Primping a little girl's hair and making her pretty for Daddy is fun and delights the heart, *providing* the child feels perfectly secure when her hair is mussed up. It is unwittingly cruel if she feels insecure, because being mussed up, being unpretty, makes her fearful of losing male approval.

Most parents love their children desperately. A few think that this is enough. Sadly, love on its own can fall short. It requires the backing of *profound* trust, an understanding on the child's part that she can depend upon the parent, come what may. Yet plain little girls are openly worried over by some mothers. Others are told they will grow up into a beautiful swan, just as the ugly duckling did. Little boys do not get hammered with such undermining messages; they do not learn that adult approval depends mainly on their looks. They are out there practicing the manly virtues upon which they base their self-esteem.

The security blanket, beloved of all children, shows parents the extent of a child's need for familiarity, for security. When, as an adult, the woman feels insecure, she searches for some familiar object to help her feel safe. Food, which is readily available, is often the answer. This starts her on the spiraling down slide of eating binges and crash diets. She cannot help it. The very object upon which she depends to make her feel secure is the very object which is most disapproved of: weight.

Control

The irony of eating disorders is that they are about control. They demand self-denial to a very high degree which, in turn, demands courage, stoicism, and fortitude. The first refusal of a cookie is not easy. The second, fifth, and twentieth can be even more painful.

191

Only a great deal of practice allows this unhealthy form of self-denial to strengthen the will sufficiently until it becomes easy. At that stage, food is the enemy. The girl has turned away from growth, from blossoming, from all within the human spirit which yearns for happiness and love.

She is seeking control. She needs to know that there is one area where she can achieve, where she can gain self-esteem. Her body is her own, and can be used for the satisfaction which comes from personal achievement. She is bombarded with messages of the new myth of thinness, and imagines that she is more appealing by losing weight. Eating disorders provide satisfying rewards; the bathroom scales show a noticeable loss of weight. The more she practices and develops her extraordinary skills of self-denial, the more her self-esteem depends upon her body image.

* * *

The point to understand is that lack of self-esteem in early childhood can create tremendous problems for parents at puberty. Even if a girl is not slim and has a normal body weight, problems can arise if her self-esteem depends, to a great extent, upon her looks. Then, the only way she can gain the rewards of personal achievement is by gaining the approval of boys. A pubertal girl in this insecure condition can seek male approval by early sexual activity, with all its attendant risks.

Studies show that the lower a girl's self-esteem when she enters puberty, the more likely that she will become estranged from her parents later. Reward a little girl's achievements in spheres other than her looks, and gain the rewards of a healthy, happy adolescent.

* * *

A healthy baby's appetite is voracious. At the toddler stage, appetite normally drops for a while. Parents may believe that their little girl has become a finicky eater; this is rarely the case. Imagination is developing, and some foods look frightening or disgusting: the wrinkly skin on milk or tomatoes; the vivid color of carrots; the strange texture of vegetables; the chewiness of meat. The greasiness of fried foods cannot be easily digested by young systems. They should be avoided on a further count; they are rich in animal fats which provide a high level of cholesterol, and can damage the heart. If the child is not forced to eat what she dislikes, appetite picks up again by school age. Providing the diet is varied, a little girl can eat more or less what she chooses.

At pre-puberty, a daughter can seem to have "hollow legs." No matter how heartily she eats, there is always room for more. This is due to the pre-pubertal stage of rapid growth in both height and weight. If she is active and within the normal weight range for her age, avoid undue worry that she is eating too much. She needs this food to sustain her daily activities *and* to build her future curvy frame.

Summary

- Baby secretions are normal and disappear in a week or so.
- The genitals require no more than the usual daily hygiene.
- Boost a little girl's self-confidence in her own abilities.
- Encourage the pleasure which comes from personal achievement.
- Act as her appropriate role model for the "manly" virtues.
- Protect her from the new myth: fear of body weight.
- Avoid persuading her to eat foods which she dislikes.
- Praise her achievements rather than her appearance.
- If her self-esteem is high, she will sail through puberty.

CHAPTER 13

Puberty

Puberty is the time of transition from physical and sexual immaturity to maturation. The young girl's body is *feminized*, and turns into that of a woman. The process takes an average 3 years, usually between the ages of 10 and 13. By the end of puberty, the reproductive organs are functioning, and the girl is capable of having a child.

Adolescence follows puberty, and is perceived as a "catching up" process. Though the girl may be adult in a reproductive sense at 13, she lacks the skills of maturity in other respects. Adolescence is the time of mental, social, and emotional maturation. It can continue until the late teens or early 20s.

The 1990 American Medical Association's *Profiles of Adolescent Health* reports: "In hospitals, emergency rooms, community health clinics, and school-based health centers, physicians treat adolescents who are pregnant, who have sexually transmitted diseases, who are injured in car accidents, who are suicidal or failing in school, who shoot drugs and are shot with guns. They see adolescents who eat too many of the wrong foods, who starve themselves, or who are obese or get insufficient exercise...*Many of these problems can be prevented...*" (emphasis added).

Height Increase

By age 10, a girl has reached 83 percent of her adult height. She will make up the last 17 percent in a very short space of time. *Rapid growth* starts at age 10; it is a sudden increase in height due to speedy skeletal (bone) development. There is more than one spurt of rapid growth spurt during puberty. Each follows a distinct pattern of order:

- The head, feet, and hands begin enlarging to adult size.
- The arm and leg bones then grow longer and stronger.
- The trunk is the last to develop to full female size.

It is not unusual for a girl to grow 1 1/2 inches within 8 weeks. The bones get harder, more solid and less flexible. Under pressure, they fracture rather than break. Skeletal growth stops around age 14, though there can be a slight height increase later. In one study, the most rapid growth was at 12 years, but 10 percent of girls grew their fastest at age 11, and 10 percent at about 13 1/2 years.

Weight Increase

In terms of percentage body weight of fat tissue, little girls are plumper than little boys. In the pre-pubertal years, both genders tend to increase their body fat. During rapid growth, this slows down. Yet in girls, there remains a steady increase in the fat content of the body. Fat is mainly deposited on the trunk and female sexual contours: breasts, lower abdomen, hips, and thighs, and not so much on the limbs.

At age 10, a girl has reached 53 percent of her adult weight. There follows a rapid increase in weight, with changes in the ratio of fat cells to muscle and bone. Appetite is hearty; it should be equal to, or larger than, an adult's. This is important as heart weight nearly doubles, lung capacity increases, and muscle and bone develop at a very rapid rate. Some parents worry that their daughter is building fat tissue, but she is building her entire frame. A *big weight increase is normal and to be expected*, because it is dependent upon the process of puberty. By the time her first period arrives, weight and height increase are almost complete.

Stretch marks occur in 25 percent of girls between ages 12 and 14, usually after the rapid growth in height and weight. They appear as pinkish or purple parallel lines on the upper thighs, buttocks, or breasts. It takes a few months, sometimes a few years, before the color fades. The stretch marks then turn smaller and white, though they do not entirely vanish.

Acne is more common and the spots are more severe in girls who have colored stretch marks; the reason why is unclear. Nor is it known if the lost interest in sports makes the condition worse; in rare cases, thin girls get stretch marks too. There has been a constant plug for exercise throughout this book. It benefits women in more ways than any beauty cream or aid can. Exercise is very important at puberty to assist a smooth passage through the rapid growth stage. If a girl dislikes contact sports, encourage dancing, swimming, bicycling, gymnastics, and so on. A word of warning: a girl with an eating disorder can over-exercise as part of her obsessive/compulsive disorder. For early avoidance of eating disorders, see Chapter 12.

Agility

From babyhood, girls are more agile than boys, bending to touch toes, and so on. The flexibility of small children depends upon the ratio of length to bulk. Both genders achieve maximum agility between ages 12 and 14. Some girls lose interest in sports at puberty. This is a pity; bones and muscles and emerging adult frame benefit from the stamina, strength, and suppleness which exercise brings. A few girls become preoccupied with their appearance, rather than their physical and mental development.

In terms of speed and timing of reaction, human response to stimulus reaches its peak between ages 10 and 14. Awareness and responsiveness continue to improve, but the capacity to learn complex skills begins to regress after age 15, *unless there is continuing training*.

Rapid growth at puberty can result in clumsiness for a while. There is a slight loss of symmetry; hands are too large for arms, feet seem too huge and so on. Objects break, and people collide, when this awkward stage arrives. Each accident reinforces a painful sense of clumsiness, of being out of control. Avoid teasing or scolding. Explain what is happening with reassurances that growth will soon even out. Exercise improves co-ordination. Encourage a girl by telling her that young athletes rarely suffer this lack of physical grace.

Sexual Development

Breast growth is usually the first sign of sexual development. The tiny budding breasts look like small round bulges *behind* the nipple; the gland tissue and fat cells start to develop in this one place. The areola swells too, and the effect looks slightly odd: cone-shaped hillocks which cause the nipple bud to be raised up. The breasts do not always develop at the same time. In 10 percent of girls, there is a time lag of a few months before the second one develops. Parents who notice this one-sided growth may fear cancer and take a daughter to the physician to check that it is not an abnormal growth.

- Breasts take, on average, 4 years to develop. This can vary from 1 1/2 years to 6 years.
- Pubic hair appears some 9 months after the breasts; underarm (axillary) hair can be a year later. Body hair takes 2 or 3 years to fully develop. This can vary between 1 and 4 years.
- The inner and outer folds of the labia enlarge. By menarche they meet and cover the inner organs.
- The vagina grows rapidly in length, and the walls become robust. It is about 11 cm long at menarche.
- The inner vulva and vagina become paler in color, changing from red or shiny pink, to a duller and thicker pink.
- The cervix becomes more clearly defined, and the cervical glands start to produce mucus.
- The uterus grows from pea-size in a child, weighing 2 grams, to the strong muscular organ weighing about 80 grams in a woman.
- The ovaries develop from nubs of inactive tissue to ripe, round structures the size and shape of almonds.
- The oviducts lengthen and the fringed fimbria spread. Inside the tubes, the cilia commence their rhythmic beat.

Apart from body hair, all these female organs are estrogen-dependent for growth. They cannot develop without estrogen from the ovaries. In fact, the first (unseen) pre-puberty change occurs in the ovaries, which begin developing at about 8 years and increase in size by about 4 times in the next 4 years.

During childhood, the production of female hormones is low. A low volume of androgens (male hormones) is secreted by the adrenals. As puberty nears, androgens promote the growth of pubic and underarm hair, and are involved in rapid bone growth. The sebaceous glands are also stimulated by androgens. Some girls at pre-puberty break out in facial spots. It is now thought, though not proven, that these spots could be one of the earliest signs of puberty.

The Whites

From 3 to 12 months before menarche, a girl may notice cream in her underwear. It is a thick, clear, greyish-white fluid which lacks odor. The distinctive sea aroma of a mature vagina does not begin until after menarche. In some girls, the "whites" are profuse. This is perfectly normal. Underwear should be of cotton to absorb the fluid, and keep the area dry.

If the "whites" cause pain, soreness or itching, there could be a vulva infection. A worm infestation from the anus could also be the cause; lax hygiene habits when using school toilets can cause outbreaks of such infestations. More rarely, foreign matter or dirt get into the vagina and cause inflammation. Usually, however, a vulva infection is due to lax habits. Now is the time to instruct a daughter in genital hygiene.

Little girls are rarely concerned with cleansing routines. At the approach of menarche, they benefit from a fairly serious chat on feminine hygiene. The "whites" should be removed daily to avoid risk of infection. Towels and body cloths should be kept separate and really clean. (Wash cloths tend to hold germs; clean hands are effective.) Cotton panties should be changed frequently; panty liners are useful to mop up discharge if it is profuse. Worm infestation is transmitted by hand from lax toilet habits before handling food. Hand-washing before meals, and after using the toilet, reduces this risk.

Menarche

The first period, menarche, occurs about 18 months after the phase of rapid growth. In America, the average age is 12.3 years. In Britain, it is 13.3 years. Girls who eat less stay thinner and often have a later menarche than those who eat well. There is a big possible range of 18 months or more either way. Some 10 percent of girls menstruate before age 11, and 10 percent after age 14. A smaller height increase of 2 1/4 inches (5.8 cm) remains after menarche, within an inch or so more or less.

On average, menarche starts 2 1/2 years after the first signs of puberty; breast development is well advanced. This interval can be only 6 months or up to 5 1/2 years. The first periods are non-ovulatory; no egg is sprung from the follicle. As the ovaries produce more estrogen, LH is released from the pituitary with FSH, and the two hormones trigger the rupture of the follicle. Ovulation begins 3 to 12 months after menarche, yet occurs in only half of all periods. It takes about 2 years to be regular and consistent. By this time, the uterus has reached full adult proportions and sexual maturity is attained.

The first periods are naturally irregular. They can come for a few months, then stop, or be unevenly spaced. This irregularity takes a while to settle down. On average, a 16-year-old knows when to expect her flow, knows it will last 4 to 5 days, knows it will be heavy at first, then slow to mild spotting on the last day. Even painful periods tend to be regular (though she may perceive them as *always* coming early if dread of pain clouds her time-keeping).

A young girl can imagine that she is losing a great deal of blood. This is because blood looks very dramatic and stains very vividly. Average blood loss is between 3 and 9 tablespoons (50 to 175 cc). Reassure a girl who considers her flow to be abnormal. Give her a diary to record the dates, duration, and type of flow. Check her diet for sufficient iron to avoid anemia. Sleep, and more sleep, are of great benefit. If appropriate, a visit to the physician will bring her peace of mind.

Monthly Protection

In 1982, the Institute of Medicine Committee cautioned women, especially young women between the ages of 15 and 24, to avoid the use of high absorbency tampons to lessen the risk of Toxic Shock Syndrome. It seems that mothers automatically give their daughters sanitary napkins at menarche. Girls are content to use them for the first year or so. Later, they begin to perceive the benefits of tampons. It is especially hard to carry bulky napkins on public transport.

"I don't want you to use tampons until you are older."

"But, Mom — "

"What?"

"This awful thing happened today."

"If it's about tampons, I'm not listening."

The boys had grabbed her school bag. On the bus. They were looking for essays to read aloud, so they could jeer. They did it to all the girls. Nobody stopped them. It was awful. Today, when they found her napkins, they went silent for a bit. Then some horrid "boy" thing made them start up again. They pulled out their penknives and started cutting them up. She wanted to die.

"It's for *your* health," she heard her mother say. "You'll thank me when you're older." Yet parents rarely get thanked for harm which does not occur. Try to avoid arguments over sanitary napkins versus tampons. At this stage, arguments tend to end in parental defeat. The less defeat a parent suffers, the more a girl will accept other advice.

Not Too Early...

Precocious puberty is very early sexual maturity. Puberty is considered precocious if development begins at age 8. In most cases, early developers are healthy and normal. For some unknown reason, the hypothalamus, pituitary, and ovaries simply switch on before the norm. Check for early menarche on *both* sides of the family. The phenomenon of precocious puberty accounts for those sensational tabloid tales of 5-year-old girls giving birth. It can happen!

A girl who matures much earlier than her agemates can feel isolated from them. If her breasts grow large, they cannot be entirely hidden. Hair on the arms or legs, and underarm hair with its special odor, make her feel different, not one of the gang. Carrying napkins to school, having nowhere to deposit used ones, being fearful her flow will start at an inappropriate time, all these factors increase her feelings of being odd.

Problems of mental adjustment can arise because the girl looks more mature than she actually is. Adults can easily forget her social and emotional skills have not kept pace with physical precocity. The girl may be given responsibilites or tasks she is too young to cope with. Other children, especially siblings, often tease cruelly about her height, spots, gangly movements, extravagant breasts.

Individuals who experience precocious puberty can (and often do) become mothers at very early ages. This statement by a woman gynecologist is not carved in stone! In fact, the shock of early development causes some girls to withdraw into themselves. Others find their new state a challenge. They flaunt their breasts, and flash their charms in a manner which makes adults cringe. If not handled with great tact, and reassured that they are loved, they look for something to put in isolation's place. Unfortunately, that something is all too often the male organ. A girl who is desperately seeking recognition will take on any man who appears to offer love.

Counsel your little "grown" girl. She is still a baby, after all. Explain to her exactly what is happening, but without too much detail. Encourage a withdrawn daughter to feel better about her emerging charms (she cannot be proud of them yet). Explain to a "jail bait" daughter that this phrase is a *sneering joke* among certain men who know how to exploit her *and despise her* at the same time. If the parent/child relationship is not close, seek professional help and counseling.

Precocious puberty can be due to hormone or brain disorders. There are usually signs of other things seriously amiss. In most cases, no reason is found for precocious puberty; the girl is perfectly healthy. A physician's all clear sets everyone's mind at rest.

Not Too Late...

The medical indicators for *delayed puberty* are no breast development by age 13, and no menarche by age 14 or 15. Until then, the girl is considered a late developer. Like precocious puberty, it is an inherited tendency, and there is no cause for alarm. If the girl is plump and *neither* sign has appeared by age 13, a visit to the physician is advisable. Thinner girls tend to menstruate late, and there are some benefits to this.

Boys show a fairly standard correlation between their state of maturity and physical performance. Girls who mature late are usually superior to their agemates in terms of strength, speed, and agility. Thinness can be a great advantage in many sports. Late maturers who are thin often excel in physical activities. This success fuels their interest for a longer time, which allows for more improvement of a skill which, in turn, increases their motivation to remain interested in sports.

Primary amenorrhea occurs when menarche does not start within the average time range after breast and pubic hair development. It could be due to a genetic disorder. One in 5,000 girls is born without a uterus. In very rare cases, the hymen is imperforate. The tendency to go on crash or fad diets should be considered. A certain level of fat cells is necessary to support estrogen production. However, in most cases, late developers are perfectly healthy. If there are no signs of puberty by age 14, visit the physician for a check-up.

Abbie's Daughter

"Why are you wearing that awful old jacket?" Abbie asked.

Her daughter, Franny, was embarrassed. "You know. It covers my — you know."

Abbie did know. Only too well. Her daughter's breasts were over-growing, just as hers did when she was 13.

Franny raged. "Why won't they stop growing? It's *gross*. I *hate* them."

Abbie let her daughter storm on. She wanted to gauge just how strongly the girl was affected by her size. She herself had had breast reduction surgery six months after Franny was born. It had been a satisfying experience. Yet, there had been drawbacks.

Franny raged on, "All the boys snigger. They make jokes behind my back. The girls act like I've grown them on purpose. To show off. But I *hide* them all the time. And my bra straps cut into my shoulders. I *hate* sports. Men stop in the street to stare. *Everybody* stares. *I hate my breasts*. They're *deformed*. They're *ruining* my life!"

Abbie had hoped that Franny would grow very tall. Her breasts might then seem more in proportion. Yet even at model height, they would still be abnormally large. Men would still stare, and women disapprove. It seemed like some ghastly trick of nature, especially at Franny's age. Later, at pregnancy, the problem would become much worse. She said, "I had my breasts reduced after you were born."

Her daughter was quick, very quick. With a scream of delight, Franny flung her arms around Abbie's neck. "Yes! Yes! Oh, please! *Please!* I'll work. Save money. Help with the cost."

"It's not simple," Abbie said. "You must know the drawbacks."

"I don't care," Franny retorted. "Nothing in the whole world can be as bad as this."

Abbie wondered if a 13-year-old was capable of making such an important decision. "The surgery is long and complicated. There is always a risk with anesthesia. They cut under the breast, and then up to the nipples. Sometimes, they remove the nipples first, and graft them on afterwards. Or they leave them, and they get transposed."

"Transposed?"

"Otherwise the nipple would be in the wrong place. It's like a slice of cake they cut out, then draw the sides together and sew them up. You can see that the nipples have to be moved."

"So there's scars — ?"

"Yes, darling. The ones under the breasts don't show. But the others come right up to the nipple and go around each areola. The scars fade, but remain because the healed surfaces are dead."

There were other drawbacks, too, serious health risks. Abbie knew she must warn her daughter before a decision was made.

Breast Reduction Surgery

The condition of oversized breasts in young girls is *virginal hypertrophy*. For some unknown reason, breast growth does not switch off at the usual time. If *breast reduction* is an option, keep in mind that the larger the breasts, the greater the risk of problems with surgery. The nerves to the nipples can be damaged during their transposition, with total loss of sensation. Grafting the nipples back rather than transposing them adds to this risk. After breast reduction, even with minimal nerve damage, sensation is reduced in both the nipples and the breasts.

Breast reduction reduces the chance of breast-feeding. One option is to wait until child-bearing is over, but a young girl then has to endure years of misery and pain. Make it clear to a daughter that she could have regrets later on. Franny was disappointed with the results. "They're still too big," she wailed. She and Abbie had viewed the "before and after" photographs in the surgeon's office. Franny had chosen a B-cup. Her breasts were now C, and one was slightly larger than the other.

Keep in mind that any type of cosmetic surgery does not always provide the expected outcome. This is particularly so with breast tissue. If Franny wants to keep her C-cup size, she must avoid putting on weight. Fat is stored in the breasts, and reduction surgery will not stop them increasing in size.

In about 4 percent of cases, reduction surgery damages the blood supply to the areola-nipple complex. If this occurs, they die; tissue cannot live without blood. Artificial nipples are then constructed from genital tissue, and attached to the breasts. Obviously, there is no sensation left. To date, there are no reports that breast reduction carries a cancer risk. Women over age 35 should have a mammogram first.

A girl whose breasts remain small after puberty may plead for *breast augmentation*. This is not generally advisable until she is older. There is now considerable controversy over the health risks of silicon gel implants.

Self Esteem

"I like the way I look."
"I feel happy the way I am."
"I like most things about myself."
"I wish I were somebody else."

A study from the American Association of University Women found that the majority of girls age 9 were confident, assertive, and felt positive about themselves. By the time they reached high school, less than one-third felt that way. The others had also suffered a drop in self-esteem. Mothers know this, often from past personal experience. The benefits of self-esteem are now better understood, and most parents do their best to boost a daughter's confidence through puberty. Yet these findings were published in 1991. What is still going amiss?

The study found that boys also suffered a drop in self-esteem. Perhaps this drop is a reasonable part of growing up. The child loses what remains of egocentricity; she stops believing that the world revolves around her. For example, a 4-year-old thinks that the stars come out at night solely for her delight. A 14-year-old accepts that they do not, and has a diminishing sense of her own stature by comparison. Peer pressure is at its highest, and teens measure themselves against harsher critics than those at home.

Such events do not necessarily lower self-esteem. Yet puberty is a friable time; anything can alter anything for a while.

Body Image

Though a drop in self-esteem might be considered normal after puberty, the boys ended up with far more self-assurance than the girls. In answer to the question "How often do I feel happy the way I am?" 67 percent of the younger boys and 60 percent of the younger girls answered "always." By high school, 46 percent of the boys still felt that way. Only 29 percent of the girls did.

One curious finding from the study concerned racial factors. Far more black girls, than white and Hispanic girls, remained self-confident in high school. White girls lost self-esteem earlier than Hispanic girls. The survey raises questions about the effects of culture on self-concept. It also raises queries about the role of schools, both in the drop in self-confidence and in the role of intervention.

One of the great disappointments for a boy at puberty occurs if he does not grow tall. A girl can worry over her entire body image; she must also learn to cope with the monthly flow. It has become acceptable at menarche to tell a girl that her periods are a wonderful phenomenon to celebrate. She is now part of Mother Earth, at one with the moon, her glorious womanhood has arrived, and she should rejoice. This is a very grown-up response to menstruation, and one which only an adult mind can accept. Many girls dislike their periods; they feel diminished by the monthly flow. If they suffer cramps, the problem is compounded. They then face a quandary: either they cannot trust their mothers to tell them the truth, or they themselves are unnatural monsters to dislike their periods so.

For whatever reasons, self-esteem is put to its greatest test at puberty. Even a girl with a healthy self-concept can find it is shaken at times. A close friend suddenly turns enemy for no reason, an easy subject becomes difficult, a group she wishes to join rejects her. If her self-esteem is high, she is unlikely to blame herself for such failures or rejection. If her confidence is low, she may not bounce back easily. Studies show that the lower a girl's self-esteem when starting puberty, the more likely she will become estranged from her parents later.

Betsy's Tale

"I can't have babies," the girl complained into camera.

Deirdre, the interviewer, blinked in amazement. "You are on this program because you have AIDS."

"I know," the girl spoke petulantly. "What really ticks me off is my tubes are infected as well. Now I can't have babies."

Deirdre drew in a sharp breath. The girl, Betsy, was HIV serum positive, yet here she was, asserting her rights to *give life*.

"Can you warn other girls your age? Help them to avoid AIDS?"

"Nah. Cos if you hurt as a teenager, you don't care, not even about tomorrow. It's called lack of self-esteem."

They had chosen Betsy from four other girls, all with HIV. She was the prettiest, and came from an average, regular, American home; that was important too. She looked fresh and sweet, the kind of girl any parent would be proud to have as a daughter. And smart. She had good grades. Deirdre watched in dismay as the girl tossed her long blonde locks and smiled for the cameras.

She prompted gently, "How can you help?"

Betsy pouted, "You can't." She was still soft with puppy-fat. She's just a *child*, Deirdre thought. A little *girl*, who has been told that sex is OK. By *us*, *by adults*. She wondered if those teen movies were partly to blame, the ones which showed young girls indulging in wild sex parties without any apparent risk.

She said, "What about the boy? How is his health?"

The girl's mood darkened. "He's ill. Serve him right. He lied about this other disease in my tubes. Now I can't have a baby."

"Is he going to die?"

"I spose."

Deirdre spoke to camera. "There are now 2,000 teenagers with AIDS. Most of them will die. This number is doubling every 14 months. The spread of AIDS through the heterosexual population will be far more rapid than through other high-risk groups. This evening we have seen the tragic case of Betsy, a sweet and trusting young girl whose very life is now in jeopardy. Betsy, would you like a final word?"

"Teen girls will do anything if a guy says *I love you*."

"But if he doesn't mean those words?"

"Doesn't matter. You can have his baby. Someone to love."

Deirdre, shocked, tried to smile into camera.

It was the saddest interview of her entire career.

The Double Standard

"If you loved me, darling, you would let me."

"If you say no, I can find someone who'll say yes."

"I'll protect you from harm. Slay dragons for you."

Yes, but dragons are mostly out of season.

The double standard, one code of sexual behavior for boys and the opposite for girls, has been pilloried, and most people believe that it no longer exists. Yet studies show that, for teen boys, there is still subtle pressure from parents to "prove their manhood" by becoming sexually active with girls. Many parents are unaware that they apply this pressure, and might be upset to know. If they withdrew it, then young boys might put a little less pressure on girls. The syndrome of encouraging a boy to "sow his wild oats" has its roots in the unconscious fears of a homosexual son.

Moral values aside, the health risks of early sexual activity are *always much greater for the girl*. By her anatomy, she is more likely to contract sexual disease and AIDS than a boy. Few teens use contraceptives at first. When they do, it is sporadic and often inadequate. Though the babies of teen girls have better health at birth, this deteriorates in the first year, except where the infant lives with its grandmother...!

A U.K. study found that the highest rates of depression were among unskilled young women looking after children. These women were married and had planned their families. They worked solely in the home, devoting their time to raising children. The four factors which brought these mothers to clinical depression were boredom, isolation, frustration, and resentment. How much greater is the risk of depression for a girl who, unmarried and caught in the trap of an unintended pregnancy, drops out of school?

More and more teens are becoming sexually active at younger ages. More and more girls are resorting to abortion. Those who choose to raise their infants alone face a struggle against tremendous odds. All these issues appear a disturbing trend for the health and happiness of our nation's future mothers *and* their infants. Until these trends become reversed, perhaps parents can apply pressure on their sons as well as their daughters to avoid early sexual activity, or to take preventive measures.

Awful Adolescence?

"Who am I?
"What am I here for?
"Where am I going?"

The primary task in the teens is to find out who the self is. A girl struggles to assess herself realistically: to discover her strengths and weaknesses, to learn what she wants in life, to establish her own belief system. She may look for help to female teachers, women in various careers, pop stars, heroines from the past, and so on. More often, she looks to her peers; girlfriend attachments become very close.

An adolescent can be an exquisitely sensitive plant. Parents are excused if they sometimes forget this when faced with an over-critical, self-centered youth! Such unattractive behavior is a defense mechanism to conceal flaws which the girl perceives in herself. Mood swings, often attributed to hormones, are due to fears of an unacceptable body image, and attacks of self-doubt.

Spurning parental advice and criticizing their lifestyle are all part of the search for autonomy. Denial of adult values seems an appropriate way to find her own. There is no excuse for obnoxious behavior nor is there any need to tolerate it. Yet a girl's struggles for independence are a critical factor in the maturation process. If serious conflicts erupt, consider whether adult reins are appropriate for her age group. If so, check that they are consistently held. Reins which are too slack one day and too rigid the next can result in her taking tremendous risks — in case she has the right day. Youth is a time of risk-taking; teens regard themselves as invulnerable and life as ever-lasting.

If the early parent/child relationship was satisfactory, this stormy stage soon passes. If the relationship was unsatisfactory, consider professional help. Unconsciously, the girl is seeking revenge; she wants to return hurt now that she is old enough to do so. She also wants something of her own which nobody can take from her. Unsuitable boyfriends and pregnancy can be the answer.

Adolescents perceive issues in terms of black and white; there is rarely, if ever, an acknowledgment of grey. They lack the skills and maturity to accept that adults, *particularly parents*, are mixtures of frailities and strengths. Keep in mind that teens and parents both are learning new roles. They are equally capable of making mistakes. Guiding a daughter through adolescence can be the ultimate test of parenthood. Even difficult daughters stay close friends. One survey found that 87 percent of girls put down "Mom" as their best friend.

Summary

- On average, puberty occurs between ages 10 and 13.
- There is a wide variety in the times when puberty starts.
- Reassure a daughter she is not "late" or "early."
- Counsel her in hygiene and its value in sexual health.
- Period cramps can be relieved with modern medication.
- Encourage use of sanitary napkins; avoid conflicts over tampon use.
- Explain clearly the health risks of early sexual activity.
- Unacceptable behavior can be due to an unhappy body image.
- Where appropriate, boost her confidence and self-esteem.

CHAPTER 14

The Climacteric

At this critical time of life, the female sex are often visited with various diseases of the chronic kind... Pain and giddiness of the head, hysteric disorders, colic pains, and a midlife female weakness...intolerable itching at the neck of the bladder and contiguous parts...Women are sometimes affected with low spirits and melancholy.

—John Leake, British gynecologist

Baby boomers, menopause approaches. There are more than 35 million women over age 50 in this country, and that number is expected to top 50 million by 2010, when more women will be experiencing menopause than at any time in history.

Question: Between now and 2010, when all these women begin having hot flashes, what effect will this have on global warming, melting the polar ice cap, the greenhouse effect etc?

Answer: The same effect caused by those millions of Baby Boom men using epoxy-based hair spray to hold their few remaining hairs in place over their expanding bald spots, which have already reached the same combined total acreage as Wyoming.

—Dave Barry, *The Miami Herald*, 1991

No man in his right mind would be interested in a menopausal woman.

> —Advertisement for estrogen replacement, 1991

After 50, a man's performance is of poor quality, the intervals between are wide, and its satisfactions of no great value
to either party. Whereas his great-grandmother is as good as
new.

> —Mark Twain, in his old age

The Climacteric

Menopause is a time of transition at the end of which a woman's
child-bearing years are completed. The ovaries cease to produce
eggs, and estrogen is gradually withdrawn. Menopause is generally considered to begin two years before the last period, and end
two to three years after it. A woman can expect to be beyond
childbearing when her periods have ceased for a full year between
ages 48 and 53.

The first signal of approaching menopause occurs when periods
become erratic. As estrogen levels begin to decline, the monthly
cycles become shorter, and the flow is heavier. When there is not
enough estrogen to stimulate a cycle, a period is missed. Once
menopause is over, the ovaries are small and shrunken, *but*, and a
very important *but*, they continue to produce androgens, the hormone of the libido, and very small amounts of estrogen. PMS after
age 40 can also be a signal of gradual estrogen withdrawal.

This gradual withdrawal of estrogen is all perfectly normal.
Many women are hardly aware of it; others are thankful that their
periods will soon cease. Some women suffer from heavy bleeding
problems. Check that there is sufficient vitamin A in the diet; a
dietary deficiency is linked with heavy flow. Increase the amount
of iron-rich foods to avoid anemia; the RDA is 10 milligrams for
women age 51 and over. Keep a record of period dates, flow patterns, heavy clots, and so on. There is a slight risk that heavy
bleeding can signify precancer changes in the endometrium (uterus
lining). Visit the physician for a check-up.

The Bad News

Estrogen seems to protect women from heart disease; it is not

212

fully understood how. When estrogen production wanes, this protection is removed. By age 65, women have the same risk of heart disease as men. The annual rate at ages 45 to 54 is 31 per 10,000 women. This rises to 95 per 10,000 between ages 55 and 64. Of women who have a heart attack, 45 percent will die within the first year, compared with 20 percent of men. After recovery from an attack, the recurrence rate is 40 percent for women and just over 10 percent for men. In 1990, some 250,000 women died of atherosclerosis (coronary artery disease). Women are more likely to have *angina* (chest pain), which is an early warning signal. Yet often there are no warning signals at all. The same risk factors for men apply to women:

- Family history of heart disease.
- Smoking.
- High blood cholesterol.
- Weight gain.
- Lack of exercise.
- Stress.
- High sugar intake.

The following are specific women-only risks:

- Early menopause before age 45.
- Surgical menopause.
- Low estrogen levels.
- Use of the birth control pill.

Cardiologists now stress that all women at midlife should be aware of the risk of heart disease. The key factor is *screening*. The *treadmill test* involves walking at an increasingly brisk pace on a treadmill to monitor blood pressure, heart and breathing rate. *Angiography* uses X-rays on a television screen to show how advanced heart disease might be. Early diagnosis is a must. Keep in mind that exercise and a healthy diet reduce the risk of heart disease *and* most symptoms of menopause. Now is the time to get fit, and stay fit, before sailing serenely through midlife.

The Good News

Male hormones such as testosterone fuel the sex drive *and* promote a sense of well-being. The ovaries continue to produce testosterone into old age, as do the adrenal glands. When estrogen levels drop, some effects of testosterone start to show through. Facial hairs appear, particularly on the chin; sometimes on the chest and abdomen. Head hair becomes thinner, loses its color, and when it falls out, is replaced more slowly. Are hair loss and an increased risk of heart disease an appropriate price to pay for testosterone? How much do women gain from an increased sense of well-being?

Stress is defined as "an emotional state which affects the body." When a person is faced with a challenge, the adrenals pour out stress hormones (adrenaline and noradrenaline), which speed up the heart and breathing rate. More oxygen can be rushed to the muscles; extra fats and sugars enter the blood for fuel. The mouth dries, the pupils dilate, sweating stops. All systems not needed to cope with the challenge shut down. This is known as the *fight or flight* syndrome. The extra energy available helps to either to fight the challenge and win it, or to take flight from the challenge if it presents too much of a threat.

Testosterone has been called the winner hormone, because the level in the blood rises when a challenge is won, or a difficult problem solved. The relaxed mood which follows winning shuts down the further secretion of stress hormones. There follows a natural surge of testosterone, with its high, a strong sense of well-being. The testosterone surge helps convert the extra fats and sugars back into stored energy. All body functions return to their normal pace. It can be seen that stress hormones and testosterone work in opposition.

However, in some cases, the person remains stressed, even if the challenge is won. The stress hormones continue to pour out, and no natural surge of testosterone can then occur. A few women cannot relax. They remain tense, anxious, and uptight. It is now thought that testosterone secretion might be blocked by such *prolonged stress*, and that the ravages from those unabated stress hormones can damage the cardiovascular system, thus speeding up the aging process. The sequence of events goes something like this:

- The stress hormones continue to pour out, and fats and sugar remain in the blood...
- This causes an unhealthy build-up of sugar and cholesterol in the blood...
- This unhealthy build-up increases the risk of *plaque* forming in the blood vessels...

- Plaque formation speeds up the aging of the cardiovascular system...
- The results can include hardening of the arteries, high blood pressure, and heart disease.

Learn to relax! By midlife, most women have accepted the fact that nobody wins all the time. For those who have constantly lost, (sadly this happens), avoid looking back on painful events. Reliving past miseries can increase the ravages of stress, and suppress testosterone. Practice yoga, take regular exercise, do whatever activity helps relax the mind and produces a sense of well-being, a testosterone "high."

Many women find that they have an increased zest for life after menopause. They feel more feisty and experience a greater sense of well-being. Often, they become more assertive at work and in their relationships. This increase in feistiness may be, in part, due to the male hormones now showing through. Keep in mind the words of Margaret Mead: "The most creative force in the world is the menopausal woman with zest."

More Good News

The ovaries continue to produce small amounts of estrogen for 10 years or more after menopause. Long before they slow down, estrogen is produced in the adrenal glands and fat cells. After menopause, the adrenal glands are the main source of estrogen. They produce a type of androgen which is converted to estrone (a type of estrogen). This conversion process is complicated. Two factots help to speed it up:

- Exercise.
- Having "a little flesh on the bones."

In his novel *The Bonfire of the Vanities*, Tom Wolfe refers to the fashionable ladies of New York as "X-rays." They are thin to the point where their hip bones jut out. Being proud of such skinniness, they flash their bony charms in evening gowns sculpted to show the maximum effects of constant dieting. Though being skinny may be admired in voguish circles, it carries a price in terms of bone loss and other midlife problems.

Keep in mind that a certain amount of fat cells is necessary to support hormone activity. Being underweight for age is never advisable, and particularly not at midlife. The good news is that women with "a little flesh on the bones" experience less symptoms of menopause.

"Everything you see, I owe to spaghetti," says Sophia Loren on dieting.

Hot Flashes

Hot flashes are the most common symptom of menopause. They are also known as hot flushes because they are like sudden waves of heat, with sweating over the face, neck, chest, or throughout the body. A hot flash feels like a tiny charge of electricity. A mild flash lasts less than one minute, may produce no sweat, and does not upset normal activity. A moderate flash causes sweating for two to three minutes, with a desire to stop activity and cool down. A severe flash involves heavy sweating for three minutes or more. There can be shivering, nausea, and palpitations. Severe flashes can cause distress, irritability, and a feeling of being unable to cope.

On average, hot flashes last less than two years, but a few unlucky women have them for five years. Keep in mind that most estrogen withdrawal is gradual, and most hot flashes are mild to moderate only. Wearing jackets or other outer clothing which can be removed during a hot flash helps to keep the body cool. Exercise helps to raise the body's tolerance to sudden heat. An increase in exercise makes it possible for many women to just shrug off the discomfort and carry on.

With moderate to severe flashes, there is heavy sweating at night. Drink plenty of liquids to replace what is lost. Night sweats can cause great strain on a woman's general health. Waking up drenched several times each night is not pleasant. Worse is the exhaustion which comes from the lack of sleep. Severe flashes are due to a *sudden* drop in estrogen. If the quality of life is seriously affected, consider *estrogen replacement therapy*, ERT. ERT is very effective at relieving the symptoms; it replaces the natural estrogen which is being withdrawn.

Osteoporosis

"Osteo" means bone, and "porosis" comes from Greek for porous. Osteoporosis is loss of bone density; the bones become thinner and fracture more easily. Women (and men) begin losing bone

216

mass at around age 35. Women have lighter bones to start with, so have a higher risk of fracture. One reason why exercise programs carry a warning to start *slowly* is to avoid fracture.

Apart from aging, there is no specific cause of osteoporosis. Estrogen withdrawal seems to speed up the process. So does being underweight with no fat cells to produce estrogen. Booklets in the physician's office are devised by drug companies to sell ERT. They over-stress estrogen withdrawal and plug into a woman's fears of becoming frail and helpless. With exercise and increased calcium in the diet, the risk of osteoporosis can be reduced.

Risk factors to avoid:

- Diet low in calcium.
- Physical inactivity.
- Cigarette smoking.
- Being underweight.
- Heavy use of alcohol.

Calcium: Calcium is essential for bone formation. Women (and men) tend to consume only one-third of the calcium they need. Calcium works best if obtained from food. Check that there is sufficient Vitamin C and D in the diet because they help increase calcium absorption. Avoid fluoride and calcitonin supplements; they can be toxic. Find and stick with a reliable diet plan; these are detailed in most magazines.

Milk is a good source of calcium. Two glasses daily supply 500 mg of calcium. If there is milk intolerance, or the taste is disliked, be sure to eat the dietary calcium equivalent. The RDA for calcium is 1,500 mg; the equivalent of one and one-third quarts of milk per day. Calcium supplements can be taken: 1 gram per day from age 35 until menopause; and 1.5 grams daily after menopause. Reduce the amount of alcohol, caffeine, and carbonated drinks; avoid excessive intake of protein.

Inactivity speeds up the rate of calcium loss. Inactivity is a known factor in thinning bones. Lifting weights thickens bone by increasing blood flow, which stimulates the bone-building cells. Studies on 80-year-olds and over in weight-bearing programs found that their strength, stamina, and endurance increased enormously. Lost flexibility and grace of movement returned. Stretching programs avoid shortening of the spinal bones, and the risk of compression fractures. These can be seen on elderly women (and some men) who were unaware of the benefits of exercise, and developed what was known as a "dowager's hump." As their bone loss increased, they also lost body height.

According to the director of the physiology laboratory at the Human Nutrition Research Center on Aging at Tufts University: "The single, most compelling, reason for women to get stronger is to lower the risk of osteoporosis. Women who have exercised all their lives never will have the low bone density that ultimately results in osteoporosis."

- Dump the frail image.
- Go lift some (light) weights.

Smoking/drinking: Cigarette smoking and over-use of alcohol are choices. Though dependency may be real and urgent, any addiction can be broken if the addict *truly* desires to be rid of it. Local hospitals or clinics run free programs to help. The findings of a recent study show that it is never too late to give up smoking. Not only is the risk of osteoporosis reduced, but that of heart disease and certain cancers as well.

The first five years after menopause are said to be the time of maximum bone loss, though this is not proven. It could be that some midlife women are overwhelmed with work or depressed, and so become physically inactive. A recent study found that combining exercise with low doses of estrogen was the most effective way of preventing bone loss. If there are family members with fractures, consider a bone density scan. New drugs, such as tamoxifen, are being explored as another protection against osteoporosis.

Vaginal Changes

Estrogen plumps up the reproductive organs, keeping them soft and moist. With estrogen withdrawal, the tissues gradually lose some of their moisture. The first place this may be noticed is in the vagina. The walls become thinner, shorter, and less robust. Less cervical mucus is produced, which can add to *dyspareunia*, painful intercourse. If there is sudden estrogen withdrawal, a woman as young as 50 can find that she no longer desires to make love because it hurts.

Try external lubrication first, and check for infection or a yeast condition which is asymptomatic. If the pain persists, the vagina can be made more robust with estrogen creams. These are available by prescription only. They must not be used as a sexual lubricant; the skin of the penis can absorb estrogen and some men have developed breasts. Relief from the symptoms occurs within a month. For some women, the creams are not sufficient; in these cases, ERT will bring effective relief.

Dyspareunia is not inevitable at menopause. Its medical name is *vaginal atrophy*; the very term offends. Just as some mature vaginas cannot sustain very prolonged thrusting, so some mature penises cannot sustain very prolonged erections. The point is that a woman is often made to feel less feminine, less desirable, by the natural changes at menopause. The very threat of vaginal "atrophy" can be overwhelming, and stampede her into ERT when a little lubrication is all that is required. Mature men tend to be treated with more dignity. It is rare to hear offensive terms about erection loss, and then only in jokes. With the approach of old age, *all tissue starts to atrophy*, regardless of gender and estrogen loss.

The Big Debate

To take estrogen replacement therapy, or not? That is the big debate for women at midlife. The four conditions of menopause for which ERT is recommended are:

- Protection against heart disease.
- Protection against osteoporosis.
- Protection against hot flashes.
- Protection against vaginal dryness.

The following is a list of *possible* risks of ERT:

- Cancer of the uterus.
- Cancer of the breast.
- Severe bleeding and blood clots.
- Liver problems and gallstones.
- Raised blood pressure.
- Surgery, if appropriate, to reverse some of these effects.

According to Dr. Elizabeth Barrett-Connor and Dr. Trudy Bush in a 1991 report in the American Medical Journal: "Many physicians who prescribe estrogen replacement therapy for postmenopausal women suggest it will protect them from coronary disease but such benefits have yet to be proven scientifically. Failing any randomized clinical trials, a large number of women in this and other developed countries may be prescribed estrogen replacement therapy to prevent cardiovascular disease, but without the supporting data usually required for the widespread use of any other drug recommended for disease prevention."

For severe hot flashes, and/or early surgical menopause, ERT can be a blessing and a boon. Exercise and an appropriate diet, plus natural estrogen produced from the adrenal glands and fat cells, all reduce the risk of other problems. The following is a list of benefits claimed for ERT:

- Mental tonic effect.
- Improved short-term memory.
- Enhanced sexuality.
- A more robust vagina.
- Increased sexual sensation.
- Stronger pelvic floor muscles.
- Improved bladder tone.
- Smoother, less wrinkled skin.
- Firmer, plumper breasts.
- Improved general muscle tone.
- Less general body deterioration.
- Altogether, an enhanced quality of life.

Well, that sounds terrific! Why not go for it? Advertisements for ERT use the term "supplements." This makes them sound rather like vitamin or mineral supplements, something which is fairly harmless to take as a booster. ERT works by delaying menopause. The body is tricked into responding as if there were no natural withdrawal of estrogen. So the breasts swell, the vagina produces fluids, and cervical mucus is profuse at mid-cycle. The uterus lining builds up and breaks down, with no cessation of periods. Most women do not appreciate having periods almost unto the very grave. Try to avoid ERT until periods have altogether stopped.

In the 40s and 50s, ERT was taken long before menopause. The estrogen given was in high doses, and without progesterone. This high level of "unopposed estrogen" caused the uterus to go on building a hard thick lining. Without progesterone, the lining could not soften and break down. This was found to cause cancer of the uterus. Physicians are now aware of this unhappy outcome, but just

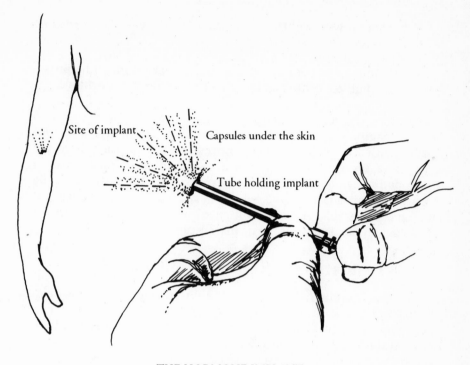

Site of implant

Capsules under the skin

Tube holding implant

THE HORMONE IMPLANT

in case: if taking ERT either before or during menopause, make sure that progesterone is also prescribed.

Today, low doses of estrogen with progesterone are given. Some studies show that taking ERT for 15 years or more, or in high doses, can slightly increase the risk of breast cancer. Other studies show no such effect. It is all very confusing. Keep up-to-date on the latest findings, which are usually well reported in the press.

All female tissue is "estrogen-dependent." It grows in response to estrogen. Unfortunately, so do female cancer tumors, and such benign growths as fibroids and endometriosis. ERT is still in the experimental stage. Not everything is known about its effects. The fears are that it could turn out to be another terrible mistake, as was DES. ERT is not for women with:

- Known or suspected cancer in any of the reproductive organs.
- Family history of estrogen-dependent cancers.
- Other estrogen-dependent growths, fibriods & endometriosis.
- Irregular, severe or unexplained bleeding.
- Chronic jaundice or any other liver disease.

- Severe varicose veins.
- Diabetes mellitus.
- Very high blood pressure.
- Previous or present thromboembolism, or thrombophlebitis.
- Very high concentrations of fat or cholesterol in the blood.

Yet ERT is splendid for controlling severe hot flashes and to relieve vaginal dryness. It is highly effective after surgical menopause with the very sudden withdrawal of estrogen. Where the quality of life is reduced by the mental and physical distress of menopausal symptoms, ERT may be well worth the known risks. Be very conscientious and have regular Pap smears, pelvic exams, and mammograms. ERT is powerful medication. Like most difficult decisions in life, it is an issue of risk/benefit ratio.

Testosterone Replacement Therapy

There is a recent, on-going debate about whether to give women testosterone as a supplement hormone at menopause. The two groups under consideration are women who suffer loss of libido after hysterectomy and those whose ovaries have been removed. It could be a very long debate: the case for giving testosterone replacement therapy (TRT) to midlife men who suffer a drop in libido is far from being resolved. Some of these men argue that as ERT (with its risks) is readily available to women, it is only reasonable that TRT should be available to men.

Women who take TRT for other reproductive ailments report that they have more energy and a greater sense of well-being. However, the side effects can be a problem: more and heavier facial hair growth, a deepening of the voice, shrinking breast tissue, and other masculine effects. These can sometimes be avoided by a lower dosage. The problem with taking TRT or ERT is that they interfere with the natural production of sex hormones.

Skin Changes

Skin changes at menopause are due to the normal aging process. The deeper layer of skin loses some moisture and elasticity, and starts to shrink. The surface skin is now looser than the inner layer, so it hangs or creases. Blood circulation slows, and the skin can become blotchy, with broken capillaries. Enlarged pores add a rougher texture. Exercise improves blood circulation, which helps nourish the skin and create moisture. However, skin changes can be made worse by sudden estrogen withdrawal.

Some skins age faster than others; it is not known why. There might be an inherited tendency. Studies show that smoking adds to the risk. It can be upsetting to know that skin thins and the tissue underneath dries. Yet this happens to men as well; notice the jawline on the average midlife male. Keep in mind that thinning skin and sagging bits happen to both genders, regardless of estrogen withdrawal.

Retin-A, the new dream cream, removes tiny surface wrinkles and light brown pigment spots. The results are remarkable in some women, giving a more youthful appearance after one full year's treatment. Retin-A can cause redness, and an allergic response. Before considering Retin-A, see a dermatologist for examination, prescription, and follow-up care.

For deeper wrinkles and aging folds, a facelift or eye surgery removes the offending bags and sags. Consult an otolaryngologist or general plastic surgeon. Some women prefer the fascination of a face which tells of a well-lived life. Plastic surgery is an issue of esthetics and choice...and cost...and risk. Not all cosmetic surgery is a success.

Exercise tones up the circulation which, in turn, tones and improves the skin. An appropriate diet is another factor to help delay the aging process. Keep "a little flesh on the bones." The absence of fat cells means less estrogen to plump out and firm the tissues. According to Barbara Cartland, the doyen of romantic fiction: *"A woman can lose her figure or her face. She cannot maintain both."*

Changes After Menopause

The following changes do not begin until some years after menopause. Many women do not experience them. A few find that they start earlier. Most of the changes are a normal part of the aging process, and not due to estrogen withdrawal. The following descriptions of the reproductive organs as they move into extreme old age are a "worst case" scenario. It is not reading for the fainthearted.

Vulva Changes: The vulva and its contents start to shrink. The plump tissue of the outer lips (labia majora) begins to disappear.

The thin inner lips (labia minora) become very small. Pubic hair grows straighter and more scanty. In extreme old age, the vulva has a glazed or shiny look.

Vagina Changes: The walls of the vagina become shorter, thinner, narrower. There is a loss of elasticity, and the ridges flatten out. A reduced blood supply makes the lining less robust, with a risk of dryness, itching, and pain at intercourse. There is an increased risk of infection due to a change in the acidity.

Uterus Changes: The uterus gets smaller as the walls get thinner. The lining still responds to estrogen if taking ERT. The oviducts cease to function; this appears to have no health effect.

Pelvic Floor Changes: The whole support system can weaken as the muscles and ligaments become more flaccid. There is an increased risk of prolapse from the bladder, rectum, uterus, or vagina itself.

Bladder & Urethra Changes: The walls become thinner and lose some elasticity. The tissue is more at risk of bladder infections and stress incontinence.

Breast Changes: The gland tissue shrinks. The support ligaments lose some of their elasticity so the breasts droop. The nipples become smaller and flatter and can lose their ability to erect.

Changes in Men: These are not so obvious because men do not have tissue moisture and plumpness in the first place. Nor do they lose their slight production of estrogen. There is a gradual decline in testosterone at about age 40. Later, the effects of estrogen can show through as male breasts and a general softening of the skin. The non estrogen-dependent effects of aging equally apply to the male genitals.

Perhaps the main difference between midlife women and men is that most men would avoid reading about the effects of aging!

Self-Care

A vagina which feels dry can be dampened with K-Y Jelly, baby oil, or vegetable oil. Avoid the use of other lotions or creams; they interfere with the vagina's ecology and yeast can flare up. Love making and masturbation help to maintain the vagina's robust muscle tone. Do Kegels exercises daily. Itchiness can be soothed and relieved by applying bancha tea or Vitamin E oil topically to the vulva and vagina area. The risk of urinary and vaginal infections can be reduced by wearing loose cotton underclothes. A hot, moist environment encourages germs and infections. Keep the area as cool and dry as possible.

Some women report that they can reduce most of the symptoms of menopause by herbal therapies; others choose acupuncture. Vitamin and mineral supplements are another route. Vitamin E may help reduce hot flashes. Vitamin C, D, and calcium are essential for bone formation. Vitamin A deficiency has been associated with heavy bleeding. Magnesium and vitamin B complex may reduce edema, help with relaxation, and ease stress. *Warning!* Never take any supplements in high doses. They can be toxic. Also, they can interfere with the absorption of healthful nutrients in the diet.

> I'm intending to go to my grave as a sexy old lady.
> There'll be plenty of time for propriety after I'm dead.
> So if heaven has answered my prayers,
> I expect to be found, around eighty, upstairs
> With my sexy old husband nestled beside me in bed.
> —*Forever Fifty* by Judy Viorst

Theory Land

According to a report in the Archives of Sexual Behavior, there are clear-cut benefits to regular sexual activity. "It may help reduce or stop some menopausal symptoms. Women who maintain a consistent sex life are less likely to experience hot flashes. There is a close association between increasing irregularity of menstrual cycles, hot flashes, declining estrogen levels, and declining frequency of intercourse.

"Regular sexual activity might have a protective action against lowering hormone levels and therefore its absence is associated with the disruption of cycles. The discomfort of hot flashes and other associated symptoms might have an inhibiting effect on sexual behavior...But the association between hot flashes and reduced frequency of intercourse may result from some common third variable."

Another theory concerns the hormones in a partner's ejaculate. These might be absorbed through the vagina walls and keep them more robust. It is suggested that this is why women who enjoyed love making before menopause continue to do so afterwards, and may be even more keen than before. It is an interesting theory because the male hormones in ejaculate contain prostaglandins, and an excess of prostaglandins can cause the uterus to contract with period cramps.

Yet another theory suggests that freedom from the risk of pregnancy heightens a sense of freedom in bed. This was a popular theory until a few women reported that the risk of pregnancy has been a sexual "turn on." Now it was gone, they were no longer as excited or keen.

Use It or Lose It?

Does the "use it or lose it" maxim apply to the vagina? Maybe. When any muscle group is not worked over a long period of time, it *atrophies*. First, it loses strength and stamina. Then, and only after very prolonged time, it withers and dies. This is true for tissue, nerves, blood vessels, all the body organs, including the vagina. The more any tissue is exercised, the less risk there is of "disuse atrophy."

Midlife men have the same risk, only to a greater degree. A penis which is not regularly exercised will rapidly succumb to disuse atrophy. This rarely happens. The penis erects at night during REM sleep, and stays erect for 20 minutes or more at intervals during each night. Even in extreme old age, men without partners (and some with) masturbate to relieve sexual tension and because they enjoy the activity. By these methods, the penis is regularly exercised and kept healthy.

The same phenomenon occurs with clitoral erection. The vagina is not involved, though it may produce the sweating phenomenon during REM sleep; research is still needed. Be wary of indulging in excess sexual activity in order to avoid the risk of vaginal atrophy. Keep in mind that other maxim: moderation in all things.

Neither menopause nor aging changes sexual desire of itself. Of far more relevance are the level of activity before menopause, expectations of continuing activity, general state of health, and the

226

presence of an active partner. At midlife, a woman can find her partner has erection problems. She may be divorced, widowed, or otherwise on her own. Marriage to an older man carries a risk of early widowhood because men die five to seven years earlier than women. In some cases, and often cruelly, a woman can be abandoned by her spouse at midlife.

Sexual activity can improve after menopause if there have been troublesome periods, constant infections, or fears of unintended pregnancy. Self-pleasure (masturbation) is the natural outlet for women on their own. It is not unknown for a woman who has a selfish partner to become assertive and stop all activity if she perceives him as boorish and unloving. Could this new and feisty attitude be due to the effects of testosterone showing through?

According to one study, nearly half of the women involved said that they masturbated in their 50s. This fell to one-third at age 70 and over. Two-thirds of the men in their 50s masturbated; this fell to just under half at age 70 and over. Those having orgasms ranged from 83 percent of women in their 50s to 74 percent in their 70s and over. 91 percent of men had orgasms in their 50s; and 73 percent in their 70s and over.

Sex is like fine wine. It gets better with aging.

Exercise

If exercise is a loathsome thing
Dance, or frisk on a trampoline.

Apart from all the benefits of exercise already listed in this chapter, vigorous physical activity stimulates the production of *endorphins*. These are morphine-like compounds secreted by the brain. Endorphins are the body's natural pain-killers. They also provide sensations of a high, with enhanced self-image and self-esteem. Other benefits of exercise include:

- Speeds up the metabolic rate for up to 24 hours afterwards.
- Builds muscle which keeps bones strong and ligaments taut.
- Burns fat for fuel and increases fat-burning efficiency.
- Continues to burn extra calories after exercise stops.
- Relieves symptoms of stress and can control depression.
- Reduces the risk of heart disease and osteoporosis.
- Relieves some symptoms of dysmenorrhea and PMS.

- Tones up the skin and improves body outline.
- Slows down the aging process.
- Increases energy levels.

In short, if exercise could be bought and taken in tablet form like vitamin supplements, would you buy and consume it?

Target Heart Rate

Age	Beats per min	Maximum beats per min
20	120-150	200
25	117-146	195
30	114-142	190
35	111-138	185
40	108-135	180
45	105-131	175
50	103-127	170
55	99-123	165
60	96-120	150
65	93-116	155
70	90-113	150

Fitness can be maintained by doing aerobic exercises for 20 minutes or more at least 3 times per week. The intensity of the activity should raise the heart rate to between 60 and 75 percent of the maximum heart rate. Average maximum heart rate is determined by taking 220 and subtracting present age. The target heart rate is the appropriate percentage of that rate. Women with a history of heart disease, who are over 45, or who are obese should not exceed 75 percent of their maximum heart rate. Consult a doctor before embarking upon an exercise program.

Warning! Avoid jumping, jogging, and bouncing if there is the slightest tendency to prolapse. "Jumping Jacks" can start urine leakage where none existed before. Bouncing adds nothing to the goals of aerobic exercise. It can overstretch the muscles and ligaments and hurt the knees. Try walking. Start slowly and gradually speed up the pace over a few weeks.

There has been so much emphasis on exercise that women who are disabled could feel dismayed. If confined to a wheelchair, or lying prone in bed, small weights can be lifted, stretching programs achieved, and isometric exercises accomplished.

One phenomenon of menopause is that many women believe they are now free of the physician's office. The risk of pregnancy is

228

over, periods have ceased, all is well. And so it is. Keep in mind, however, that cancers and heart disease are to be guarded against after menopause. Regular mammograms, Pap smears, pelvic exams, breast screenings, and treadmill tests bring that greatest of all health benefits — peace of mind.

Happiness

The main trend revealed by studies of popular attitudes is although some women in western societies have an overall negative image of menopause, it is not as widespread as was previously thought. Today, the vast majority of women at midlife do not express regret at reaching menopause, do not report more symptoms or poorer health status, and do not increase their use of medical services. The negative attitudes that do exist appear to be the province of younger women and seem to be based on an outdated stereotype of the menopausal woman.

—Utian & Jacobowitz, 1989

Though midlife may seem like a fearful turning point, it is rarely fearsome when it actually arrives. One theory suggests that menopause was touted as "dreadful," an "end of life," to keep women humble and in their place. Grandmothers were led to expect the most horrible symptoms *together with* intense feelings of depression, a heightened sense of having no more function in life, being useless, washed up.

Do women in the 1990s perceive their sole function as child bearing? As children reach the teens, are not most mothers aware that all good things come to an end? Many women who stay home to raise families are heavily involved in volunteer work, without which the voluntary services would surely collapse. It has been suggested that the resultant crisis would seriously affect the nation's economy.

The findings of a study into happiness quotients show that they are highest in youth. They drop in the early 20s and rise again after marriage. They drop after the birth of the first child and stay low, dropping even further when children reach puberty. They rise back to the youthful high peak once the grown-up children leave home. It seems that the "empty-nest" syndrome is a new myth; *happiness quotients soar once children have flown the nest.*

Summary

- Get fit and stay fit *before* menopause.
- Check diet for vitamins A, C and D, and calcium-rich foods.
- Avoid becoming too thin; put a little flesh on the bones.
- Do stretch exercises morning and night to keep supple.
- Lift weights to increase stamina and grace of movement.
- Reduce bone loss by exercise and an appropriate diet.
- Have regular screenings on the health of the heart.
- PMS after age 35 could be a signal of early menopause.
- Consider ERT if hot flashes reduce the quality of life.
- Consider ERT with early or surgical menopause.
- Consider ERT if self-care cannot cope with vaginal dryness.
- Sexual activity is a splendid form of exercise.
- Concentrate on the benefits from self-made testosterone.

CHAPTER 15

Sexually Transmitted Diseases

The most important fact of STDs is they are not contracted by people who have only one partner.

At the Clinic

Some clinics which specialize in the diagnosis and treatment of sexual diseases are free. Others charge for their services. Some are walk-in; others require an appointment to be made first. Many women opt to visit a health clinic rather than a family physician. They prefer the anonymity of their surroundings. When the infection is cured, there is no record in the family files.

Some STDs are "notifiable." By law, they must be reported to the local health authorities. This varies from area to area, and from time to time. Other STDs are anonymous; a number instead of a name is used. Still other diseases are confidential; name, address, and telephone number are kept in secret files. Again, this varies with the area and the time.

Some STDs have more than one name. Others have their names changed as more is discovered about them. They then get placed in their own special category; they no longer belong to the group they were originally designated. In much the same way, therapies and medications vary from clinic to clinic and from time to time. Though this can seem confusing, it shows an increase in medical knowledge of the disease. Also, environmental conditions and the endemic nature of the infection in one particular area are taken into account.

In towns and cities, there are hot lines to call for advice, help and information. There are telephone tapes which are useful too. In isolated areas, look for notices in public locales, such as town halls, libraries and rest rooms. Consult the phone book. Entries might be under V for venereal disease or S for STD. Above all, avoid delay in seeking help.

Little Visitors

Visitors include fleas, mites, ticks, jiggers, bedbugs, scabies, and lice. They are all parasites, as they all suck blood. They do this through tubes which help keep the blood free-flowing. One tube injects saliva into the host's skin. The saliva contains a substance to prevent blood clotting. This allows the other tube to suck up blood. The anti-clotting factor causes itching, which announces the presence of little visitors in the home.

These parasites are *infestations*, not sexual diseases. Though most are passed by infested animals, scabies and lice are usually transmitted by sexual contact. The first symptom is an itch. Avoid scratching the genitals, which damages the skin, making it more vulnerable to *secondary* infection. Examine the area for red, swollen bumps, which may be due to pubic lice. Scabies are more common where the skin is thin and folded: under the breasts, at the belt line, in the groin, and between finger and toe webs.

Pubic Lice are common; they look like miniature crabs. They live on the genitals, fastening onto a new host by sinking their mouth parts into the skin and gripping a pubic hair with their claws. The female louse lays 8 to 10 nits (eggs) per day. She cements the nits to a hair shaft with glue from her body, which makes them difficult to dislodge. The nits hatch within 10 days; the lice spread out to feed and start the next breeding cycle. It is usually only at this stage, when the itching becomes intense, that the person is aware of something amiss.

On close inspection, the tiny crabs and nits can be seen. The crabs are gray or pink in color; the nits glued to pubic hair are dark brown. Check the infested area thoroughly. Pubic lice can migrate to body hair, even up to the eyebrows and lashes; this is more common in men. Avoid panic. An infestation is a problem which can be resolved.

Scabies are particularly partial to soft, female skin. The female burrows beneath the surface of the skin to lay her eggs. These burrows can be seen as thin dark lines in a skin fold near the groin or under the breasts. The eggs hatch within a few days, and the mites crawl out to feed and mate with the males who live on the surface of the skin. In this way, large areas of the body can become infested. Itching is intense, especially at night.

Some women consult a physician. Others prefer to cure themselves. Kwell destroys both scabies and lice. In some countries, Kwell is a prescription drug. In others, it is over-the-counter. It contains 1 percent gamma BHC (benzene hexachloride), or malathion. This can produce serious allergies. Follow the instructions very carefully. Keep to the precise recommended timing. WARNING! Avoid Kwell if there have been skin allergies in the past. EXTRA WARNING! Pregnant women must *not* use Kwell; gamma BHC can be absorbed into the blood and appear later in breast milk. Both groups should consult the physician.

High Risk Behavior

High risk sexual behavior includes:

- Sex which is paid for.
- Constant change of heterosexual partners.
- Heterosexual anal sex which is unprotected.
- Sex with an intravenous drug user.
- "Tough" sex which causes lesions, bruises, bleeding.
- Male sex (anal homosexual intercourse).

AIDS is transmitted by the HIV virus in blood, semen, and vagina fluids. It can be passed in skin sores and genital lesions too tiny to be seen with the unaided eye. It is also passed from mother to child in breast milk. Infected blood and semen contain the highest concentration of the virus. Vagina fluids have a lesser concentration. HIV may be present in sweat, saliva, and tears, but the concentrations are usually too weak for there to be any risk.

STDs, however, pass in very low concentrations. One germ can be enough. Studies suggest that syphilis and herpes are significant risk factors in the transmission of HIV. The sores of either disease can be on the mouth or inside the rectum, as well as on the genitals. In women, HIV is linked with a history of genital warts. It seems likely that STDs, which disrupt epithelial (lining) tissue, are important factors in the transmission of HIV. An appropriate way to avoid infection is to avoid direct contact with a partner's semen, blood, or sores anywhere on the skin. Condoms provide some protection.

Anal Sex

Anal sex carries specific health risks for all lovers, be they heterosexual or homosexual. Feces contain highly infectious matter. The walls of the rectum are only a few cells thick. They are not designed to resist the pressure of a thrusting penis. They tear easily, and microscopic bleeding occurs. If the penis is not washed *immediately* after anal sex, whatever germs are in the bowel are thrust directly into the vagina. Infected semen, blood, or feces can then pass directly into the blood system. Repeated attacks of yeast overgrowth can also occur this way.

Whatever the moral stance, hygiene is top priority. The penis should not touch the vulva, nor should it *ever* enter the vagina straight from the bowel. Hands, particularly fingernails, are an added danger in anal sex. Wiping with a tissue is *not* enough. Penis, hands, mechanical toys, all must be thoroughly scrubbed. It is strongly recommended a condom be used during anal sex, and immediately discarded afterwards.

Oral Sex

Specific micro-organisms inhabit the mouth, just as they inhabit other body orifices (openings). They rarely cause problems within their natural ecology. If they are transmitted to other orifices, they can cause infection. One typical example is a harmless bacteria of the mouth which can come in contact with the penis. The germs enter the urinary tract, and cause male UTI.

The membranes which line the mouth are naturally subjected to tiny lesions. It has been estimated that there is gum bleeding after brushing the teeth in at least one-third of any given population.

Small ulcers can be present at the sides of the mouth. The tongue can be sore for a variety of reasons. All these factors can make the mouth an "unsafe" place for sex.

Diseases known to be transmitted by oro-genital infection are: the herpes virus cold sore, yeast infections, AIDS, gonorrhea of the throat, and syphilis chancre of the lips. At least two cases of AIDS have been contracted this way. It would seem unlikely that a woman would wish to kiss a partner with a sore on the mouth, or that she would perform oral sex on a penis with a "drip". Yet all infections have an *incubation period*. There is a time lapse between contracting a disease and the appearance of symptoms. Incubation periods vary widely with different STDs; they can take years for AIDS. With a new partner, the incubation period must be taken into account.

In some cases, both partners are asymptomatic. There are no signs of disease to remind lovers that oral sex can be hazardous. Avoid direct mouth contact with semen. Where there is high risk sexual activity, one option is to completely avoid oro-genital sex. If this is unacceptable, wait until a new partner has been tested and is known to be infection-free.

Tricky Trichomonas

Trichomonas vaginalis, or trich, is caused by a one-celled *protozoan* which grows rapidly within the vagina. Some women have an immediate and painful reaction to trich. Many more have asymptomatic trich; it is often only found if there are tests for other problems. The symptoms include a thin, foamy discharge which is yellow, green, or gray; there is intense itching and soreness, especially if the vulva is scratched. Trich can infect the urinary tract, causing burning, urgency and frequency. No tiny, one-celled creature should be able to cause such misery. But it does.

Trich can be passed on damp material: towels, bathing suits, washcloths, and toilet seats. This is rare. In most cases, it is transmitted by direct sexual contact. Metronidazole in Flagyl destroys trich. It has side effects, and should not be taken if there is any risk of pregnancy. A partner must be treated. Eschew douches and tampons. Avoid a flare-up recurrence by following the same "cool and dry" regime as for yeast overgrowth.

Vaginitis

There are many other organisms which can attack the area. They come under the generic terms *nonspecific vaginitis* and *vulvitis*. Nonspecific refers to conditions in which the cause is uncertain. They may be due to sexual infection, or they may not. The symptoms are often the same as for yeast and trich, with a profuse, foul-smelling discharge, intense itching, soreness, and in some cases, severe pain. Again, like yeast and trich, none of these attacks seem to affect the cervix. Yet they can cause real misery, and greatly reduce the quality of life.

Have a test for diabetes or a prediabetes condition first. Check diet and general health; try to boost the immune system by getting more rest, more profound sleep. Many women are run down and exhausted without realizing how deeply tired they are. Once yeast and trich are ruled out, a course of antibiotics may be the answer, though a yeast overgrowth may then have to be treated. If attacks of vaginitis or vulvitis do recur, be extra scrupulous with genital hygiene. Keep the entire area cool and dry.

Gonorrhea

Gonorrhea is a bacterial infection which affects one million people each year in the United States. It is believed a further one million cases each year go unreported, because the disease is asymptomatic in 10 to 15 percent of men, and in 50 to 80 percent of women. Of the women with mild symptoms, 40 to 60 percent ignore them, believing that they are due to some other minor problem. The cervix is the most common site of gonorrhea.

Symptoms appear 3 days to 2 weeks after sexual contact. There is a thick, yellowish discharge. The cervix looks red, with small bump-like pits which are erosions. The urine tract often becomes infected, with the classic symptoms of UTI: stinging pain, frequency, and urgency. The infection can spread to Skene's and Bartholin's glands. With oral sex, gonorrhea can spread from the penis to the throat, with sore throat and swollen glands, or it is asymptomatic. Discharge from an infected vagina or anal sex can infect the rectum with itching anus and discharge.

Untreated gonorrhea can lead to pelvic inflammatory disease (PID). Some 1 to 3 percent of women develop "disseminated gonorrhea," which spreads throughout the system. It can cause arthritis and, in rare cases, heart disease. The infection can be passed to a baby during birth, causing serious infection and possible blindness. Therapy is by antibiotics. *Protect the cervix.*

Chlamydia

Chlamydia is the most common STD in the U.S. today, with as many as 4 million new cases each year. It causes about half the known cases of NGU (non-gonococcal urethritis) in men. It breeds on the cervix in women. The symptoms are often mild, and frequently go unnoticed. They are the same symptoms as for gonorrhea and can be confused with it. However, they appear a little later, within 1 to 3 weeks of sexual contact. More rarely, chlamydia can be passed by a hand infected with the discharge from parent to baby.

If left untreated, chlamydia can lead to PID and infertility. Tests involve taking swabs from the cervix and culturing a specimen. The antibiotic of choice is tetracycline. *Protect the cervix.*

Herpes

The first attack of the herpes virus is the most painful and takes the longest time to heal. Within 2 to 20 days after infection, there is a mild tingling or itching. This can be on the labia, clitoris, or vagina opening; more rarely on the vagina wall, the cervix, the buttocks, thighs, or anus. It develops into one or more watery, painful blisters in the next few days. There can be burning or pain on urination, with swollen lymph nodes in the groin. There is an increase in discharge, or a feeling of pressure in the pelvic area. In some cases, the entire body reacts with flu-like symptoms: fever, headache, and chills.

Ninety percent of women develop sores on the vagina and cervix during a first infection. The blisters burst quickly, and shed highly contagious viruses everywhere. The now-empty blisters turn into shallow ulcers, which can be painful. The ulcers form into crusts, which heal spontaneously within 1 to 5 weeks. Visit the physician as soon as the symptoms appear. At an early stage, diagnosis can be made by sight alone. Help can begin immediately, but a culture test is very expensive.

At least 5 types of herpes virus are known to affect humans. The Epstein Barr virus and cytomegalovirus cause infectious mononucleosis, also known as glandular fever. The varicella virus causes chicken pox in children, and shingles in adults. There are 2 types of *herpes simplex virus*. HSV 1 causes cold sores on the lips or nose, also called fever blisters. HSV 2 causes genital ulcers, also called genital herpes.

By adulthood, most people have been infected with the cold sore virus, HSV 1. They develop antibodies against it, and only a few actually get cold sores. Fewer adults have HSV 2 antibodies because the virus is spread by sexual contact. The findings of a recent study suggest that 99 percent of prostitutes have HSV 2 antibodies in their blood, compared with 3 percent of nuns and 29 percent of women in a committed relationship.

About 50 percent of those with HSV 2 have no symptoms. The recent increase in genital herpes is thought to be partly due to this, and partly due to an increase in the practice of oro-genital sex. In some cases, *both HSV 1 and HSV 2 cause genital herpes.* If suffering from a cold sore, avoid kissing, and any facial or genital contact. This applies to a partner as well.

Not all HSV 2 die after a first attack. The virus coats itself in the person's own protein substance and retreats along nerve endings to the base of the spine. Here it sets up a permanent home, staying inactive for varying lengths of time. When the virus becomes active again, it usually returns to the same place as the previous attack. Recurring outbreaks can be virulent and painful, or very mild. If mild, a woman may be unaware that she is shedding highly contagious germs.

HSV 2 is particularly dangerous for women. It is linked with cancer of the cervix. The virus can cause miscarriage in the first 3 months of pregnancy. If shed during birth, 1 in 2 babies will be infected. Two out of 3 of those infected babies will die. Half the others suffer brain damage, or visual defects. These horrors are now avoided by Caesarian birth. The baby is lifted from the uterus and thus avoids contact with the virus.

As yet, there is no drug to destroy the herpes virus. The drug acyclovir helps reduce the pain of an attack; it may even lessen the number of recurrences. One of the miserable factors of herpes is the permanent risk of passing on the disease. Some physicians believe that this is only during the active phase; others strongly disagree. An infected person cannot be free of this worry.

* * *

AFFLUENT, attractive, educated man with herpes seeks similar sexy lady 25-40. Life is *not* over for us. Let's make whoopee.

This type of advertisement places herpes in perspective. In the 80s, the media over-reacted, and reported the disease at ludicrous length and in gruesome detail. Yet herpes is not new; the word comes from Ancient Greek "to creep." Avoid letting HSV 2 reduce the quality of life. Boost the immune system by keeping fit and healthy.

Genital Warts

Molluscum Contagiosum: There are two kinds of warts, simple and genital. Both can infect the genitals; it is crucial to recognize the difference. Simple warts are the kind which appear on the hands of children. They are small, dimpled *papules*, which look like spots with a drop of pearly fluid inside. They are highly contagious, as their Latin name shows. They can be transmitted to the genitals by self or partner from warts on the hands and elsewhere. The virus enters the skin through invisible lesions which occur during sexual activity. The warts appear some 30 days after contact. Attacks of simple warts on the genitals are rare, being most likely in the teens and 20 to 30 age group.

If the penis is infected with simple warts, some men try self therapy. This is *not* advisable for women. Simple warts can be painful if rubbed, otherwise a woman is unaware of them. They are not life-threatening, nor do untold damage, but they are highly contagious. Visit the physician or clinic. Therapy varies.

* * *

Human Papilloma Virus: HPV is specific to the genital area. It is transmitted by direct sexual contact. The warts appear 3 weeks to 3 months after contact, but the incubation time can be up to 8 months, even more. The warts can be single; usually, they grow in clusters like grapes. With their raised, bumpy tops, they look like miniature cauliflowers. They grow on the labia lips or anus, inside the vagina, or on the cervix. In many cases, they are asymptomatic, and the woman is unaware that she is infected.

The warts are painless, but easily irritated by rubbing, and some-times they itch. If there has been anal contact, they can grow inside the rectum and around the anus. More rarely with oral contact, they infect the linings of the mouth. If the warts breed in colonies on the cervix, the disease may not be detected until a Pap smear is done. *Women with HPV have a five times higher risk of cancer of the cervix.*

Larger warts, especially on the cervix, may be vaporized by laser therapy, but it is difficult to know if they have all been destroyed. The healing process takes 6 weeks. Repeat therapy is necessary if they flare up again; avoid losing patience as laser therapy usually works. Other therapies include burning the warts off by electric cautery, or freezing them with dry ice. The physician then snips them off. External warts can be painted with the drug podophyllin. It takes 3 or 4 weekly treatments for the warts to dry up and drop off.

HPV infection is also called *condyloma*. The prescription drug Condylox has just been made available for home treatment, which means that patients no longer need to have a physician apply the therapy. At least 56 different types of the virus have been identified. In 1989, HPV was officially diagnosed in 6 percent of U.S. adults. Research suggests that the undiagnosed number is nearer 30 percent. In America, the peak ages for HPV are 15 to 25. In Europe, the peak ages are 25 to 35. Due to the increased cancer risk, HPV is particularly dangerous for women. *Protect the cervix.*

Syphilis

The corkscrew shaped bacteria of syphilis penetrate the skin of the vulva and within 30 minutes reach the glands in the groin. Thirty-six hours after infection, the bacteria have doubled in number. They double again every 30 hours. It takes an average 3 weeks (10 to 50 days) for the first symptoms to appear. By then, there are countless bacteria in the blood stream.

The first symptom is a *chancre*, an ulcer which starts as a pimple and then develops into an open sore with a hard rim. It is painless and self-healing. Once the sore disappears, bacteria travel in the blood, rapidly multiplying. Second stage syphilis occurs 2 to 6 weeks later. The symptoms include a skin rash over the body, swollen glands, and a flu-like condition; but often the disease is asymptomatic. Syphilis continues to wreak its havoc in the vital organs. In later years, the tertiary (third) stage is devastating: heart and brain disorders, joint inflammation, and sometimes early death.

Only about 10 percent of women who get chancres notice them. They can be hidden in the folds of the labia, under the hood of the clitoris, inside the vagina or rectum, on the cervix itself. The bacteria enter through any tiny skin lesion. The sores can appear anywhere, the most usual places being the mouth, nostril, tongue, even the finger. Avoid sexual contact if sores appear on any skin parts. The same applies to a partner.

Antibiotics destroy the bacteria of syphilis. Regular blood tests are necessary for the next two years to check for lingering germs. Keep all follow-up appointments to ensure that the disease has finally gone. Syphilis is 3 times more common in men than women; it is rare in female homosexuals. It can be passed to the fetus after the 20th week of pregnancy, so a blood test for syphilis is now a routine part of prenatal care.

The incidence of syphilis declined in America until 1985, when a decade long trend suddenly reversed itself. In 1987, the incidence rose by 25 percent. According to the CDC, the number of primary and secondary syphilis cases diagnosed in 1990 increased 9 percent over 1989. The level of syphilis in the general population is now the highest since 1949: 20 cases per 100,000 people.

Hepatitis

Hepatitis A and B are caused by virus infection of the liver. The virus breeds in waste matter from the bowel and is common where there is poor sanitation. It is passed in contaminated food and drink; less usually, by sexual contact; more rarely, by transfusions of infected blood. Hepatitis is on the increase, probably due to more foreign travel. When visiting areas with poor sanitation, observe strict personal hygiene. Drink bottled water, eschew ice cubes. Avoid anal and oral sexual contact.

The symptoms of both A and B are the same: fever, nausea, headache, fatigue, loss of appetite, and chills. *Jaundice* shows as a yellow tinge to the skin, fingernails, and whites of the eyes about a week later. Urine can be dark in color; stools almost whitish. A few people are asymptomatic. With hepatitis A, the symptoms are mild. The defense system builds immunity to the virus, but it remains in the blood and can be transmitted.

The hepatitis B virus (HBV) produces severe symptoms, which start suddenly 1 to 6 months after contact. If liver damage is extensive, death occurs in 5 to 20 percent of cases. The B virus is transmitted in blood and blood products during sexual contact: semen, vagina secretions, saliva, and feces are suspect. It is also passed by IV drug users sharing infected needles. The incidence of HBV is rising rapidly, perhaps due to more foreign travel *and* IV drug use. Male homosexuals, heterosexuals with multiple partners, travelers, and drug addicts are high risk groups. There are some 300,000 HBV cases yearly in America, *mainly in young adults.*

Pelvic Inflammatory Disease

PID is a generic name for any infection of the uterus, tubes, and ovaries. These are normally germ-free. Their position keeps them safe from infection, with added protection from the cervix, and its mildly antiseptic mucus. Sexual disease is very dangerous once it reaches the cervix, because PID often starts with a cervical infection which travels to the uterus lining, then to the uterus muscle, then the tubes (salpingitis), the ovaries (oophoritis), and out into the pelvic cavity (peritonitis).

Consider the extent of damage which can occur. These normally germ-free areas, organs, and tissues are now *inflamed*, swollen with pus and disease. Symptoms include: fever, chills, lower abdomen pain, irregular bleeding, spotting, pus-filled discharge from the vagina, and pain during or after intercourse. The more severe the infection, the worse the pain and other symptoms. About 100,000 women each year become infertile as a result of PID.

Visit the clinic or physician promptly. Therapy is urgently required to reduce the extent of damage. Hospitalization is necessary for the first PID attack, so that antibiotics can be given intravenously (IV). If the infection is widespread, PID may not respond to antibiotics. Surgery is then required to drain an abscess or pus-filled cavity, or to remove infected tissue. One attack of PID gives no immunity against further attacks.

Other causes of PID include miscarriage and abortion. Surgery is required to remove fetal or placental tissue still in the uterus. The infection is associated with intrauterine devices, and the IUD should be removed. Birthing and endometrial biopsy also open the cervix and increase the risk of PID. Some women are more vulnerable to PID after a period. In others, the risk seems higher after intercourse. It is thought that germs on sperm proteins might be carried through the uterus and out to the pelvic cavity via the tubes, but this is not proven.

The cervix is the last defense against PID. Use barrier methods such as condoms and diaphragms where there is any risk. A significant number of PID cases are due to gonorrhea; keep in mind a partner can be asymptomatic. Chlamydia, which breeds on the cervix and causes PID, can also be asymptomatic. *Protect the cervix.*

AIDS

AIDS stands for Acquired Immune Deficiency Syndrome.

Acquired: it is passed on, but not inherited.
Immunodeficiency: the immune system grows weak and deficient.
Syndrome: a group of symptoms of which the cause is unknown.

However, it is now known that AIDS is caused by the human immunodeficiency virus (HIV). The word AIDS is still used to avoid confusion. The virus does not kill, but it damages the immune system, leaving the person vulnerable to rare infections and cancers which are life-threatening. If death occurs, it is not from AIDS, but from one of these opportunistic diseases.

HIV is transmitted in body fluids: blood, blood products, semen, vagina secretions, breast milk. It does not appear to be easily transmitted in saliva. When the U.S. outbreak was first recognized in 1981, almost all cases were among white, middle-class, homosexual men and blood transfusion recipients. By 1989, more than 11 percent of all new AIDS patients were female; 23 percent were intravenous drug users, and 43 percent were blacks or Hispanics.

According to a 1991 study, "Up to 80,000 women in the United States of child-bearing age may be infected with the virus that causes AIDS." This means 1,500 to 2,100 babies could be born with the human immunodeficiency virus in the United States each year. The study looked at the results of blood tests from more than 1.8 million infants born from 1988 to 1990 in 38 states and the District of Columbia. Of these babies 2,382 tested positive for HIV antibodies, showing that their mothers had the virus. It is estimated that one-third to one-half of babies born to these mothers will develop the virus as well.

As of March 31, 1991, a total of 171,876 cases of AIDS had been reported to the CDC. Most are attributed to the usual risk factors. In 6,474 cases, the mode of transmission was not known. Nor is it known how many other people are infected with HIV, but have not yet developed AIDS.

Although some women in rural areas were infected, the greatest numbers were in the inner cities. The four areas with the highest rates of infected women were the following states:

- New York with 5.8 per 1,000
- New Jersey with 4.9 per 1,000
- Florida with 4.5 per 1,000
- Washington DC with 5.5 per 1,000
- In Connecticut, the rate was 3.0 per 1,000
- Montana and New Hampshire reported none.

Call the government AIDS hotline: 1-800-324 AIDS to find the location of a center nearby for anonymous testing.

* * *

A man who allegedly had sex with a female acquaintance without telling her that he was infected with AIDS boasted that he would take all the women he could with him.

Mr. B, age 25, was charged in April 1991, with assault with a deadly weapon. He set out to "ritually infect future sex partners out of spite," said the assistant district attorney.

The Oakland man was ordered held without bail.

HIV-POS Woman of up to 50 sought by slim caring male.
Let's enjoy what's left. It's a lot!

The Future

Scientists using an experimental AIDS vaccine have succeeded in changing the way the body fights the AIDS virus. The discovery could open the door to new ways of treating the disease. By giving the vaccine to 30 men and women infected with HIV, researchers found that they were able to prompt the immune systems of most in the group into mounting a more sophisticated counterattack against the virus. It is too early to know if this response will help HIV-infected people to survive the ravages of the disease.

The study's results counter the long-standing and pessimistic conviction of many AIDS researchers that there is little to be done to improve upon the immune system's battle against the HIV virus. According to the National Institute of Allergy and Infectious Dis-

ease: "This is not a breakthrough. But it is a very interesting observation which needs to be pursued."

New therapies such as the use of the antiviral drug AZT early in
infection and inhaled pentamidine to prevent an AIDS-caused
pneumonia will delay the time when HIV infection develops into
full-blown AIDS. The World Health Organization estimates that
AIDS cases in North America and Europe will begin to level off
around the middle of the 1990s. Its rise is predicted to continue in
Africa with no plateau in sight. Another estimate suggests that the
number of Americans with AIDS will level off at between 60,000
and 67,000 a year in the period 1990 to 1995. The number of those
with advanced stage HIV disease, but without a diagnosis of AIDS,
will grow by 40 percent during the next 5 years. The HIV infection
rate among homosexual men peaked in 1984, and has declined
since. For IV drug users, the infection reached its highest mark in
1986 and has since dropped. However, the heterosexual epidemic
of AIDS is still growing. It could more than double from the 3,700
new cases in 1990 to 8,700 in 1995. The estimated current number of
infections from heterosexual transmission is between 75,000 to
125,000.

Dear Ann Landers: I am a successful executive woman. A
year ago I applied for life insurance. I was required to take
an HIV antibody test. To my complete shock, it came back
positive.

I am not a prostitute. I am not promiscuous. I am not and
have never been an intravenous drug user. I am not a member of a minority group. I am not indigent nor am I home-
less. I have not slept with a bisexeual.

I am a suburban, nonsmoking, non-drug using, successful
American woman. I got HIV from a man I am in love with
and have been seeing for five years. He is not homosexual
or bisexual. He has never used intravenous drugs. He had
no idea he was carrying the virus. He believes he may have
been infected six years ago by a woman with whom he had a
brief, meaningless relationship.

We are both in excellent physical condition and look terrific. In my ignorance, I thought people who carried the AIDS
virus looked emaciated. I now know it can take years for
HIV infection to progress to AIDS...

AIDS has become a party joke. People who would never

kid about cancer, cerebral palsy, mental illness or tuberculo-
sis think AIDS is fair game. They don't realize I could be
their sister, friend, co-worker, niece, daughter or cousin.
They treat AIDS differently because it is sexually transmitted.

Please, Ann, print this letter to sensitize people to the
hurt they cause when they make thoughtless comments.
Many of us look like everybody else.

Summary

- Try to avoid all high risk sexual activity.
- Though not 100% safe, the condom *does* act as a barrier.
- It must be worn until ejaculation is complete.
- Insist on condom use if there is high risk sexual activity.
- Avoid the exchange of all body fluids in high risk behavior.
- A change in male partners should involve condom use.
- The diaphragm and spermicides provide some protection.
- Urinating after sex helps *very slightly* to flush out germs.
- It is possible to have asymptomatic STD and be contagious.
- Always have a check-up after high risk sexual activity.
- One STD infection gives no immunity against further attacks.
- Stop sexual activity if a disease is detected or suspected.
- Inform a partner so he can have simultaneous treatment.
- The earlier the therapy, the quicker and easier the cure.
- Be very vigilant. *Protect the cervix.*

Index

abortion, 110, 152, 165, 208, 242; induced, 164, 165; spontaneous,
115, 152, 170, 185
abscess, 134, 135
abstinence, 155; periodic, 156-157
acne, 196-197
Acquired Immune Deficiency Syndrome (AIDS), 36-37, 38, 206-207,
208, 233, 235, 243-246; rates of infection, 244; transmission of, 243;
treatments for, 245; vaccine, 244-
245
adhesions, 105, 108-109, 174, 179
adolescence, 195, 208-209
adrenal glands, 45, 214, 215
adrenaline, 214
amenorrhea, 43, 48; primary, 43,
202; secondary, 43, 55-56
American Cancer Society, 100-101,
143
Amiel, Barbara, 85
ampulla, 105, 106, 107, 108
anal sex, 34, 233, 234, 236, 239-240,
241
androgens, 45, 110, 198, 212, 215
angina, 213
angiography, 213
anorexia, 189, 190
anorgasmia, 81
anovulation, 171
antiprostaglandin inhibitors, 51
anus, 72, 239; baby, 183; hygiene,
30, 42

apocrine glands, 16, 17
apocrine sweat, 30
areola, 71, 120-121, 132, 198, 204;
hair, 123-124; infection, 134; removal of, hair, 124; *see also* areola-
nipple complex; nipple
areola-nipple complex, 121, 122,
127, 136, 204; *see also* areola; nipple
artificial insemination by a donor
(AID), 178
atherosclerosis, 12, 213
avoiders, 9, 186
AZT, 245

baby, 181-186; development of geni-
talia, 183-184; secretions, 183,
193; and UTI, 184
barrier methods *see* fertility control; specific types of methods
Bartholin's cyst, 19
Bartholin's glands, 18-19, 20, 236
basal body temperature method
(BBT), 156
biological therapy, 115
biopsy, 141; fine-needle, 141, 142;
surgical, 141
birth defects, 170, 185
bladder, 61, 64, 68, 69, 224; infections, 59, 60, 224; and UTI, 61-62
"boarding school synchrony," 48
body image, and puberty, 205-206;
and self-esteem, 205-206, 208

intrauterine insertion (IUI), 177
intravenous pyleogram (IVP), 114
in vitro fertilization (IVF), 176, 177, 178, 179, 186

Kegels exercises, 23, 68, 69-70, 225
Kwell, 233

labia, baby, 183; effects of puberty on, 198; majora, 16-17, 31, 32, 59, 71, 223; minora, 17, 31, 32, 224; at orgasm, 73; and STDs, 237, 239, 241
Lanson, Lucienne, 88
laparoscopy, 97, 175
laser surgery, 97
libido, 44, 47, 100, 164, 212, 222
lice, 232; pubic, 232-233
life expectancy, 13, 147
ligaments of crupa, 128

love making see sex
Love, Susan, 126, 128
lumpectomy, 148, 149
luteinizing hormone (LH), 46, 48, 103, 154, 171, 200

mammograms, 115-116, 143, 150, 204, 222, 229; safety of, 144
mastalgia, 137; cyclic, 137
mastectomy, 149; radical, 142-143
Masters and Johnson, 18
masturbation, 80, 225, 226, 227; and orgasm, 78
meatus, 59
menarche, 44, 199-200, 202, 206; early, 201; see also menopause
menopause, 9, 49, 94, 102, 110, 136, 211-230; breasts at, 127; changes after, 223-224; and diet, 212, 220, 225, 230; effects of on vagina, 24, 218-219; egg production and, 153, 212; and estrogen withdrawal, 112, 212, 214, 216; and exercise, 227-229, 230; happiness and, 229; and menstruation, 212; self-care after, 224-225; sex and,

225-226, 227; and sexual desire, 226-227; skin changes at, 222-223; surgical, 230; symptoms of, 216; see also menarche; premenstrual syndrome
menorrhagia, 43
menses, 44
menstruation, 31, 34, 43-58, 115, 163, 170, 186, 209; blood loss during, 43; and blood spotting, 49; breasts during, 131; dysfunctions of, 43, 48, 49-51, 55, 56; and exercise abuse, 55; and fertility control, 161; irregular, 56-57, 102, 171; irregular, and fertility problems, 171-172; length of flow, 43; loss of, 55-56; menopause and, 212; and nipples, 122, 131; pain relief, 50-51; and PMS, 43-44, 51-54; and sex, 225; timing of, 48-49; and UTI, 65-66; see also menarche; menopause
mental retardation, 170
Mifepristone, 164
milk ridges, 182
mini-pill, 161
miscarriage, 110, 164, 179, 238, 242
mittelschmertz, 103-104, 156
molluscum contagiosum, 239
mons veneris, 15-16, 31
Montgomery's glands, 121
morning after pill, 161
mucus method, 156
myomectomy, 95

National Cancer Institute, 101, 147, 148, 149
National Coalition for Cancer Survivorship, 101
needle aspiration, 140
nipples, 71, 72, 117, 121, 125, 132, 150, 198, 203, 204; care of, 121, 122; discharge, 136-137; during pregnancy, 127; erection, 122-123; extra, 123, 182; extraverted, 122; inverted, 122; itchy, 135-136; lack of, 183; and menstruation,

93, 102, 116, 155, 195, 208, 231-
246; asymptomatic, 37, 42, 63-64,
246; contraceptives and, 39-40,
246; and fertility, 167; and fertility
control, 39-40, 152, 157, 160, 166;
high risk behavior and 233-234,
246; and oviducts, 167; prevention of, 37; symptoms of, 41; and
UTI, 63-64, 66; *see also* specific
diseases
sexual stimulation, 19; *see also* masturbation
Silber, Sherman, 167-168
Skene's glands, 19, 20, 68, 236
Sloane, Ethel, 19, 27
smegma, 18, 30, 35
sperm, 25, 26-27, 31, 58, 75, 105,
106-107, 153, 154, 156, 161, 170,
172, 173, 175, 176, 177, 179; capacitation, 107, 173; counts and
fertility, 173; defective, 173, 177,
179; donation, 178, 179; production, 153, 169, 172; quality, 168;
survival rate, 106, 154-155; washing, 173, 177, 179
spermicides, 31, 39, 40, 42, 65, 153,
157, 158, 159, 165, 246
sphincters, 61-62
sponges, 65, 153, 165
sterilization *see* tubal ligation; vasectomy
stress, and cancer, 146-147; and fertility, 172
stress hormones, 165; and heart disease, 214-215
stretch marks, 196-197
surrogacy, 178-179
sweating phenomenon, 24-25, 31
symptothermal method, 156
syphilis, 36, 37, 39, 234, 235, 240-
241; secondary, 240, 241; tertiary,
240

tampons, 21, 57-58, 59, 65-66, 200,
201, 209, 235; and vagina, 57-58
tart's wash, 30

testicles, 45, 46, 87, 169, 173; embryonic, 181
testosterone, 44-45, 131, 213-215,
224, 227, 230; blood levels, 45, 46-
47
testosterone enanthate (TE), 164
testosterone replacement therapy
(TRT), 222
toxic shock syndrome, 57-58, 159,
200
transvaginal ultrasound, 98, 171
treadmill test, 213, 229
trichomonas vaginalis, 39, 235
tubal ligation, 163
tubes see oviducts
Turner Syndrome, 185-186

ultrasound, 112, 113, 115; transvaginal, 98, 171
underwear, 29, 42
urea, 61
urethra, 59-60, 61, 63, 65, 66, 75,
224; infections, 60
urinalysis, 66
urinary incontinence *see* incontinence
urinary tract, 59-70; infection, 11,
40, 60-68
urinary tract infection (UTI), 11, 40,
60-68, 69, 157, 235; in babies, 184;
bladder and, 61-62; chronic, 68;
cranberry juice and, 62, 63; curing, 67-68; diagnosing, 66-68;
diet and, 62-63; E. coli and, 62-
63, 66; fertility control and, 64-
65, 159, 165; male, 234;
menstruation and, 65-66; perfume and, 63; prevention of, 61-
62, 67, 70; STDs and, 63-64, 66;
symptoms of, 60, 236
urine, 61, 63, 66; leakage, 33, 68-69;
retention, 64; static, 61, 64
uterus, 25, 26, 27, 47-48, 49-50, 51,
56, 57, 72, 74, 87-102, 107, 108,
109, 116, 153, 164, 168, 171, 176,
177, 178, 226, 242; absence of,
185; anteflexed, 88; baby, 183,